Useful Acronyms for Personal Online Communications

ACRONYM	MEANING	ACRONYM	MEANING
AAMOF	as a matter of fact	IMHO	in my humble opinion
BFN	bye for now	IMO	in my opinion
BTW	by the way	IOW	in other words
BYKT	but you knew that	LOL	lots of luck *or* laughing out loud
CMIIW	correct me if I'm wrong	NRN	no reply necessary
EOL	end of lecture	OIC	oh, I see
FAQ	frequently asked question(s)	OTOH	on the other hand
FWIW	for what it's worth	ROF	rolling on the floor
FYI	for your information	TIA	thanks in advance
HTH	hope this helps	TIC	tongue in cheek
IAC	in any case	TTYL	talk to you later
IAE	in any event	TYVM	thank you very much
IMCO	in my considered opinion	<G>	grinning
WYSIWYG	what you see is what you get	<J>	joking
		<L>	laughing
<Y>	yawning	<S>	smiling

Useful Emoticons for Personal Online Communications

EMOTICON	MEANING
:) *or* :-)	Expresses happiness, sarcasm, or joke
:(*or* :-(	Expresses unhappiness
:] *or* :-]	Expresses jovial happiness
:[*or* :-[	Expresses despondent unhappiness
:D *or* :-D	Expresses jovial happiness or laughing
:e *or* :-e	Expresses disappointment
:I *or* :-I	Expresses indifference
:-/ *or* :-\	Indicates indecision, confusion, or skepticism
:Q *or* :-Q	Expresses confusion
:S *or* :-S	Expresses incoherence or loss of words
:@ *or* :-@	Expresses shock or screaming
:O *or* :-O	Indicates surprise, yelling, or realization of an error ("uh oh!")

E-Learning Companion

A Student's Guide to Online Success

Custom Edition

Ryan Watkins, Michael Corry

CENGAGE
Learning

Australia • Brazil • Japan • Korea • Mexico • Singapore • Spain • United Kingdom • United States

CENGAGE
Learning™

E-Learning Companion
A Student's Guide to Online Success
Custom Edition

E-Learning Companion: A Student's Guide to Online Success, 3rd Edition
Ryan Watkins, Michael Corry

© 2011, 2008 Wadsworth Cengage Learning. All rights reserved.

Executive Editors:
 Maureen Staudt
 Michael Stranz

Senior Project Development Manager:
 Linda deStefano

Marketing Specialist:
 Courtney Sheldon

Senior Production/Manufacturing Manager:
 Donna M. Brown

PreMedia Manager:
 Joel Brennecke

Sr. Rights Acquisition Account Manager:

 Todd Osborne

Cover Image:
Getty Images*

*Unless otherwise noted, all cover images used by Custom
Solutions, a part of Cengage Learning, have been supplied
courtesy of Getty Images with the exception of the Earthview
cover image, which has been supplied by the National
Aeronautics and Space Administration (NASA).

For product information and technology assistance, contact us at
Cengage Learning Customer & Sales Support, 1-800-354-9706

For permission to use material from this text or product,
submit all requests online at **cengage.com/permissions**
Further permissions questions can be emailed to
permissionrequest@cengage.com

This book contains select works from existing Cengage Learning resources and
was produced by Cengage Learning Custom Solutions for collegiate use. As such,
those adopting and/or contributing to this work are responsible for editorial
content accuracy, continuity and completeness.

Compilation © 2010 Cengage Learning
ISBN-13: 978-1-111-74193-8

ISBN-10: 1-111-74193-X

Cengage Learning
5191 Natorp Boulevard
Mason, Ohio 45040
USA
Cengage Learning is a leading provider of customized learning solutions with
office locations around the globe, including Singapore, the United Kingdom,
Australia, Mexico, Brazil, and Japan. Locate your local office at:
international.cengage.com/region.

Cengage Learning products are represented in Canada by Nelson Education, Ltd.
For your lifelong learning solutions, visit **www.cengage.com/custom.**
Visit our corporate website at **www.cengage.com.**

Printed in the United States of America

Contents

1   Selecting the Right Opportunities for Success Online   1

2   Create a Plan for Online Success   16

3 Technology Tips for Online Students   38

4 Time Management Strategies   79

5 Developing Positive Online Relationships   90

6 E-Learning Vocabulary   106

7 Maintaining Motivation in an Online Course   127

QR Quick Reference Guide   137

How-To Tutorials   T1

Praise for the E-Learning Companion

"*E-Learning Companion* is a comprehensive learning tool that provides a foundation for all online learners. It is an invaluable reference book that all online learners should use throughout their studies." —Wendy Rybinski, Bisk Education

"The *E-Learning Companion* provides tutorials that cover several course management systems and operating systems, making it good for students, no matter what platform they are using." —Amber M. Epps, The Art Institute of Pittsburgh

"The *E-Learning Companion* is a supplemental text that would be a great addition to any online introductory course. The Companion addresses common concerns and roadblocks distance students typically encounter: time management/procrastination, technology issues, and online student-instructor relationships." —Melissa Vosen, North Dakota State University

"I like the binding and size. A very handy guide chock full of useful information." —Caroline Lieber, Post University

"Excellent, excellent. [The chapter exercises] provide pertinent practice that will set a strong foundation for the course. Fabulous!" —Diana Nystedt, Palo Alto College

About the Authors

Ryan Watkins, Ph.D.

Ryan Watkins, Ph.D., is an Associate Professor in the Educational Technology Leadership Program at The George Washington University in Washington, DC. Dr. Watkins has also been a visiting researcher with the National Science Foundation (NSF) and has served as vice president representing the United States in the Inter-American Distance Education Consortium (CREAD). Besides the *E-Learning Companion*, Dr. Watkins has authored six additional books, including *75 E-Learning Activities: Making Online Courses More Interactive* (Wiley/Jossey-Bass, 2005); *Performance by Design: The Systematic Selection, Design, and Development of Performance Technologies* (HRD Press, 2006); and *Strategic Planning for Success: Accomplishing High-Impact Results* (Wiley/Jossey-Bass, 2003). For more information, visit http://www.ryanrwatkins.com.

Michael Corry, Ph.D.

Michael Corry, Ph.D., is an Associate Professor and Director of the Educational Technology Leadership Program at The George Washington University in Washington, DC. Dr. Corry is intimately involved with the course design, delivery, and management of this pioneering program delivered via distance education. Dr. Corry's research interests include distance-learning theory, distance-learning policy, faculty development, asynchronous learning, the integration of technology into K–12 and higher-education settings, instructional design, and human–computer interaction. He has numerous publications and presentations related to his research interests, including *Distance Education: What Works Well* (Haworth Press, 2003), for which he was the lead editor. He has also designed and delivered faculty-development workshops involving technology. Dr. Corry holds a doctorate degree from Indiana University in Instructional Systems Technology. Before coming to George Washington University, he taught at Indiana University, as well as at the high-school level in Utah.

To Instructors

Keys to Success in Online Learning

The online classroom is a new learning environment for almost all students. Although many students have been very successful in the traditional classroom, the online learning environment presents them with an array of obstacles and opportunities that must be addressed in order for them to succeed. The *E-Learning Companion* is intended to provide strategies and tactics for achieving success with any online coursework, whether it is for an entirely online course or for a course that simply uses online tools to supplement on-campus learning. Throughout this text, we address specific steps that can be taken by all students to realize their goals and gain the most from their online courses.

Based on our years of experience in both taking and teaching online courses, we have identified two fundamental skills that are essential to the success of online students. Each chapter in this book guides and assists students in developing these skills as they apply to e-learning success.

Online Success Skill 1: Adapt Old Skills and Habits from the Traditional Classroom for Use in the Online Classroom

Students enter the online classroom with a range of learning skills and study habits that they have developed through their years of experience in the traditional classroom. Some of these skills and habits are not useful in achieving goals (for example, daydreaming while giving the appearance of paying attention to the instructor!), but many of them will provide students with an excellent foundation for adapting to the new characteristics of the online learning environment. In this book, we build upon these existing skills and habits whenever possible.

Online Success Skill 2: Develop and Apply New Skills and Habits for the Online Classroom

Success in online coursework requires the effective integration of online strategies and student success skills (see the figure on the next page). By combining the learning skills and study habits that are necessary for success in any college course with the distinctive skills and habits required in online learning environments, your students will develop the expertise to be successful in any online coursework that may be required throughout their college education.

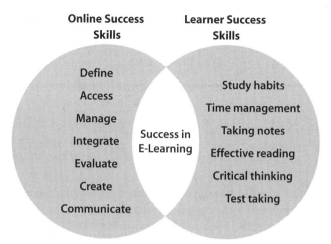

The integration of online skills and student success skills[1]

What Has Changed in the Third Edition?

Since we wrote the second edition of the *E-Learning Companion*, the knowledge and skills required for successful online learning have shifted somewhat to keep current with today's high-tech college experience. For example, several new e-learning technologies have emerged, while the growth of e-learning in high schools has often improved the baseline e-learning study skills of incoming students. The opportunity to write a third edition of the *E-Learning Companion* has enabled us to update, expand, trim, and edit our earlier work to ensure that it remains relevant for today's college students. We have made numerous changes throughout this edition, including:

- *(New)* **Try Something New** features identify free Web-based tools that you and your students can use to improve communications, manage time, share resources, and stay organized.

- *(New)* **Emerging e-learning technologies** such as social networking, online file sharing, wikis, and blogs are discussed throughout the book.

- *(New)* **How-To Tutorials on Google Docs** join the existing tutorials on Blackboard, WebCT, and eCollege.

- *(New)* **Tips for Online Security and Privacy** have been added to Chapter 3.

- *(New)* **Tips for Using Apps** on a smart phone (such as iPhone, G1, or BlackBerry) or iPod to improve study skills have been added.

- *(Updated)* **Tips for avoiding plagiarism and copyright violations** have been expanded, including a new worksheet and more examples in Chapter 3.

- *(Updated)* **A Quick Reference Guide** collects a variety of tips and recommendations on such topics as email, online discussion boards, listserves, online exams, and e-research in one convenient place.

- *(New and Updated)* **Resources on the E-Learning Companion Premium Website** include links to numerous resources on topics ranging from plagiarism and personal safety to time management and troubleshooting technology problems.

- *(New and Updated)* **Resources on the E-Learning Companion Premium Instructor Companion Website** include an answer key for the chapter activities in the book, guidance on using the Tutorials, Integration Guides for using the E-Learning Companion along with other Cengage Student Success titles, and links to additional instructor resources.

Key Features of This Book

E-Learning Readiness Self-Assessment

The E-Learning Readiness Self-Assessment on page xxii helps students evaluate their readiness for online success. Students can use the self-assessment to guide their own preparation. Alternatively, instructors can use the quiz as a group evaluation for identifying which e-learning study skills they should emphasize in their course. An online version of the self-assessment is also available on the *E-Learning Companion* Premium Website.

Students who have completed the E-Learning Readiness Self-Assessment may use their results to guide them to the appropriate chapters to expand on their previous e-learning study skills as well as to develop new skills for ensuring their success in using information and communication technologies.

"Stay Focused" Chapter Objectives

Each chapter in the E-Learning Companion addresses several of the critical skill areas identified by Educational Testing Services (ETS) in the Information and Communication Technology (ICT) Literacy assessment.[3] ICT literacy is defined by the International ICT Literacy Panel as "using digital technology, communications tools, and/or networks to access, manage, integrate, evaluate, and create information in order to function in a knowledge society." ICT literacy therefore represents an essential range of skills for college students whose classes, reports, exams, and social lives are more intertwined with technology than ever before. ETS further defines the cognitive and technical skill areas of ICT literacy as define, access, manage, integrate, evaluate, create, and communicate.[5] Accordingly, each chapter of the book begins with a series of "Stay Focused" learning objectives that relate the chapter's contents to the critical skill areas of ICT literacy. "Did You Stay Focused?" questions at the end of each chapter allow students to quickly assess their understanding of these objectives.

Try Something New

This new feature to the third edition identifies free Web-based tools offering unique technologies that can be used to improve study skills and support student success in college. Each *Try Something New* feature provides an overview of the tool and a short description of how it can be used to improve student success—for free.

Student-to-Student Tips

Included in this book are more than 50 tips that we have collected from successful online students from around the world. Each recommendation is based on students' real-life experiences in completing online course assignments and activities. From effectively using email to communicate with college instructors to improving time management skills, these student-to- student tips ground the recommendations found in this book with actual student experiences.

Activities

A variety of activities are offered throughout the book to give students an opportunity to practice many of the strategies and skills of online success. By completing these activities as they read through each chapter, students will build their comprehension and increase the likelihood that the skills discussed in this book will become successful study habits throughout their college experiences.

Chapter Exercises

In addition to the activities in each chapter, there are also longer exercises at the end of each chapter. While the chapter activities may be done without any additional resources, many of these end-of-chapter exercises require students to use a computer that has Internet access.

How-To Tutorials

At the end of this book are 47 How-To Tutorials that provide students with step-by-step instructions for completing many of the online skills that are discussed in each chapter. The How-To Tutorials icon (shown in the margin) appears throughout the book to indicate which topics have an associated tutorial on the skills being discussed. For quick reference, an index of the How-To Tutorials is provided on the inside front cover of this book. The How-To Tutorials are also available on the *E-Learning Companion* Premium Website.

QR Quick Reference Guide

Because many of the tips and techniques in this book are most valuable when students are actively engaged in e-learning activities, they have been collected in a new Quick Reference Guide that enables students to easily get help on specific topics while working online. The Quick Reference sections serve as go-to-guides on how to effectively use Internet technologies such as email, chat rooms, discussion boards, e-research tools, and other resources. The Quick Reference icon (shown in the margin) throughout the book identifies topics for which the guide provides additional tips, suggestions, and resources for improving e-learning study skills.

Glossary

In each chapter, words or phrases with which students may be unfamiliar are clearly identified first in **boldface** type and then with <u>underlining</u> on subsequent use. These key terms are also collected in a Glossary at the end of the book. In addition, online flashcards for glossary terms are available on the *E-Learning Companion* Premium Website.

Premium Website

Each chapter of the book contains references to resources for students that are available on the *E-Learning Companion* Premium Website, accessible at http://www.cengage.com/success/Watkins/ELearning3e. The Premium Website icon (shown above) appears throughout the chapters next to topics for which additional resources are available online, such as interactive versions of the E-Learning Readiness Self-Assessment and chapter activities; interactive Flashcards with the terms from the Glossary; the complete set of Tutorials from the book; information on avoiding plagiarism and evaluating online sources; a social-networking safety quiz on how to limit the risks involved in using sites like MySpace and Facebook; web links for additional e-learning and Student Success resources; Video Skillbuilders, interactive video and exercises that showcase real students talking about their struggles and successes in college; and more. To gain access to the password-protected content on the Premium Website including the How-To Tutorials and Video Skillbuilders, students will need either a Printed Access Code (PAC ISBN: 0495810509) that can be bundled with the text or an Instant Access Code (IAC) that can be purchased online at http://www.ichapters.com. Talk to your Cengage Sales Representative for more information. Need help finding your rep? Visit http://academic.cengage.com.

Instructor Companion Website

Instructor resources available on the *E-Learning Companion* Instructor Companion Website include an answer key to the chapter activities in the book; a guide to using the Tutorials; and a set of Integration Guides showing how to smoothly integrate the *E-Learning Companion* into courses that use some of Cengage Learning's most popular College Success titles.

Assessment Tools

If you're looking for additional ways to assess your students, Cengage Learning has additional resources for you to consider. For more in-depth information on any of these items, talk with your sales rep.

College Success Factors Index: This pre- and post-test determines student's strengths and weaknesses in areas proven to be determinants of college success.

CL Assessment and Portfolio Builder: This personal development tool engages students in self-assessment, critical thinking and goal setting activities to prepare them for college and the workplace. The access code for this item also provides students to the Career Resource Center.

Noel-Levitz College Student Inventory: *The Retention Management System™ College Student Inventory* (CSI from Noel-Levitz) is an early-alert, early-intervention program that identifies students with tendencies that contribute to dropping out of school. Students can participate in an integrated, campuswide program. Cengage Learning offers you three assessment options that evaluate students on 19 different scales: Form A (194 items), Form B (100 items), or an online etoken that provides access to Form A, B, or C (74 items). Advisors are sent three interpretive reports: The Student's Report, the Advisor/Counselor Report, and The College Summary and Planning Report.

The *Myers-Briggs Type Indicator® (MBTI®) Instrument*[1] is the most widely used personality inventory in history—and it is also available for packaging with *the E-Learning Companion*. The standard Form M self-scorable instrument contains 93 items that determine preferences on four scales: Extraversion-Introversion, Sensing-Intuition, Thinking-Feeling, and Judging-Perceiving.

College Success Planner

Package your textbook with this 12-month week-at-a-glance academic planner. The College Success Planner assists students in making the best use of their time both on and off campus, and includes additional reading about key learning strategies and life skills for success in college.

Cengage Learning's TeamUP Faculty Program Consultants

An additional service available with this textbook is support from **TeamUP Faculty Program Consultants.** For more than a decade, our consultants have helped faculty reach and engage first-year students by offering peer-to-peer consulting on curriculum and assessment, faculty training, and workshops. Our consultants are educators and higher education professionals who provide full-time support helping educators establish and maintain effective student success programs. They are available to help you to establish or improve your student success program and provide training on the implementation of our textbooks and technology. To connect with your TeamUP Faculty Program Consultant, call 1-800-528-8323 or visit http://www.cengage.com/teamup.

Acknowledgments

We would like to express our appreciation and gratitude for the encouragement that we have received from our friends and family throughout the writing of this book. We would especially like to thank the following people for their support: Christina and Jordan Gee; and Deborah, Brandon, Rachel, Ryan, Madison, Murray, and Donna Corry.

We are also grateful to the many colleagues and students who participated in the development of the strategies and tips offered in this book.

In addition, we would like to acknowledge the following people whose feedback and guidance have helped shape this book:

REVIEWERS OF THE FIRST TWO EDITIONS

Cathryn Balas, Terra Community College

Marla Barbee, South Plains College

Cecelia R. Brewer, University of Missouri—Kansas City

Amy Feistel, Duke University

Elaine Gray, Rollins College

Amy Hawkins, Columbia College

Gary L. Heller, University of Phoenix—Idaho Campus

Kristel Kemmerer, Albright College

Dana Kuehn, Florida Community College—Jacksonville

Kristina Leonard, Mississippi State University

Jennifer Lindquist, Thomas University

Katie Lynch, Mississippi State University

Donna Matsumoto, Leeward Community College

Mary McKenna, Kaplan College

Pamela Patrick, Capella University

Jennie Scott, Pima Community College

Derek Stanovsky, Appalachian State University

Jason Steinitz, Erie Community College

Robert A. Stuessy, Midlands Technical College

Lynette Teal, Western Wisconsin Technical College

Karla Thompson, New Mexico State University

Kimberly J. Verdone, University of Pittsburgh

Kate E. Wrigley, University of Connecticut—Storrs

REVIEWERS OF THE THIRD EDITION

Melissa Vosen, North Dakota State University

Amber M. Epps, The Art Institute of Pittsburgh

Dr. Andrea Goldstein, South University

Caroline Lieber, Post University

Diana Nystedt, Palo Alto College

Wendy Rybinski, Bisk Education

Lastly, we would like to express our gratitude for the support and guidance provided by the staff of Cengage Learning, especially the following individuals who made significant contributions to this book: Shani Fisher, Daisuke Yasutake, Cat Salerno, and Alison Eigel Zade.

Ryan Watkins
Michael Corry

Notes

1. Based in part on Anderson and Kanuka, 2003; Educational Testing Service, 2003.
2. See Educational Testing Service, 2003; International ICT Literacy Panel, 2002.
3. See http://www.ets.org/ictliteracy/.
4. International ICT Literacy Panel, 2002, 2.
5. See Educational Testing Service, 2003; International ICT Literacy Panel, 2002.

To Students

College professors are increasingly using online technologies to supplement, or even replace, many of the course activities that used to be confined to the classroom. As a result, achieving success in today's college courses requires you to develop not only effective learning skills and study habits for use in the on-campus classroom but also the skills necessary for success when your courses use online technologies such as real-time chats, online discussion boards, and email. The *E-Learning Companion* is intended to be a course resource and quick-reference guide to help you develop those skills so that you can succeed in any college course that uses online technology. You may find parts of this book useful for your classroom-based college courses as well. The resources, tools, ideas, activities, suggestions, tips, examples, and recommendations included in this book may even be useful to you in graduate school or on-the-job training after college. As a result, this book is likely a value tool for your learning... today, tomorrow, and into the future. As you read and apply many of the skills discussed in the book, identify ways that they can be used in many places that you learn.

What Is E-Learning?

The use of online technologies for course assignments and activities has become widespread at colleges and universities. From required online discussions with your instructor to Internet-based quizzes, the use of these technologies to move education outside the boundaries of the classroom will require you to sharpen many of your skills and learn some new ones. This combination of good study habits and technical skills is not only essential to your success in college, it is the foundation of *e-learning*. Specific examples of e-learning include the following:

- Using resources from the Internet to define which content elements should be included in a term paper
- Using your college's Web portal to review a course syllabus
- Using instant messaging to organize a group project
- Using your computer's word-processing software to edit a collaborative research paper
- Using the Internet to assess the usefulness of research articles available through your college's online library system
- Using email to contact your professor with a question on an upcoming assignment

- Developing an online portfolio of your English (or other course) papers to share with friends at other colleges

How Do I Know if This Book Is for Me?

You will benefit from the *E-Learning Companion* if you are any of the following:

- *A student or prospective student taking a college-level distance education course*—You will find this book a helpful guide to both adapting your existing study skills for online courses and learning new skills. Even if you are buying this book midway through your college experience, it is never too late to start fostering new and useful study habits that can ensure your success in the emerging online classroom and provide you with the skills necessary for a successful transition to using technology in the workplace.

- *A high school student preparing for the rigors of college*—This book will help you prepare for success in online college coursework. Although some of the examples and suggestions may not directly apply to your present educational setting, you will learn useful skills for any online activity.

- *An employee who is or will be taking an online training course*—This book will enable you to be successful in online training or work-related activities. Although some of the book's examples, suggestions, and tips may not directly apply to your current situation, many of them are as useful in the workplace as they are in the classroom.

How Should I Use This Book?

Complete the E-Learning Readiness Self-Assessment

The E-Learning Readiness Self-Assessment on page xxii will provide you with individual feedback on your readiness to successfully complete online course assignments and activities, helping guide your path as you develop necessary skills and habits. This individualized feedback can also help you determine where you should focus additional time and energy to most effectively develop your skills. You may also complete an interactive version of the Self-Assessment on the Premium Website.

Don't Be Afraid to Write in This Book

Fill in each of the activities, checklists, and exercises with your responses. Take notes in the margins and update any information that you may find to be slightly different at your own college or university. You should use and customize this book so that it will become a useful resource for each of your college courses.

Use the How-To Tutorials

The How-To Tutorials in the back of the book provide step-by-step instructions for completing many of the tasks required for being successful in your online coursework, such as attaching files to an email or participating in an online chat. When you see the How-To Tutorials icon in the margin, refer to the related tutorials section at the end of the book for easy steps to help you develop that skill. Online versions of the How-To Tutorials are also available on the Premium Website. The online tutorials are password-protected, but you can access them through an Instant Access Code (IAC) that can be purchased at http://www.ichapters.com.

Apply the Skills Whenever You Can

None of us were born with all the skills and knowledge for succeeding in college. For most of us, developing these skills and turning them into successful study habits requires a good deal of practice. Be sure to take the time to apply the techniques, tips, and methods described in this book whenever you can, even when using the Internet for activities that have nothing to do with your courses. By practicing these skills, they will become familiar study habits to help you throughout your college education.

One Size Does Not Fit All

Applying each study strategy that we describe in this book may not be beneficial for everyone. If there are tips and techniques that do not seem to work for you, skip over them and move on to the next. After all, your individual success is the goal. Remember to come back to this book as the online demands of your courses change each semester and throughout your college experience. The strategies and tips that may not sound useful this semester may be very helpful a year or two from now.

Use the Resources on the Premium Website

On the Premium Website for the *E-Learning Companion* (http://www.cengage.com/success/Watkins/ELearning3e), there are a variety of resources that you can use to assess, build, and expand your preparation for online success. From online versions of the E-Learning Readiness Self-Assessment and How-To Tutorials to an interactive version of the chapter activities and exercises, you will find many tools for developing valuable study skills on the Premium Website.

After Reading the Book, Keep It Nearby as a Resource

The *E-Learning Companion* is intended to be a resource that you will use throughout your college experience. Keep this book near your computer or in the book bag that you take to the computer lab. You never know when you will want to refer to a chapter, illustration, or tutorial for help with completing online activities and assignments!

E-Learning Readiness Self-Assessment

Self-assessments are valuable tools that we can use in developing learning skills and study habits for college success. Take a few minutes now to complete the E-Learning Readiness Self-Assessment starting on the next page.[1] The E-Learning Readiness Self-Assessment will provide you with individual feedback on your readiness to be successful in online course assignments and activities, helping guide your path as you develop necessary skills and habits. This individualized feedback can also be useful in determining how to use this book and where you should focus additional time and energy in developing necessary skills for success.

After completing the E-Learning Readiness Self-Assessment, follow the guidelines provided at the end of the assessment for scoring and interpreting the results; make special note of those chapters which may require that you spend some additional time and energy studying the strategies and suggestions provided in this book. By using the Self-Assessment as a guide to your development of online study skills, you will better be able to build on your prior experiences in order to improve your online proficiencies.

🌐 An online version of the E-Learning Readiness Self-Assessment is also available on the *E-Learning Companion* Premium Website (http://www.cengage.com/success/Watkins/ELearning3e).

Introduction

For each item in the assessment, indicate your agreement with the statement by circling the corresponding value. For each category of statements, calculate your average response by dividing the total value of your responses by the number of items. When you have calculated your average response for each category, complete the interpretation table provided at the end of the Self-Assessment.

1 = Completely disagree

2 = Strongly disagree

3 = Not sure

4 = Strongly agree

5 = Completely agree

TECHNOLOGY ACCESS AND PROTECTION

I have access to a computer with an Internet connection.	**1 2 3 4 5**
I have access to a fairly new computer (for example, 1 Gig or more of RAM, speakers, CD-ROM).	**1 2 3 4 5**
I have access to a computer with adequate software (for example, Microsoft Word 2007 or newer, Adobe Acrobat 6.0 or newer).	**1 2 3 4 5**
I have access to a computer with up-to-date antivirus protection software (for example, McAfee, Symantec/Norton, AVG).	**1 2 3 4 5**
I can update my computer's antivirus protection software (for example, McAfee, Symantec/Norton, AVG).	**1 2 3 4 5**
Average response (total ÷ 5)	

TECHNOLOGY SKILLS

I have the basic skills to operate a computer (for example, saving files, creating folders).	**1 2 3 4 5**
I have the basic skills for finding my way around the Internet (for example, using search engines, entering passwords).	**1 2 3 4 5**
I can download software and software updates to my computer from the Internet.	**1 2 3 4 5**
I have the skills to upload files to the Internet.	**1 2 3 4 5**
I can copy-and-paste text between files or Internet websites.	**1 2 3 4 5**
I can send an email with a file attached.	**1 2 3 4 5**
I am comfortable evaluating the reliability, quality, and usefulness of online resources.	**1 2 3 4 5**
I think that I would be comfortable using a computer several times a week to participate in a course.	**1 2 3 4 5**
Average response (total ÷ 8)	

ONLINE RELATIONSHIPS

I think that I would be able to communicate effectively with others using online technologies (for example, email, chat, instant message).	**1 2 3 4 5**
I think that I would be able to express myself clearly through my writing (for example, precision, mood, emotions, humor).	**1 2 3 4 5**
I think that I would be able to use online tools (for example, email, chat, Google Docs) to work on assignments with students who are in different time zones.	**1 2 3 4 5**
I think that I would be able to schedule time to provide timely responses to other students and/or the instructor.	**1 2 3 4 5**
I think that I would be able to write clearly in order to ask questions and make comments.	**1 2 3 4 5**
Average response (total ÷ 5)	

MOTIVATION

I think that I would be able to remain motivated even though the instructor is not online at all times.	**1 2 3 4 5**
I think that I would be able to complete my work even when there are online distractions (for example, friends sending emails, Facebook messages, YouTube videos).	**1 2 3 4 5**
I think that I would be able to complete my work even when there are distractions in my home (for example, television, children, roommates).	**1 2 3 4 5**
Average response (total ÷ 3)	

ONLINE VIDEO/AUDIO

I have watched online video clips in the past.	**1 2 3 4 5**
I think that I would be able to relate the content of short video clips (1–3 minutes typically) to the information that I have read online or in books.	**1 2 3 4 5**
I think that I would be able to take notes while watching a (1- to 3-minute) video on the computer.	**1 2 3 4 5**
I think that I would be able to understand course-related information when it's presented in video formats.	**1 2 3 4 5**
I can download music, MP3, podcast, or other audio files to play on my computer, Apple iPod, or MP3 music player.	**1 2 3 4 5**
Average response (total ÷ 5)	

ONLINE DISCUSSIONS

I can send and receive email messages.	**1 2 3 4 5**
I think that I would be able to carry on a conversation with others using the Internet (for example, Internet chat, instant messaging).	**1 2 3 4 5**
I think that I would be comfortable having several discussions taking place in the same online chat even though I may not be participating in all of them.	**1 2 3 4 5**
I think that I would be able to follow along with an online conversation (for example, Internet chat, instant messaging) while typing.	**1 2 3 4 5**
I sometimes prefer to have more time to prepare responses to a question.	**1 2 3 4 5**
I would be comfortable posting my questions and comments to a discussion board for later responses from other students and the instructor.	**1 2 3 4 5**
Average response (total ÷ 6)	

IMPORTANCE TO YOUR SUCCESS

Regular contact with the instructor is important to my success in online coursework.	**1 2 3 4 5**
Quick technical and administrative support is important to my success in online coursework.	**1 2 3 4 5**
Frequent participation throughout the learning process is important to my success in online coursework.	**1 2 3 4 5**
I feel that prior experiences with online technologies (for example, email, Internet chat, online readings) are important to my success with online course.	**1 2 3 4 5**
The ability to immediately apply course materials is important to my success with online courses.	**1 2 3 4 5**
Average response (total ÷ 5)	

Scoring and Interpretation

After completing the E-Learning Readiness Self-Assessment, calculate your average response for each section of the assessment. This is calculated by dividing the total (that is, sum) of each section by the number of items included in that section. Based on your average score in each section of the Self-Assessment, there may be particular chapters of this book where you should focus more of your time and attention (see the table on the next page).

Relating Self-Assessment Results to Chapters in the *E-Learning Companion*

YOUR AVERAGE	SECTION OF SELF-ASSESSMENT	FOCUS CHAPTER(S)
_____	Technology Access	Chapter 6, How-To Tutorials, and Quick Reference Guide
_____	Technology Skills	Chapter 3, How-To Tutorials, and Quick Reference Guide
_____	Online Relationships	Chapter 5 and Quick Reference Guide
_____	Motivation	Chapters 1, 5, and 7
_____	Online Video/Audio	Chapter 3, How-To Tutorials, and Quick Reference Guide
_____	Internet Discussions	Chapters 3, 5, How-To Tutorials, and Quick Reference Guide
_____	Importance to Your Success	Chapters 1, 2, and 5

We recommend that for any section of the Self-Assessment in which your average response score was a 3 or below, you would benefit from spending additional time studying the strategies and suggestions provided in the related chapters of this book.

In addition, students frequently benefit from creating a study plan for how they are going to improve their e-learning study skills based on the results of their self-assessment. Include in your plan the specific actions you will take to improve your study skills. For example, if your lowest average score was for items related to Motivation, then include in your study plan for the next two weeks to (a) read chapters 5 and 7, (b) complete all of the activities in Chapters 5 and 7, and (c) search the Internet for additional recommendations on how to increase (or maintain) your motivation throughout the semester. Create a plan that is based on your self-assessment results, has defined deadlines, and includes explicit activities that you will complete.

When you have completed your initial reading of the learning skills and study habits discussed throughout this book, we suggest that you again complete the E-Learning Readiness Self-Assessment to evaluate your progress and to help you further develop strategies for strengthening the skills necessary for success in online college coursework.

Note

1. Based in part on Watkins (2003) and Watkins, Leigh, and Triner (2004).

1 Selecting the Right Opportunities for Success Online

STAY FOCUSED

By the end of this chapter, you will be able to

- *Evaluate* your preparedness for e-learning success.
- *Identify* ways to integrate your e-learning activities with your personal, work, and academic commitments.
- *Create* a plan for fitting e-learning into your schedule.

Most of us enjoy movies that take us on a journey with someone who struggles to overcome obstacles or challenges in pursuit of goals and ambitions. Some of the stories are of athletes who were challenged by the prejudices of society, and others are about writers who struggle with the inner obstacles of adding meaning to their words. But it is neither the character nor the context of the story that is most often central to providing us with inspiration. It is the struggle, the struggle to overcome the obstacles that others and we have placed in our path toward success. Success in your college courses is no different; you must overcome challenges, from technology problems to study group members who do not pull their weight, to achieve your goals.

Even though the journey to success in college is filled with many challenges for all students, to be a successful student you don't necessarily have to overcome as many obstacles as you might think. For most of us, through our decisions, we frequently make the path of success much more of a challenge than it has to be, whereas successful students make decisions to ensure that the path toward success in school is not made more difficult by obstacles that they can control.

Often we try to do too much, and regularly each of us selects the wrong opportunities, or we select the right opportunities but at the wrong times. No matter the circumstances or the reasons, throughout the *E-Learning Companion,* we will focus our attention on making decisions that will provide us with the best opportunities for being successful in our studies.

1

Increasing the Odds of Your Success

Too often in life, we put ourselves in situations where the odds of being successful are not in our favor. We do this by taking too many courses in a given semester, by enrolling in courses for which we have not mastered the prerequisite skills, by signing up for more than one challenging course in the same semester, or by committing to many outside activities in the weeks leading up to final exams; the list could go on for pages.

There are few opportunities in college (or life) where success is guaranteed, so each of us must learn to play the odds. We will want to make decisions that put us in situations where all the support necessary for our success is in place. Although there will be obstacles to our success, we can make decisions that minimize the barriers and increase our chances of achieving our academic goals.

E-Learning Experiences

It wasn't until my junior year in college that the importance of selecting the right opportunities became very clear to me. At most universities and in most majors, students commonly agree that a particular course (often with a particular professor) is used to "weed out" those students who are destined to graduate in the major from those who will have to search elsewhere for a career. For my major, that course was calculus, and passing calculus was one of my barriers to success.

Given my course of studies within my major, I had mistakenly decided, without the input of my academic advisor, to enroll in calculus during the fall semester of my junior year. Now to me, this seemed like a great time to take this course, which I knew would be a challenge; after all, I had already passed a few other courses in my major. But when you go to a university with a top football program and each weekend brings family and friends to town for the games, the fall semester is not the best time to take your most challenging courses. By the fourth week of the semester, our football team was on a winning streak, but I was falling behind in my studies as fast as they scored touchdowns. At the end of the semester, my less-than-ideal study habits were matched by my less-than-passing grade. Though I did go on to pass calculus the following semester, the lesson I learned about taking courses when you are most likely to succeed has stayed with me much longer than any of the mathematical formulas.

Now for you, the distractions of college life may not be related to athletics, and they may not be confined to a single semester. For each of us, however, there are always many distractions that can lead us away from success in our courses. Making decisions about what opportunities to take and when, however, will be essential in your success in college. Courses that require online study, whether for a completely online course or for additional activities in an on-campus course, require the same careful analysis as any other college course. Don't be fooled; just because you have the opportunity to complete some or all of your assignments using online tools doesn't necessarily mean that the course will require any less time, concentration, or effort.

We want to avoid anything less than success whenever possible. As a result, we will work on making better decisions about what courses to take and when, and balancing our academic, personal, and work commitments. This way we can enter each semester with the best possible odds at being successful.

In selecting the opportunities that offer you the best prospects for success, you want to consider not only the amount of time a course requires, but also the timing of the course with your other obligations. It is essential for success to keep these two elements of your time in balance. Nonetheless, we often only think of the first. Being able to negotiate stability across these two elements of time is typically the critical factor determining a student's success.

Be Realistic with Your Time

The time necessary to complete the requirements of online **coursework** (for example, class time, time working on assignments, time discussing topics with the instructor and other students, and time studying for exams) will be roughly equal to the time that you would spend on traditional classroom assignments and activities. But when and where you will spend that time will likely be dramatically different.

In the conventional course, the majority of the discussion concerning course topics and concepts takes place two or three times a week in the lecture hall, lab, or classroom. However, with online coursework, it is more typical that you will be expected to discuss the course materials in small chunks of time throughout each week of the semester. This often means that you will be online posting messages and responding to **emails** every day, or every other day, throughout the semester.

Of course, you may be online for only a few minutes each day. Yet by the end of the semester, you will have spent approximately the same amount of course time as you would in a traditional classroom course. Although this may sound like a small change with little impact on your study habits, the shift from concentrating on a particular course for an hour on Tuesday and Thursday afternoons to being actively involved in class discussions each day of the week for the entire semester can be a major obstacle to success.

Although online courses and coursework will typically require about the same amount of your time as a conventional classroom course, the flexibility of online coursework does offer many advantages (and some disadvantages) that should be considered when selecting the courses in which you are most likely to be successful.

For example, if you are planning to take an overload (typically, more than 12 to 15 credit hours in a given semester) and also participate in extracurricular activities (a theater production, fraternity or sorority events, intramural athletics, and so on), then the flexibility of a course that offers opportunities for the <u>coursework</u> to be done online could be to your advantage. However, if you already have trouble staying on task and maintaining your motivation throughout the semester, then the flexibility of online <u>coursework</u> may be dangerous because there is often no set schedule for you to follow as there is in conventional classroom courses.

There is, unfortunately, no easy formula to give you for determining whether or not you have the time for successfully completing all the requirements of any college course. Throughout this book, we will, however, provide you with several tools for assessing your unique situation and selecting the opportunities that offer you the best odds for being successful.

Review Distance-Learning Options

The use of technology to enhance your college education is not limited to the **Internet** and other online offerings. Distance-learning courses and programs commonly use a variety of e-learning technologies to support your education.

A Little History: Carnegie Units

So how do colleges and universities decide on how much time you should spend studying for each of your courses? Here is a little background information that can help explain. In 1909, while defining what constitutes a course in order to assess college professor pensions, the Carnegie Foundation for the Advancement of Teaching established a standardized measure of academic equivalency. This definition established a measurement of work based on time in the classroom. According to the board's definition, a standard of 750 minutes with a qualified instructor was equivalent to 1 hour of academic credit, or a Carnegie unit. This unit of measurement has since become a standard throughout American education and is the reason why the typical 3-credit-hour on-campus course meets three times a week for 50 minutes each time, over a semester of approximately 15 weeks. This gives students 2,250 minutes of time with a qualified instructor for each 3-credit-hour course.

Of course, professors typically add to this the expectation that you will study 2 to 3 hours on your own for each hour you spend in the classroom, thereby requiring roughly 4,500–6,750 minutes (or 75–112 hours) of studying for each 3-credit-hour course. In courses requiring online <u>coursework</u>, however, you won't typically interact with the instructor or other students during three prescribed time periods in each week. Rather, many of your 75–112 hours will be spent watching, listening to, or reading lecture materials provided by the instructor; discussing course topics with other students online; completing online activities; and/or doing other course assignments that can be facilitated using online technologies.

ACTIVITY 1-1   Analyze Your Time

🌐 Complete the following table based on your experiences in the last 6 months. Although there are no *correct* answers to the questions, by examining your response to each question, you can evaluate the effectiveness of your current study habits as you develop new learning skills for online <u>coursework</u>.

	NEVER	SOME OF THE TIME	MOST OF THE TIME	ALWAYS
1. Do you keep up with course readings even when there are no required deadlines, quizzes, or assignments?				
2. Do you say "no" to friends when you have <u>coursework</u> to be done?				
3. Do you study effectively after 10:00 P.M.?				
4. Do you have time set aside each day (outside of class) for your studies?				
5. Do you typically procrastinate on completing <u>coursework</u> until the day before it is due?				
6. Do your friends and family support your efforts to be successful in your courses?				
7. Do your friends and family keep you so busy on weekends that you don't have time to study?				
8. Do you schedule your personal commitments around your course commitments?				
9. Do you plan to study and then find other things to do?				
10. Do you often feel like you have committed yourself to too many activities?				

You should identify and assess all available distance-learning options. This will increase the likelihood of finding the right match between your expectations and the offered learning opportunities.

Online

Given the number and variety of online communications tools available with <u>Internet</u> tools, online distance learning has become a popular course delivery option. Adequate access to the <u>Internet</u> is necessary for this format of e-learning, but the growth of <u>Internet</u> access in recent years has made online learning an option for many students.

CD-ROM or DVD

Many topics do not require **synchronous** (real-time) communications between students and instructors in order to provide valuable learning opportunities. If you believe that this may be the case for your learning interest, then you should search for CD-ROM/DVD learning opportunities. After all, these may offer additional flexibility to your schedule and accomplish the same learning goals as other e-learning options.

Telecourse

Video-based courses (whether using satellite, <u>Internet</u>, or cable transmissions) offer students and instructors the opportunity to interact in a <u>synchronous</u> classroom environment. These interactions are valuable in accomplishing learning objectives and may be preferred by many students and instructors. Telecourses do, however, require access to video-conference equipment and do not offer the flexibility in scheduling as other e-learning options.

Hybrids

Generally, no single e-learning technology (for example, online, telecourse, or DVD) can provide all the characteristics that students and instructors require to create a successful learning experience. As a result, many colleges and professors are using a combination of e-learning technologies to deliver an array of learning opportunities to students. These courses will often use some combination of online, classroom, telecourse, CD-ROM/DVD, and other e-learning technologies in order to find an adequate balance between achieving the learning goals and offering students the flexibility necessary for their situation.

Consider the Timing

Closely related to assessing whether there is enough time in your day to complete all requirements for your courses is comparing the timing of your college courses to that of your other commitments. For each of us, there are a variety of events that add meaning to our lives beyond the boundaries of our studies (for example, artistic expressions, music, and athletics). Yet their impact on your success in school, both positive and negative, cannot be underestimated. In deciding on the best opportunities for your success, you will want to consider the timing of courses (as well as specific activities, assignments, projects, exams, and so forth) in relation to these other events.

Developing a timeline of courses that you plan to enroll in over the next two to three semesters is an essential step for comparing the timing of courses. Based on the requirements for graduation at your college or university (and the advice of your academic advisor and other successful students), you should create a list of what courses you plan to take in future semesters. In making the timeline, be sure to consider which courses should be taken during the same semester, any prerequisite requirements, and what outside events that may distract you from your studies. Also include any other personal variables that you may consider important.

The idea behind viewing your schedule of courses over several semesters is to negotiate a balance of commitments between your studies, friends, family, work, and other obligations each semester. For example, if you are interested in auditioning for a college theater production of *Hamlet* in the spring, it may not be an ideal time to also enroll in two of the more difficult courses required for your major. Maybe one of the more challenging courses can be taken the following summer. You can also add some flexibility to your schedule for the spring semester by taking an elective course that meets only once a week and that uses online technologies for the other <u>coursework</u> requirements.

Planning in advance can help ensure that you are selecting the course opportunities where you are most likely to be successful. Knowing your commitments and your ability to manage (that is, balance or negotiate) your commitments will be essential. Two primary categories of commitments that you likely have in addition to your academic commitments are work commitments and personal commitments. Both of these will have substantial influence on selecting the right opportunities for your success in college.

Balance Your Academic and Work Commitments

For most students, the increasing cost of a college education requires the negotiating of course demands with the commitment to work full or part time.[1] For many students, it is this requirement for flexibility in scheduling around work commitments that persuades them to look for courses that either use online technologies to supplement the classroom experiences or even to investigate courses that are offered completely online. Without this flexibility, in fact, a college education would be beyond the reach of many college/university students.

In selecting the opportunities that offer the greatest likelihood of success, one of the major variables that you should consider is the balancing of your educational and work commitments. Depending on your specific situation, you may or may not have these competing demands on your time, but whatever your situation, the competing requirements for your time and attention do not have to be a barrier to success. By understanding the conflicting demands for your time, you can make a decision that puts you in the best possible situation to be successful.

A few of the variables that you will want to identify and consider in planning your course of studies include the following:

- ☐ Does your work schedule remain the same throughout the semester?
- ☐ When during the semester will your courses require the most attention (for example, midterms, finals, major assignments)?

☐ Do you have access to the <u>Internet</u> at work?

☐ Can you complete online <u>coursework</u> at your workplace when you have completed your work requirements?

☐ How can online activities and assignments that add flexibility to your course demands be used to ensure that you can meet your work commitments?

☐ How many hours will you have committed to work and school if you add together the time required for studying and the number of hours you are planning to work?

☐ Knowing your past success and study habits, is it realistic to attempt to study and work each week throughout the semester?

Clearly, you may not have all the information for answering each of these questions at this time. But by taking the time to talk with instructors of the courses that you are considering for next semester, along with your employer, you can make better informed decisions and increase the likelihood of your success.

Balance Your Academic and Personal Commitments

Because you are a college student, a primary distracter from your studies will more than likely be your many personal commitments. Whether they are plans for a ski vacation with friends, dinner with co-workers, or a sorority/fraternity social event, the personal commitments to friends and family will take time away from studies throughout any semester. Although these social activities are important to your success in college, they too must be balanced with the requirements of your <u>coursework</u>.

In negotiating your study times with your other personal obligations, the flexibility and individual control of online <u>coursework</u> will likely be attractive, although the total number of hours spent studying for each course should be about the same as a traditional course. The advantages (and disadvantages) that are inherent with individual control and flexibility should also be considered as you select the right courses and extracurricular opportunities for a successful college experience. Finding this equilibrium does nevertheless require that you carefully assess your learning skills and study habits. Without knowing your strengths and weaknesses, making decisions about how to manage your time in college is next to impossible.

> **STUDENT-TO-STUDENT TIP**
>
> Set a specific time at least three to four days a week to do your regular communications such as **discussion board**s, <u>emails</u>, and **instant messaging.**

ACTIVITY 1-2 **Plan with Your Commitments in Mind**

🌐 Complete the following table for the next three semesters with the best estimates that you can make at this time.

COMMITMENTS	ACADEMIC (COURSE HOURS/WEEK)	PERSONAL (HOURS/WEEK)	WORK (HOURS/WEEK)
Fall			
Spring			
Summer			

Get Your Feet Wet: Take an Online Course of Personal Interest

Today there are a variety of <u>Internet</u> sites that offer a diverse array of online learning experiences that you can participate in for free. From wine tasting to the chemistry of the human brain, these free courses can provide you with an assortment of experiences while allowing you to develop some basic learning skills and study habits for being successful in online <u>coursework</u>. At the same time, they can help you assess your readiness for further courses that use online technologies. Typically, these courses are short (5 to 6 weeks) and can be taken at a variety of times throughout the year, including summer.

www.cengage.com/success/Watkins/ELearning3e

By building on your experiences with online technologies outside the classroom, you can be better equipped for success when your college course requires that you use technology. Online sources for free courses include the following:

http://www.free-ed.net

http://u.about.com/

http://www.newsu.org

http://www.hp.com/go/learningcenter

http://www.word2word.com/course.html

http://www.docnmail.com

http://www.fathom.com

Review Prerequisite Requirements

Most college and university courses will require that you have a range of prerequisite skills and knowledge. These requirements are typically identified by the instructor in the course syllabus and are often included as a component of the course registration system. Prerequisite requirements, both those related to previous courses as well as technical skills, should be considered when making your decision about what courses to take and when to take them (for example, having mastered college algebra requirements prior to taking chemistry or being able to send <u>email</u> with an **attachment** prior to taking a course that uses online technology).

Prerequisite requirements are selected by professors to help students gauge their preparedness for success in a college course; therefore you will want to check the prerequisite requirements for any course in which you are considering enrolling (especially those courses that may require that you use online technology). Not having even one of the required skills greatly reduces the likelihood of your success. Particularly for courses in your major, you will want to contact the professor prior to enrolling in the course to ensure that you have met the prerequisite requirements.

STUDENT-TO-STUDENT TIP

Making sure that you are grounded in the prerequisites is absolutely essential to having an enjoyable and successful experience. Once the prerequisites are satisfied, you can concentrate all your efforts on the task at hand versus having to expend extra energy in getting prepared for the learning experience.

Verify Your Support Services

Although success in college rests primarily on your shoulders, without adequate support services from the institution, achieving your goals will be much more difficult than it has to be. From offering librarians who work with students online to technology support and financial aid, the support systems of the institution should be examined carefully to ensure that you are making the best use of the resources available to you.

College Computer Labs

Most colleges provide computer labs that are available to students. On many campuses, different computers feature specialized **software** for students who most often use that particular lab. For example, a computer lab located near the statistics department will commonly feature specialized <u>software</u> for making statistical calculations, whereas a computer lab in the main campus library may only provide access to a limited range of <u>software</u> applications used for searching databases and locating resources. Campus computer labs will also routinely offer differing hours of operations, some being open 24 hours a day while others close in the early evening. You should become familiar with the variety of computer labs available to you as a student and verify the <u>software</u> available in each lab that you may use throughout the semester. The technical support provided at most computer labs is limited, though the staff is often more than willing, to the best of their ability, to help you resolve any technology problems you may have.

Online Library Services

Colleges and universities today typically offer a range of online services through their libraries. These services are designed to help you manage your time and get the most from the library resources. You will most likely have to contact your institution's library to find out the range of services available, though descriptions of the services are often available on the **World Wide Web** or through your dormitory.

Services available without having to go on campus typically include online searchable databases for identifying resources without leaving your apartment or dorm, as well as completely online journals, newspapers, and magazines. All the resources that you may require in college will not be available online; you will still have to go to the library. Many libraries offer orientation sessions for students where an information specialist will help you identify and use both the online and on-campus library services.

Technical Support

Your college or university will commonly offer a variety of technology support services that you should take advantage of while registered as a student (also discussed in Chapter 3). From helping you troubleshoot why your <u>email</u> account is not working to providing you with access to virus scan <u>software</u>, most institutions

STUDENT-TO-STUDENT TIP

Being able to contact the institution for assistance and support on any problems that come up can make all the difference, leading to a positive learning experience and success.

typically offer many technology support services to students. When taking a course that requires use of online tools (for example, **chat** rooms, <u>discussion boards</u>, and online readings), the likelihood of the availability of these services goes up. Because these services are typically included in your tuition, you should not look for outside technical support that may cost you hundreds of dollars.

When you first enroll in a course that uses technology, you should contact the college or university technology support services to identify all resources available to you. Make a list of essential phone numbers, email addresses, **website**s, and office hours that you can keep next to your computer. When a technology crisis happens, the last thing you want to spend your time doing is chasing down the phone number of the right person to contact.

Student Training Courses

As a student, you may be able to enroll in many of the training courses offered by the college. These courses will typically provide you with foundational skills for using specific <u>software</u> programs (such as Microsoft Word or Microsoft Excel) and are often as short as 2 to 3 hours. These training courses can provide you with an excellent opportunity to practice many of the skills that you will later be required to use in completing your online <u>coursework</u>. It is often worth your time to contact your college's technical support services to see what training courses are available and when.

Career Counseling

Many institutions now offer both on-campus and online career-counseling services. From conducting job searches to getting feedback on your résumé, these support services are often very useful (yet underutilized). By visiting the career-counseling center <u>website</u>, which most college and universities now have available, you should be able to identify the spectrum of services available to you as a student.

Financial Aid

As the price of a college education has increased, financial assistance has become a common requirement for most students. Though applying for and receiving financial assistance may still require your presence on campus, many institutions now offer some limited services through the <u>Internet</u> or automated phone systems. Before going to the financial aid office at your institution, it is likely worth your time to first visit its <u>Internet</u> site or call the office on the phone, to determine what timesaving services they may now offer through technology.

Special-Needs Accommodations

Accommodating the requirements of special-needs students is required under federal law for colleges and universities. These accommodations are not, however, limited to the conventional classroom. Online resources must also meet a standard for accessibility for special-needs students (including

---

ACTIVITY 1-3   **Did this Section Click?**

⊕ As a review, answer the following questions by circling T (true) or F (false) for each statement.

1. T F   Colleges are required by law to provide special accommodations for disabled students even when courses are delivered using online technologies.

2. T F   When doing research for course assignments and activities, you should always start by going to the on-campus library.

3. T F   The prerequisite skill requirements for a course provide guidelines on what you should be able to do before enrolling in that course.

4. T F   Online databases available through most college libraries have access to online full-text copies of all journals available at the campus library.

5. T F   Enrolling in courses where you are most likely to be successful requires more than just knowing which courses are being offered for the upcoming semester.

---

accommodations for sight and/or hearing impairments, learning disabilities, and other factors that may add to the burden of the student). Your college or university will be able to provide you with specific guidelines for applying for accommodations and ensuring that you are aware of the services available to you as a student.

Writing and Mathematics Labs

Support for students taking writing and mathematics courses is a standard support service provided at most institutions. Today, these services will typically provide you with a range of support including technology support on using <u>software</u> that is required for <u>coursework</u>. Although less common than other support services, many institutions now offer some online services through their writing and mathematics labs. From reviews of draft term papers to answering questions about college algebra, these services can be useful to students when there is no time to visit the offices on campus. Because these services are typically limited, you should contact the writing and math labs at your institution to identify what types of support are available.

Summary

Success in college requires that you choose your opportunities wisely. When planning for college experiences and scheduling courses each semester, you will want to consider a variety of factors that may impact the likelihood of your success. From personal commitments that may interfere with your study times to prerequisite skill requirements outlined by the instructor, selecting only the right opportunities for your success is a critical skill for college students.

Chapter 1 Exercise

To begin the exercise, you will want to access to the World Wide Web, using a **Web browser** (such as Netscape Navigator or Microsoft Internet Explorer).

> **STEP 1:** Identify and locate the **Web portal** for information regarding the services of your college or university. This is not typically the **educational portal** where you would find links to **real-time chats**, discussion boards, and course syllabi, but rather the website where you can locate information on the academic degree programs, faculty and staff, the library, and other support services provided to students.

> **STEP 2:** Locate and select the link to the **webpage** for the college's library. When you have identified the webpage for the college's library, determine the appropriate librarian (or library services department) who should be contacted with regards to the online services offered by the library.

> **STEP 3:** Contact, by email or phone, the librarian (or library services department) who provides the online services offered by the library. In your email (or phone call), request information on online tutorials, as well as any on-campus training that is available from the library on using the online library resources.

> **STEP 4:** Locate and select the link to the webpage for the college's *student technical support services*. When you have identified the webpage for the college's technical support for students, determine the appropriate department that should be contacted to access this support (for example, a student help desk).

> **STEP 5:** Contact, by email or phone, the department that provides technical support for students. In your email (or phone call), request information on online tutorials, on-campus training, hotline phone numbers, and other resources available for students from technical support.

Did You Stay Focused?

After completing this chapter, you should be able to do the following. If there are tasks below that you cannot do, take a few minutes to review the chapter, focusing on those areas that you may have missed the first time through.

☐ I have *created* a timeline of courses that I plan to enroll in for at least the next two to three semesters, based on the college or university requirements for graduation.

☐ I have *created* a list of my personal commitments that will have impact on my time for studying.

☐ I have *evaluated* my work commitments in selecting only those course opportunities where I have the best odds of being successful.

☐ I have *identified* at least two activities each week that can be *integrated* with other commitments in order to reduce the demands on my time.

☐ I have *identified* and contacted the library, technology, and other support services available at my college or university.

☐ I have *completed* the chapter activities.

Additional Resources

⊕ Additional resources on topics covered in this chapter are available at the Premium Website for the *E-Learning Companion*.

Note

1. See http://nces.ed.gov/pubs98/condition98/c9852a01.html.

2 Create a Plan for Online Success

STAY FOCUSED

By the end of this chapter, you will be able to
- *Evaluate* your time management skills and preparations.
- *Create* a plan for balancing your many commitments.
- *Set* goals that will guide you to success in college.
- *Manage* your time more effectively.

Roger Maris, a famous baseball player, once said, "You win not by chance, but by preparation."[1] The same is true for success in college; you succeed not by chance but by preparation. Planning for success is a significant step toward accomplishing your goals in your college courses. From visualizing your achievements to scheduling your time and creating a helpful studying environment, planning is much more than just stating that you want to be successful.

You must follow through with your plans to accomplish the results that you want to achieve. Merely developing plans will not be enough to ensure your success. Acting upon your plans is what moves good intentions to positive achievements.

Whether in the traditional classroom or in the online classroom, creating and following through on your plans will lead you to the success that you want to have in your college courses. Although this may sound fairly simple and straightforward, unfortunately, it is not for most of us. In this chapter, we discuss many strategies, tips, tools, techniques, suggestions, and recommendations for setting goals that you can accomplish, making plans that will lead to success, creating environments that support your success, and achieving your goals by following through with your plans.

Planning for Online Success

The flexibility of college courses that use online technologies can be a double-edged sword for most students. The opportunities to complete assignments or activities at times that are convenient for you can be misleading, swaying you to procrastinate or encouraging you to attempt the course without a well-thought-out plan for your success. As a result, the importance of planning for success is by no means diminished when you have the opportunity to complete your <u>coursework</u> using online tools.

You must not only set out a clear plan of activities that will lead to your eventual success in the course but also ensure that you keep to your plans. From setting time aside each day for accessing online materials to creating a study environment with few distractions, all during the course you should stick to your plans for success. As you find out more about the course requirements, the requirements of individual instructors, the goals of your fellow students, and even your preferred study habits, you will likely want to alter your plans somewhat. Always, however, remain true to your initial decisions regarding your plans for being successful in your studies.

Developing and revising your plans for success with regards to any online <u>coursework</u> involves just a few minutes each week. Starting on the first day of the course, you will want to define a clear statement of what you want to accomplish. This includes not just the grade that you want to receive but also the knowledge and skills that you would like to have when the course is complete. It could be to gain such specific skills as mastering the calculations required for algebra or creating a short story that will hopefully be published someday.

No matter the specific goals that you may set, by planning for success you can make an initial estimate of how much time the course requires, what types of study environments are best to ensure that you reach your goals, and how to balance your academic, work, and personal commitments. Making these and other decisions will be essential to your success. From this initial assessment, you will conceive a plan that outlines the major steps to be taken to accomplish your goals for the course.

Yet no matter how good the plan created, many times during a course each of us will likely want to depart from our plans; maintaining good study habits can be difficult as other interesting distractions come our way. Athletic events, homecoming events, trips home to visit family and friends—all will compete for your attention. But by staying with your initial plans, you have the best opportunities for success in the course and can establish habits that will ensure your success in later endeavors as well.

Short-Term and Long-Term Goals

Achieving success in college requires that you can both visualize and plan for your success in the long term as well as the short term. By linking together what is required for long-term success (in this instance, the goals that you have set with regard to your performance throughout your college experience) and the more immediate requirements (such as which assignments must be completed today), you will ensure that you have a holistic plan capable of guiding you on the path toward success.

However, neither long-term nor short-term planning in isolation from the other is effective. Long-term plans that do not define what must be accomplished today and throughout the week are inadequate because long-standing achievements, like your success in college, are built on a foundation of interim accomplishments (such as getting an A on your creative writing assignment). Likewise, short-term plans alone are ineffectual since they do not have the means to continuously support the motivation required during semester long courses (let alone 2- or 4-year degree programs). Only by establishing an integrated plan that includes short-term and long-term plans can you better ensure your success.

Plan for Success in College

Although a college education is merely a steppingstone toward many lifelong ambitions, to keep our focus in this book, we will limit our vision of long-term success to your college experience. This long-term perspective of what is required for you to be satisfied with your performance in college will establish the standard for the personal expectations and goals that you set each semester.

Planning for success in college requires that you first define what it will take for you to consider yourself successful at the end of your college experience. For many, graduation will define *success,* whereas for others their grade point average (GPA) within their major may be at the heart of what they consider success. Leaving college with a high-paying job may be part of your definition, as well as acceptance into graduate school. No matter how you define *success,* you should take the time now to write down on paper your definition of *success.* Merely the act of writing down what it will take for you to consider yourself successful will greatly improve the odds that your vision will be realized.

Plan for Success this Semester

Success in college typically has as its foundation your accomplishments across several semesters. Not meeting your aspirations during one or more semesters can greatly reduce the chances of meeting your overall goals for college. For example, it is much more difficult to improve a low GPA from your first year in college than it is to damage a higher GPA once it is established. For that reason, you will want to plan for your success semester by semester, course by course, setting goals for each semester that will lead to your long-term success in college.

Plan for Success this Week

While plans for success at the semester level will provide more details than you had when you defined *success in college,* the comprehensive plans for being successful in the weekly assignments and activities of your courses are crucial if long-term goals are to be realized. Creating and following through on weekly plans will help you not only align your short-term and long-term planning but also manage your time, keep track of course assignments, evaluate your course performance, schedule events with other students, plan your daily tasks, and even find time to relax.

Unlike the long-term plans that you have set for the semester and throughout college, your weekly plans will likely require more frequent revisions. For example, imagine that one goal for this week is to collect four journal articles as references for a sociology paper. However, after searching your college or university's online databases, you realize that the articles you want will require that you go to an off-campus library. Revising your weekly plan (as well as your daily plans) will be necessary because you won't be able to complete this research until next week. Revising weekly plans is common, and as long as you keep the weekly plans aligned with semester and daily plans, you should be on target to accomplish your long-term goals.

Plan for Success Today

Daily planning is at the core of the short-term successes that lead to long-term accomplishments. Each day you will want to determine what goals you must achieve to provide a foundation for weekly and semester accomplishments. You will want to write down a daily list of tasks that you should complete and goals that you want to accomplish. Each morning you should create your list, and each evening you should review your list to evaluate your success. By evaluating and tracking your progress daily, you can better ensure that your daily accomplishments lead to your weekly, semester, and long-term success in college.

STUDENT-TO-STUDENT TIP

Set up a class calendar; I did one in Microsoft Excel with all the assignments and their due dates, as well as some commitments I had for work and in my personal life. Using the calendar helped me plan how I was going to accomplish my goal of success in the class and still meet my other obligations.

ACTIVITY 2-1 **Daily To-Do List**

🌐 Complete a table like the following, with to-do lists for each day of the upcoming week. Each day should have at least three activities, which can be academic, personal, or work-related.

To-Do List

SUNDAY	MONDAY	TUESDAY	WEDNESDAY	THURSDAY	FRIDAY	SATURDAY
1.	1.	1.	1.	1.	1.	1.
2.	2.	2.	2.	2.	2.	2.
3.	3.	3.	3.	3.	3.	3.

Setting Realistic Expectations of Online Coursework

Establishing realistic expectations of online coursework can provide a practical foundation for planning your success. The preconceived ideas that you may have about online technologies and online learning (for example, the quality of instructional materials, the amount of interaction with the instructor and other students, or the value of online readings) will often define how you participate in online coursework as well as affect your achievements in the online class-room. Yet, for better or for worse, most of these *accepted wisdoms* about online coursework are not based on the realities of the course or courses that you are currently taking. Because each course at each college or university will use online technologies in its own unique way, you should build your expectations based on what you know about the current course. Although finding accurate information about what you should expect with regard to the use of online technologies within your particular course may not be easy to uncover, you should start your search by asking the course instructor.

Here are a few questions that you may want to ask your instructor in order to better define your expectations about online coursework in the class:

☐   Will I be expected to participate in a synchronous chat each week?

☐   Will the number and quality of postings that you make to the discussion board determine my participation grade?

☐   Do you require online readings or traditional textbooks or both?

☐   What types of online support services are offered by the college or university?

☐   Should I expect to receive replies from you to my emails within 24 hours?

☐   Will there be a requirement for online group activities in the course?

☐   How does student performance in online coursework compare with student performance in on-campus coursework provided by the instructor?

☐   What suggestions do you have for being successful in the online coursework?

Common Misconceptions of Online Coursework

Nevertheless, most of us will enroll in courses with several mistaken ideas about what an online learning experience is really like. Following are several misconceptions that students commonly have about online coursework.

Courses that Use Online Technologies Require Less Time Than Traditional On-Campus Courses   Unfortunately, the opposite is actually true for most students. The requirements of online coursework are typically new to students, and the primarily text-based methods for communicating online slow the learning pace for many students. When completing online <u>coursework</u>, you should ordinarily anticipate spending more time reading and writing than you would in most conventional on-campus courses.

Not Having to Go to Class Means that I Can Wait Until the Last Minute to Participate   Unlike in the traditional lecture course where your participation is commonly required only once or twice a week during a scheduled time, an online course more often than not takes place 24 hours a day, 7 days a week. This isn't to say that you will be expected to participate every day throughout the semester, but waiting until the last minute to participate in online discussions is not a strategy for success in online <u>coursework</u>. In general, you will want to participate in online discussions and <u>coursework</u> at least 3 or 4 days each week.

Online Instructors Are Always Online   You should never wait until the day before the assignment is due to <u>email</u> your professor with a question or request feedback on a draft term paper. Online instructors are not always online, nor will your message necessarily be at the top of the priority list in responding to <u>emails</u>. Many times students have the expectation that if they are awake at midnight working on an activity for class, then the instructor will also be awake and answering his <u>email</u> (or the instructor will answer <u>email</u> questions at 8:00 A.M.). This is a misconception. Teaching courses is just one of the many duties that your instructors will have at the college or university, so you should plan ahead to ensure that there is adequate time for the instructor to reply to your questions or requests before assignments are due.

You Can't Make Friends in an Online Course   Strong friendships can be and often are built online. Many students actually find that it is easier to create friendships online because the online environment doesn't have many of the social pressures that are common in the classroom (for example, body image, physical disabilities, or social cliques). In fact, so many people believe that friendships and other relationships can be developed online that during a single month in 2002 more than 18 million people visited online dating <u>websites</u>.[2]

Little Feedback is Given on Online Assignments and Activities   Like in the conventional classroom, the level of feedback that you receive on your assignments and activities done online will vary by the instructor delivering the course. Many professors who use online technologies will use the tools and resources available to provide feedback to students sooner than the long-established 5 or 7 days that many on-campus instructors have between class meetings, and other faculty members may take days before answering your <u>email</u> questions.

If I Don't Like to Participate in Class, Then Online Courses are Better for Me   Learning, either online or in the classroom, is an active pursuit. Your success in college will depend on your dynamic involvement in your <u>coursework</u>. From reading required textbooks to discussing ideas with study partners, the more you can be involved in the learning experience, the greater the likelihood that you will be successful.

For those students who do not like to participate in class due to a possible disability or social fear, then the online learning environment can offer

ACTIVITY 2-2   Did This Section Click?

🌐 As a review, mark the correct phrase that completes the following statements:

1. Goals for your success in college should focus on
   a. the long term (for example, your GPA at graduation).
   b. the short term (for example, your grade on the mid-term exam).
   c. both the long term and short term aligned together.

2. For most college students, courses that use online resources typically require
   a. about the same amount of time as traditional classroom courses.
   b. significantly less time than traditional classroom courses.
   c. almost no time because they are easier than traditional classroom courses.

3. When emailing a question to a college professor, you should expect a response within
   a. 12 hours.
   b. 2–3 days.
   c. 1 week.

shelter from many of the social pressures that are common in the classroom. Your active participation is, however, still required for learning to take place.

Online Materials are Always Available   Although online course materials are typically available to you 24 hours a day, you do not want to wait until the last minute to access the resources required to complete any college activity or assignment. Often professors will turn off the students' access to course materials for a given week, module, or lesson after the related activities or assignments are complete. And, of course, critical technology failures can (and will) happen at unexpected and inopportune times. As a result, you should plan ahead to ensure that you have all online materials that you will require (such as online readings, assignment descriptions, submission guidelines, and online library resources) well before an online course assignment or activity is due.

Clarifying Personal Expectations and Setting Goals

Once you have swept away any misconceptions or inaccurate perceptions that you may have had concerning online coursework, it is time to establish some realistic personal expectations for the course. Your expectations for any college course should be based on realistic prospects given your past performance; grades in courses with similar content; performance in similar semesters given other work, personal, or academic commitments; and performance in classes that require similar use of online technologies.

If you have few experiences with college-level courses, the basis for your expectations will have to rely even more heavily on the recommendations of your academic advisor, course instructor, and fellow students. Performance in high school courses, though of some value, rarely predicts success in college-level courses that use online technologies. Not only has the learning environment shifted away from 50-minute class meetings five times a week, but also the expectations for independent learning have increased with your move to college-level courses. It is therefore essential that you discuss your expectations and plan for success with your academic advisor and/or professor. They will be able to offer you guidance and assistance in preparing your path toward success.

Because your expectations regarding the course will provide a foundation for your course goals, here are a few questions you will want to consider when establishing course expectations:

- ☐ Does this course require that I apply skills or knowledge that I have not applied recently? (For example, was my last course in math 3 years ago?)

- ☐ Am I familiar with the online technologies that I will be required to use in completing the course?

- ☐ Is this course required for my major?

- ☐ Given the assignments and activities required in the course, how have I performed in the past when other classes had similar requirements?

- ☐ Will other courses that I am enrolled in this semester divert my attention away from my studies for this course?

- ☐ Is the topic of the course of great interest to me, or will I struggle to remain motivated?

- ☐ Have I developed the necessary learning skills and study habits to be successful in this course?

Based on your expectations of each course, you will want to set independent goals related to each course that you are taking. These goals will provide you with operational definitions of *success* for each course. In other words, by achieving these goals, you will be achieving success in your studies.

These definitions of success that you establish through your goals for each course are individual and specific to your college experience, so you shouldn't feel pressure based on the goals that others have set for themselves. They are your standards, and when you have accomplished them, you should consider yourself successful. Everyone will set her own goals and thereby her own definitions of success, but the only classifications of *success* that really matter are those that you define. Meeting the expectations of others just isn't practical; after all, they have come to different answers when analyzing their expectations for the course.

Course goals should include the final grade that you would like to receive (when appropriate) as well as the knowledge and skills that you want to take away from the experience. Though these goals may be linked, this is not always the case. Typically, in some courses you will want to focus more on the course grade (especially in courses within your major), while in other courses your interests may be more about developing or applying skills (for example, many college students will take art courses as electives, though their majors may be in the social sciences like psychology or education).

For goals to be effective tools, they should have the following characteristics:

- They should be specific to each course. Although you will have goals for your overall college experience (for example, overall GPA), you will want to set more specific goals for each course.

- They should be measurable. Define what it takes to be successful, and you will know when you are successful.

- They should be challenging yet realistic. Goals should push you to do your best while remaining consistent with the expectations that you have established for the course.

Below are a few examples of course goals that you may establish:

- ☐ I will have an average score of 85 or higher on the four exams that I am required to take for Algebra 101.

- ☐ My participation grade will be 40 out of 40 points in Public Speaking 200.

- ☐ I will score no lower than an 80 on each of my mid-term exams this semester.

Building Comprehension Skills

You should build into your plan for success the time and resources necessary for developing your comprehension skills. Research has shown that students who have built skills for comprehending greater amounts of information from readings and discussions are more likely to have higher academic achievement.[3]

By improving your comprehension skills in four areas (reading, listening, conversation, and feedback), you can be successful in all of your college coursework.

Reading Comprehension

Even with the enormous growth of technology use in education, reading proficiency and comprehension remains a foundational skill for success in the college classroom, whether online or on-campus. Improving your reading comprehension starts with becoming an active reader: previewing readings, taking notes, asking questions, anticipating materials, and summarizing what you have learned. While most of the strategies for successful reading that apply to printed works are appropriate for online readings as well, often you will want to use the resources of online technologies to improve your skills and build on these habits. In the Quick References you will find many strategies and techniques for improving your reading proficiency and comprehension when course readings are online.

Listening Comprehension

Often, daydreams or other distracters in the classroom will keep us from gaining a full grasp of all the materials covered by a professor during a lecture. Increasing your listening comprehension requires that you become an active listener: asking questions, taking notes, anticipating forthcoming topics, and so forth. Listening comprehension is an essential skill for online <u>coursework</u> that requires listening to or watching lectures that have been recorded. Though you may not be able to receive immediate responses to questions, keeping a list of questions to <u>email</u> your instructor or study partners is a good technique to increase your listening comprehension (as well as to manage your time because you will not have to review the lecture in order to clarify questions).

Conversation Comprehension

By and large, most of us are not great conversationalists. During our conversations with other students, we commonly find ourselves so eager to make our next comment or ask our next question that we fail to listen to the other people who are in the conversation with us. Or at the end of the conversation, we realize too late that we have not clarified our expectations, nor do we really understand what we are supposed to do next. The same failures to comprehend the valuable information contained in any conversation are also common in online conversation (such as in a <u>chat</u> with your study group members or in a <u>discussion board</u> conversation with your instructor). To increase your comprehension in all your conversations (online or in person), you want to be an active participant.

The ratio of "two ears to only one mouth" is important to conversation comprehension; ideally, you should listen two-thirds of the time and speak one-third. Neither dominating nor failing to participate in a conversation is an effective strategy online or in the classroom. For example, during an online <u>synchronous</u> <u>chat</u>, you should not feel pressure to respond to every line posted by other students or your instructor. Take your time to reflect upon what is being discussed, ask specific questions for clarification, and post well-thought-out items that add value to the discussion. If you are continuously attempting to respond to every posting in the discussion, you will comprehend little of the conversation and only manage to tire out your fingers.

Feedback Comprehension

A lack of meaningful feedback in previous course experiences (for example, getting only a letter grade from an instructor on a ten-page paper) has produced for many of us an unconscious reflex that reduces our comprehension when others are giving us feedback on our work. We are so familiar with negative or worthless feedback that we have learned to hear but not listen to the feedback others offer. Although you will most likely still receive meaningless feedback in some of your college courses, increasing your attentiveness to feedback and potential valuable lessons that may be contained within each statement is a hallmark of successful college students. By comprehending and applying the feedback offered by other students and your instructors, you can improve your learning skills and study habits and increase the odds of your long-term and short-term success.

Establishing Study Times

An essential element of any plan for success in online <u>coursework</u> is scheduling your study time. Dedicated study times are both an issue of time management (as discussed in Chapter 5) as well as a matter of effective planning. Developing a flexible plan for success that will keep you on task throughout the semester is the goal when creating a schedule that you can follow. You should try to balance expectations that are compatible with the goals that you have for the course with realistic time frames, given your other personal and professional commitments.

Setting aside consistent blocks of times each week for working on online course assignments and activities is one strategy for developing a regular flow to your online studies. Though it will likely be tempting to designate differing times each week for your online <u>coursework</u>, a familiar pattern of study times each week throughout a semester can help you avoid procrastination and manage your time. Too often, online activities will be postponed from Monday to Tuesday and then Tuesday to Wednesday, until the assignments are overdue and your success in the course is jeopardized.

Establishing a study schedule (for example, completing online <u>coursework</u> on Monday and Wednesday nights from 8:00 to 10:00 P.M., as well as on Saturday afternoons from 1:00 to 2:30 P.M.) for your courses will also help you develop the types of learning skills that make for success in college courses. While a certain amount of flexibility will be required to meet all of your academic, personal, and work commitments, adhering to your established study schedule can provide consistency in your study habits, help you manage your time, and improve the odds that you will stay with your plan for success until the goal is accomplished.

ACTIVITY 2-3   **Did This Section Click?**

As a review, read the following statements, then circle T (true) or F (false) for each one.

1. T F   Listening comprehension skills are not necessary for success in online <u>coursework</u>.

2. T F   Short-term goals for each course should be specific and measurable.

3. T F   Conversation comprehension is improved when we are active participants in the conversation, whether online or in person.

4. T F   You should establish regular study times that you can stay with throughout the semester.

5. T F   Most strategies used to improve comprehension when reading a newspaper or book are not effective when reading online.

For most of us, it will be important to prepare our study schedule for the entire course at the beginning of the semester to ensure that we don't have conflicts. For example, you wouldn't want to inadvertently plan a weekend at the beach before a critical research paper is due. By planning for the entire semester, you can visualize when potential conflicts may occur and plan your study times accordingly. That way, you can complete the research paper and still be able to enjoy a weekend at the beach.

> **STUDENT-TO-STUDENT TIP**
>
> It is extremely important to schedule your time to work on online course assignments and activities. Be realistic in your plans to be able to complete assignments. Always assume that something will interrupt you and/or that something may not work as you had planned and therefore delay you.

Creating an Effective Study Environment

Your study environment should be a component of your plan for success. In the conventional classroom, much of the study environment was created for you (for example, rooms with few distractions and resources for communicating with other students). In the online classroom, however, you will typically have the ability to create an individualized study environment (including both the physical environment of the room in which you access online materials as well as the online course environment that you establish on your computer). In both cases, developing a study environment that facilitates your success by minimizing your distractions will be the goal of your plan.

Physical Studying Environment

Where you study plays a critical role in your success in online coursework. Depending on the computer that you use to access the Internet (that is, laptop or desktop), you can have varying levels of flexibility with your physical study environment when completing online coursework. In the following pages are tips for creating a positive studying environment.

Find a Place with Adequate Access to the Internet and Electrical Power

A functional study environment for today's college student requires both access to electrical power as well as the Internet. Although college students do still use traditional paper, pencils, and pens in completing some assignments, the vast majority of coursework in college today requires the use of computers; from making mathematical calculations to writing term papers, the tools of success are typically functions of the personal computer. Although not all college assignments and activities will require that you use Internet resources, the availability of reference materials and other online assets can help ensure that you have all the resources that you require to be successful. Some examples are the online dictionary available at

www.cengage.com/success/Watkins/ELearning3e

http://education.yahoo.com/reference/dictionary

or the online thesaurus found at

http://www.thesaurus.com

Find a Quiet Place Where You Can Concentrate

Most of us can concentrate better on our studies when there is not high-volume conversation, music, or television in the same room. For some students, however, depending on preferences and the potential for sporadic noises, some low-volume background music may be good for concentration. If you find that this is true for you, then you should select music that is consistent (for example, a music CD is probably a better choice than the radio because there are fewer interruptions and unpredictable shifts from music to commercials to announcers). Keep it at a low volume so that you do not end up listening to the music instead of comprehending what you are reading.

Limit the Number of Potential Distractions

We can typically plan for most of the distractions that will interrupt our studies. For example, if friends like to come by your dorm room to talk, close the door before you begin to study. Don't be tempted to have a television that you can view from your desk, and turn off your cell phone (and/or the ringer on your home phone). Reducing the number of potential distractions from your studies is a relatively easy step that you can take on your path toward college success.

Take Study Breaks

Long uninterrupted periods of studying may seem like the most efficient use of your study times, but in actuality study breaks will help sustain your comprehension as well as provide your eyes, fingers, and brain with the necessary rest to avert exhaustion. Depending on your study environment (for example, the comfort of your desk and chair) and the length of time that you have been studying, the frequency and duration of your study breaks should vary. A 3- to 5-minute break every 45 minutes may be enough when you first sit down to study, but a 6- to 8-minute break every 30 minutes may be required after several hours of studying.

Study breaks should involve leaving the computer or study desk to stretch your arms, legs, and back (as well as rest your eyes). Simply moving from completing your homework at the computer to **surfing** the <u>World Wide Web</u> will not provide your body and mind with the necessary intermission from studying.

Don't Forget to Drink Water and to Eat Nutritional Snacks During Study Breaks

Your body, including your brain, requires water and nutritional snacks to function properly and maintain the heightened levels of concentration required for effective studying. Although you may not want to have these right next to your computer (to avoid distractions and possible spilling), keeping them close by (such as in your backpack, dorm refrigerator, or kitchen) can be helpful so that study breaks do not have to be extended while you go out for water and a nutritional snack.

You will also want to avoid beverages or snacks that have a large amount of processed sugars in them (for example, candy bars, sodas, and chocolate) because the energy from the sugar is quickly used up and the "sugar hangover" that follows will only reduce your ability to study.

Find Your Ideal Room Temperature

The ideal temperature for studying is generally an individual preference. Typically, however, it is better to study in a room that is a little cooler than a room that is too warm. If you are going to study in a room where you do not have control over the temperature (for example, the library, study lounge, or a friend's apartment), then you should dress in layers. This will offer you the flexibility to find the ideal comfort level for studying.

Select a Good Computer Desk and Chair

Long hours of studying at your computer can be tiring and potentially harmful for your body. Before studying, ensure that the computer desk and chair are at the correct height for your body size. Ideally, your keyboard will be at approximately elbow height, allowing the hands, wrists, and forearms to be in a straight line that is approximately parallel to the floor. For extended periods of studying, a computer with a detachable keyboard that can tilt at a slight angle can be invaluable for reducing the effort required of your fingers, wrists, and forearms. Most laptop computers only offer a flat keyboard, but another keyboard can commonly be added to the laptop when you are planning to study for longer periods (see your laptop computer's manual for instructions on attaching a second keyboard for temporary use).

A high-quality chair with adequate lumbar support for your lower back, as well as an adjustable height control for your keyboard to ensure that hands, wrists, and forearms are parallel to the floor, can increase the duration and comfort of your study times.

Have Essential Resources Close at Hand

The last kinds of interruptions that you want to have to your study time are those that you can plan for and avoid. By keeping the necessary resources for completing your assignments and activities close at hand (such as books, articles, pens, and printer paper), you can reduce the number of these distractions from your studies. If you are studying in your dorm or apartment, then having these resources close by shouldn't be a problem; keep them in or around your desk. However, if you regularly study in the library, student lounge, or in other locations away from your desk, then you will want to keep a variety of these resources in your book bag, backpack, or computer case so they will be available whenever necessary. Remember, being prepared will lead to your success.

Study Where There is Proper Lighting

Computer monitors do not provide adequate lighting for your studies, so your study environment should also include top lighting that illuminates the keyboard, books, papers, and other studying resources required to complete your online assignments. Lights should not, however, glare or reflect strongly on the computer screen, and many students prefer natural light. Additional lighting will help reduce the strain on your eyes, and research suggests lighting may also influence your attitude and academic achievement.[4]

Online Studying Environment

Like the physical study environment, the online study environment that you create for completing your <u>coursework</u> will be critical to your success. In planning for success, you will want to create an ideal online study environment that can aid in reducing distractions and increase your comprehension of essential course information.

Don't Have a Cluttered or Disorderly Computer

Although maintaining a strategy for organizing all of the course-related documents, <u>software</u> applications, and other files in your computer will require some planning, the benefits of being able to locate and access files that you want to use, when you want to use them, is essential for being successful in online <u>coursework</u>.

Organize your computer so that each course has its own file **folder** in which you keep all files related to the assignments and activities for that particular course. Each semester you should start with an empty <u>folder</u> for each course for which you are enrolled. In addition, you should use sub<u>folder</u>s for organizing assignments, keeping notes on online readings, organizing feedback that you have received on draft documents, and so forth. By including dates in the **files name**s (for example, "assignment two 10-13-04.pdf"), you can further classify which files have been submitted for grading and which are earlier drafts.

Eliminate Online Distractions

When studying or completing any type of online <u>coursework</u>, you will want to reduce the number of possible online distracters that will diminish your comprehension or keep you from your studies altogether. Just like in the physical study environment, the online environment offers a variety of potential distracters that you can avoid. For example, turn off the <u>email</u> and **instant messaging** <u>software</u> applications that you may have running on your computer. <u>Email</u>s or instant messages from family or friends are common distracters because most of us can't help but read these messages when they first arrive.

<u>Surfing</u> the web, like television, is another distraction that most of us have a difficult time avoiding. Relatively few of us can surf the <u>World Wide Web</u> for just a few minutes and then go back to our effective study habits. Instead,

5 minutes of looking for an interesting <u>website</u> quickly becomes 45 minutes of looking at <u>websites</u> that are of little interest (having an effect similar to that of flipping through numerous television channels finding nothing to watch).

Work on One Assignment or Activity at a Time

Sustaining your concentration and comprehension commonly requires that you do not jump back and forth between various online assignments and activities. Attempting to complete your biology homework while doing research for a history paper will usually reduce the amount you get done on either project. Most often, you will want to close all the files and <u>software</u> applications that are not required for the current online <u>coursework</u>. This will help you stay focused on the task at hand.

Make a Plan for Backing Up Your Files

You should have a plan and schedule for making backup copies of all the files on your computer each semester. In addition, you should also plan to **back up** the assignments and activities for your current courses each week throughout the semester. Burning copies to CD-ROM or DVD, saving copies to a floppy disk, or moving copies to a shared **server** space can all be effective techniques for ensuring that you do not lose essential files.

> **STUDENT-TO-STUDENT TIP**
>
> Many students don't think of <u>backing up</u> their files until they lose them the first time!

Install and Maintain an Antivirus Software Application

Viruses are <u>software</u> programs that are created to disrupt your use of the computer, and they can cause many of your course-related files to stop functioning. These virus programs can be sent to your computer by <u>email</u> or through <u>websites</u>; because of this, you will want to have the most recent virus protection <u>software</u> available. Many colleges and universities have site licenses for **antivirus** <u>software</u> that you can install and maintain free of charge as long as you are a student. By contacting the technical support services at your college or university, you should be able to find out more about what <u>antivirus software</u> applications they offer and support.

Install Any Required Software at the Beginning of the Semester

When planning for the semester, you should identify and install any <u>software</u> that you may be required to use in completing your <u>coursework</u>. This will give you time to ensure that the <u>software</u> is running properly before you must start work on an assignment or activity. If there are problems with the <u>software</u> or questions about how to use the <u>software</u>, having installed it at the beginning of the semester will give you the opportunity to troubleshoot or contact technical support well before any <u>coursework</u> will be due.

Don't Plan to Install Unnecessary Software During the Semester

When you have the <u>software</u> required for your <u>coursework</u> installed at the beginning of the semester, it typically isn't a good idea to risk installing new <u>software</u> unless necessary. Though the likelihood that one <u>software</u> application will disrupt the functionality of another is not always high, it typically will not be worth the risk because inevitably any troubles will come at a time when you can least afford to have computer problems.

Planning with Learning or Physical Disabilities in Mind

Planning for success in online <u>coursework</u>, like success in the classroom, requires some additional attention for students with learning or physical disabilities. Although all colleges and universities are required to provide reasonable accommodations that support students with a variety of learning or physical disabilities, the implementation of these accommodations is not always as obvious in the online classroom. Nevertheless, there is an ever-growing variety of assistive technologies (as well as <u>software</u> accessibility features discussed in Chapter 3) that can be used to ensure that you have the resources required for online success. Below are descriptions of just a few assistive technologies that may be useful in preparing for success with online <u>coursework</u>:

> *Text-to-speech* can read text at the desired speed and voice while recording it into a variety of **file format**s. A user can listen to <u>email</u>, <u>webpages</u>, eBooks, and other documents on the computer or a portable MP3 player.

> *Talking word processor* is **word processing** <u>software</u> that has built-in text-to-speech features providing auditory feedback of letters (characters), words, sentences, or whole paragraphs.

> *Voice recognition* allows a user to use his voice as an input device. Voice recognition may be used to dictate text into the computer or to give commands to the computer (such as opening application programs, pulling down **menu**s, or saving work).

> *Talking <u>Web browsers</u>* are <u>Web browser</u>s that use **plug-in**s to add text-to-speech capabilities.[5]

For more information on the accommodations and assistive technologies available at your college or university, contact your academic advisor or institution's student services department. At many institutions, however, you are required to provide confidential documentation of your learning or physical disability in order to receive accommodations. Even if you don't anticipate requiring accommodations during your college experience, it is worth your time to document your disability once you are enrolled with your college or university to ensure that there will be minimal delays if you decide later on that accommodations would be helpful.

Familiarizing Yourself with the Course Design

Planning for success in a college course is difficult when you have little information about what to expect. Most often, course syllabi (as well as access to online course resources) are provided to students on the first day of classes. When you first have access to the course syllabus and other materials that outline the structure of a course, it is important that you note the dates on which assignments are due, as well as submission requirements, test dates and formats, and other critical information regarding online technologies for planning your success.

Here are few tips of what to highlight in each course syllabus:

- What is the instructor's <u>email</u> (and phone number)?
- When are the instructor's office hours? (These may also include online office hours when the instructor is available for <u>synchronous</u> <u>chat</u> discussions.)
- When are assignments and activities due?
- How should assignments, activities, and exams be submitted for grading?
- What are the course policies regarding attendance (including online participation)?
- How can online resources be accessed (passwords or logins)?
- Is group work required? If so, how will teams be formed and facilitated?
- Which textbooks are required? Are there online resources that accompany these books?
- Is specialized <u>software</u> required for the course?
- What technical support is provided for online <u>coursework</u>?
- Will feedback and grades be provided online?

Staying in Touch

Even the best of us fall short of keeping with our plans from time to time. Unfortunately, at some point during your college experience an unexpected event that disrupts your plans, such as a computer failure or an illness, will likely occur. Therefore, staying in contact with your instructor or online project group members is essential for your success.

When unexpected events do occur, let the instructor know immediately. Typically, alternative arrangements can be made when unforeseen events disrupt your studies; however, if you wait until

> **STUDENT-TO-STUDENT TIP**
>
> Check your <u>emails</u> daily and the discussion forums regularly. Once you get a response or post something, make sure to follow up within 24 hours! This is important because it keeps the content fresh and creates a continuous dialogue among students.

after assignments are due or exams are taken, fewer options are available for the professor.

When contacting your instructor about an unexpected event that is impacting your studies, the following guidelines may be useful:

- Although you will not typically be asked to provide personal information (for example, the nature of the illness), you should be prepared to *provide specific information* regarding the impact of the event on your studies. For example, "On Wednesday, April 22, my dorm room was broken into, and my personal computer was stolen."

- In your conversation (online or in person) with your professor, *include specific dates* related to the impact of the unintended event. For example, "I have not been able to participate in the online course discussions since last Friday (November 3), but I should be able to resume my participation tomorrow (November 8)."

- *Offer to provide supporting documentation* for the expected event (such as a note from the emergency room, a receipt for the replacement of a broken computer hard drive, or documentation from an <u>Internet</u> service provider that services were not available after an ice storm).

- *Include a proposed plan of action* that includes reasonable suggestions or alternatives for getting back on track toward success in the course.

- Because unexpected events commonly influence our performance for several weeks, let instructors know that you will *keep in contact* with them throughout the remainder of the semester.

Creating an Effective Plan

By familiarizing yourself with the course structure and integrating that information into your goals and schedules, you will be better able to plan for your success. Below are several steps for developing a successful plan for online <u>coursework</u>:

STUDENT-TO-STUDENT TIP

Instructors give us a syllabus for a reason; remember that an online class typically isn't a work-anytime class. Check your due dates, set your work times, and go.

1. Define *success* for yourself. Identify your long-term goals for your college experience (including each semester). You should do this once now and then review your progress at the end of each semester.

2. Define how you will determine if you are successful in the short term. Define short-term goals for each course and each week of the semester. This will have to be done each semester.

3 After reviewing your course syllabi for the semester, establish an appropriate study schedule for the semester. Set consistent study times for each week, taking into account holidays, breaks, and other interruptions to your regular study times.

ACTIVITY 2-4

As a review, match the following word or phrase with the correct definition

1. ___ instant messaging

a. Should be studied when planning for success in any course

2. ___ success

b. Should be organized and structured to improve accessibility

3. ___ installing software

c. Should be turned off to prevent possible distractions while studying

4. ___ files

d. Should *not* be done unless necessary during the semester

5. ___ course syllabus

e. Should be defined as your first step in planning

4. Arrange for required software to be installed in your computer (as necessary). After installing the necessary software for the semester, don't install superfluous software since you don't want to have conflicts or problems.

5. Determine the ideal physical study environment for each course assignment or activity. Depending on what is required, your physical study environment may change to ensure that you have the proper resources for success.

6. Create a model online environment for your success. Turn off possible distracters from your computer (such as instant messaging) and devise a plan for organizing your course files.

7. Visit online resources (for example, Internet portals such as Blackboard or WebCT) to make certain that you have access when it is necessary. Include in your study times additional time for reviewing online resources.

8. Develop strategies for increasing your reading, listening, conversation, and feedback comprehension throughout the semester.

9. Identify potential assistive technologies that you may require for the course.

10. Contact your instructor if any unexpected events hinder you from achieving the goals that you have established for the semester.

Summary

Success in college requires that you not only create a useful plan but also follow through on that plan throughout each semester. From aligning your long-term and short-term goals to establishing an effective online study environment, achieving the success you want in college courses is within your reach. By taking the time to plan for success, you can greatly improve the odds that you will accomplish all your goals.

www.cengage.com/success/Watkins/ELearning3e

Chapter 2 Exercise

HOW TO 17

To begin the exercise, you will want to access your web-based course materials (that is, <u>educational portal</u>), using a <u>Web browser</u> (such as Netscape Navigator, Mozilla Firefox, or Microsoft Internet Explorer). In addition, you will want to open a new document in a <u>word processing</u> program (for example, Microsoft Word).

HOW TO 10

STEP 1: Locate an online copy of a syllabus for a course in which you are currently enrolled or plan to enroll. (If an online copy is not available, then you may use a paper syllabus provided by an instructor.)

HOW TO 27

STEP 2: Review the course syllabus to determine which assignments and activities will be graded during the semester. In your <u>word processing</u> document, list in a table (four columns wide) the assignments and activities that will be graded, along with the number of possible points for each and the date it is due.

HOW TO 34

STEP 3: For each graded assignment and activity, determine a goal for your grade. Based on your experiences and expectations, these goals should be aligned with your long-term goals for college success. In the fourth column of your <u>word processing</u> document, insert your goal for each assignment and activity.

HOW TO 41

STEP 4: Below the table that contains the assignments and activities for the course (along with your goals), identify five changes that you will have to make to your learning strategies and study habits in order to achieve success. These can include changes to your online study environment or study schedule, competing commitments, and other topics that have been discussed up to this point.

Did You Stay Focused?

After completing this chapter, you should be able to do the following. If there are tasks that you cannot do, take a few minutes to review the chapter, focusing on those areas that you have missed the first time through.

- ☐ I have *defined* long-terms goals for my success in college.
- ☐ I have *defined* short-term goals that are aligned with my long-term goals.
- ☐ I have measurable goals for each of my courses this semester.
- ☐ I have *defined* realistic expectations of online <u>coursework</u>.
- ☐ I can avoid misconceptions about online <u>coursework</u>.
- ☐ I can improve my listening comprehension, reading, conversation, and feedback comprehension.
- ☐ I have *created* a good online (as well as physical) study environment.

☐ I know who to contact if I have a learning or physical disability.

☐ I have *created* an effective for plan my success in college courses.

☐ I have completed the chapter activities.

Additional Resources

🌐 Additional resources on topics covered in this chapter are available at the Premium Website for the *E-Learning Companion.*

Notes

1. http://www.najaco.com/literature/quotes/planning.htm.
2. http://www.msnbc.com/news/806278.asp.
3. http://chronicle.com/free/2002/06/2002061001u.htm, *Chronicle of Higher Education,* June 10, 2002.
4. R. Dunn, J. S. Krimsky, J. B. Murray, and P. J. Quinn (1985), "Light Up Their Lives: A Research on the Effects of Lighting on Children's Achievement and Behavior," *Reading Teacher* 38(19): 863–869.
5. Based on http://www.nsnet.org/atc/tools/.

3 Technology Tips for Online Students

By the end of this chapter, you will be able to

- *Define* how e-learning can support your academic, personal, and professional goals.
- *Create* a plan for accomplishing your academic, personal, and professional goals.

Computer technologies are just one of the keys to the recent increase in the use of online coursework in many colleges and universities. Much of the growth in the use of technology in education is also a direct result of the adaptability of students. Gaining the most from the use of technology in college courses does, however, require that you become a skilled user of the many tools and resources available (for example, **podcast**s, wikis, Web portals, and discussion boards).

While much of the responsibility for developing and supporting these technologies is left to the institution offering the course, successful students must also have an adequate knowledge of technologies in order to take advantage of the learning opportunities (and to overcome some of the learning barriers) that are part of any online coursework experience. As you become familiar with many of the time- and energy-saving tips for making the best use of software applications, you can improve both the efficiency and quality of your study habits.

Tips for Before Online Coursework Begins

Most of us do not actually rely on user manuals when learning new software applications; rather, we attempt to complete a series of task using the software, learning through our successes and failures. Although this is not always considered the most efficient process for learning new software, for most of us the familiarity with other software programs (such as Microsoft Word or Internet Explorer) has provided us with many foundational skills that we can apply to most other applications. Having tasks to perform, however, is essential to learning software operations; just "playing" with the software with no goals in mind usually results in an ineffective and dull experience.

Learning how to use your college's educational portal (that is, Web portal) for completing your coursework is analogous to learning any other new software application. It is equally challenging to discover the functionality of online course resources, such as chat rooms or tools for sharing files with other students, without activities that use multiple functions of these resources.

BEFORE CLASS CHECKLIST

☐ Before classes begin, you can often access your college's Web portal for courses to *complete tutorials* and *view sample courses*. Take the time to explore the resources that will be available before the semester even begins.

☐ *Contact both the library and technical support services* to identify any training they may offer regarding the online tools used at your college.

☐ If possible, *select a single computer* that you will use for completing your online assignments and activities. If you use a computer lab, this may not be possible, but you do want to make sure that you have adequate access to computers with similar software configurations throughout the semester.

☐ *Review your course syllabus* carefully to determine when and how online resources will be utilized throughout the semester.

☐ If adequate information is not available in your course syllabus, *contact the instructor* (either by email or phone) during the first week of classes to determine how online technologies will be used in your courses. Be sure to ask when and how students will be able to access the online resources.

☐ As soon as online resources are made available in your courses, visit the websites to *verify your access*. If you have technical problems (for example, your login and password do not work properly), you will have time to get the problems resolved before online assignments or activities are required.

HOW TO
10

HOW TO
27

☐ When you access your courses' online tools and resources, *follow each link* and verify that you can access each component of your online learning environment. For example, does the chat room appear to function properly on your computer, and does the link to online lecture materials seem to function as it should?

HOW TO
34

HOW TO
41

☐ If you have not previously used one or more of the online tools that are available, you should *familiarize yourself with the functionality of each online tool* during the first week of the course. Take a few minutes to review tutorials provided on the Website, post messages to a synchronous chat room, or post your introduction of yourself to other students in the online discussion board.

☐ *Contact technical support services* if you have any problems or questions regarding the use of the online resources at your college.

Tips for Evaluating Online Resources

Both accurate and inaccurate information is readily available on the <u>Internet</u> and <u>World Wide Web</u>. As a student, you will want to develop the critical thinking skills for determining which information that you find online is of value and should be included as a resource for your online <u>coursework</u>. Consequently, evaluating online resources will be an essential skill for your success. Unfortunately, there is no formula for sifting out useful and reliable sources of information on the <u>Internet</u> from those that you would not want to use in college <u>coursework</u>.

STUDENT-TO-STUDENT TIP

Today, information on just about every conceivable topic is being posted on the <u>Internet</u> on a continuous basis. The information is easy to access but can be difficult to evaluate in terms of validity. With today's technology, individuals can easily produce what might seem to be a professional-looking <u>webpage</u>; however, upon further scrutiny you might find the site contains inaccurate information.

What follows are guidelines and suggestions for assessing the reliability, quality, and usefulness of online (as well as traditional print-based) resources. You should review these tips before, during, and after you conduct any research using the <u>Internet</u> to ensure that you have selected only the information sources that will lead to your success.[1] In addition, you should contact your college's library for assistance in identifying dependable online and print-based resources for your college papers and assignments.

Source Reliability

The reliability of the information that you have available to include when writing your term papers, reviewing for exams, making references in position papers, and so forth will be an essential ingredient to your success in college. While there is no simple formula for assessing reliability, by following the steps below you can better ensure the reliability of your sources.

- *Contact information.* Check to determine if the author's contact information is available for the selected information. This information should include name of author, title, and organizational affiliation, as well as postal or <u>email</u> addresses.

- *Author's credentials.* The credibility of an author is often related to his or her credentials. Review the biographical information provided about the author to determine if he or she is a reliable source of information. For example, has he published several scholarly articles on the topic in the research journals of his field or has she been recognized by professional organizations for her contributions to her field of study? It is also often valuable to confirm an author's expertise on a topic through examining other publications by the author and/or identifying references to the author's work in publications by other experts in the discipline.

E-Learning Experiences

While teaching a course on educational technologies a few years ago, I had a student who came across a <u>webpage</u> that he thought would be a valuable resource for an upcoming course assignment. The <u>webpage</u> title was "Parents of Nasal Learners Demand Odor-Based Curriculum." The article went on to say that parents of nasal learners, backed by olfactory-education experts, were demanding that U.S. public schools provide odor-based curricula for their academically struggling children.[2]

While most students would quickly notice the humor as they read the story on the <u>webpage</u>, in a hurry to finish his course assignment, this student eagerly wrote about the injustices of an educational system that would not equally support students with less-known learning disabilities. If he had taken the time to review the <u>website</u> for the organization that initially published the article (http://www.theonion.com), he would have promptly discovered that the organization provides daily satire on news stories from around the world and commonly makes up false stories with a humorous twist.

Accordingly, don't be fooled by everything you see or read on the <u>World Wide Web</u>. Some information is intentionally misleading, and some is inaccurate by accident.

- *Publication's reputation.* Publications (such as journals, magazines, and <u>websites</u>) build their reputation within a field of study by publishing reliable and useful information for readers. You should become familiar with the reputations of various publications within your field of study as you begin your research. You can always ask your professor or librarian to make recommendations on the reputations of various publications.

- *Blogs and <u>wikis</u>.* Online publications such as **blogs** and **wikis** are rarely reviewed for accuracy, truthfulness, or potential bias. As a result, they are risky resources for your college papers and assignments. Although these types of online publications can provide you with background information on a topic, you will typically not want to use them as references or quote them without confirming the information through a reputable research publication or periodical.

- *Sponsoring organization(s).* Many publications (such as journals, magazines, and <u>websites</u>) are sponsored by organizations such as professional societies, nonprofit organizations, and other entities with a mission behind the publications that they sponsor. Reviewing the mission of the organization that funds any <u>website</u>, journal, or other publication can provide you with information regarding potential biases or perspectives that may shape the reliability of the information.

- *Blind peer review.* The most reliable publications are typically those that are blind peer reviewed. Many, but not all, scholarly journals provide for a blind peer–review process whereby scholars in the field assess articles submitted for publication before the articles are published. You should determine which publications in your field of study use a blind peer–review process because these will often be the most reliable sources of information (this information is often located in the introductory materials on the primary <u>website</u> or in the front pages of a printed journal).

 • *Email the author.* Although the information that you find posted to public bulletin boards and other discussion forums should rarely be viewed as reliable information for use in your college courses, these resources can often provide you with useful leads to reliable information. When you find information that may be useful, write to the author of the posting to determine if he can provide you with additional references or resources where you can find reliable information for use in your assignments or activities.

Information Quality

The quality and accuracy of information that you use in college <u>coursework</u> is critical. Inaccurate or misleading information may end up costing you points toward your grade; consequently, taking the time to examine potential resources for indicators of accuracy is always worth it.

● *Broad generalizations.* Inaccurate information is commonly detectable when an author uses broad (that is, sweeping or vague) generalizations about the subject. As a result, statements like "All students . . . ," "Everyone must . . . ," or "Athletes always . . ." can be identified as indicators that overgeneralizations are being made by the author and the accuracy of the statements should be questioned. This isn't to say that all generalizations are inaccurate, but rather that generalizations are often used when the accuracy of information should be questioned.

● *Dates.* Check the date of publication, dates of references, statistics, and other resources used by the author. The timeliness of information can often impact its accuracy in the current context. For example, you would not want to quote statistics from 1990 about the number of single mothers enrolled in college courses because these numbers have grown steadily in the last decade.

● *Consistency of facts.* Examine the facts (especially the statistics) to see if there is consistency. Inaccurate information is often unintentionally added to publications (journal articles, magazines, <u>webpages</u>) when an author who is not familiar with the relationships of statistical values discusses a variety of statistics. For example, on one page the author may state that 250 subjects participated in a study, but then during the data analysis, the author may inadvertently use data from only 200 participants. Inconsistencies like these can indicate imprecise conclusions on the part of the author.

● *Grammar and spelling.* Numerous errors in grammar and spelling are often indicators that information may not be of a quality that you want to include in your college <u>coursework</u>.

- *Online databases.* Online databases are generally excellent resources for finding quality information, though each individual database should be evaluated using standards similar to those that you would use to assess the quality of information in an academic journal or other resource.

- *Biases.* If the author presents only one side of a debate or an issue, it is often an indicator that the information is not from an objective source. You should look for signs of partiality in the terms and phrases used by the author. For example, proponents of uniform testing refer to exams as "standardized tests" whereas opponents refer to them as "high-stakes testing." By examining the words the author chooses to use when describing a topic, you can often identify potential biases.

- *Comprehensive review.* Most of the scholarly resources that will provide you with quality information for your college coursework present a comprehensive review of the literature supporting the many viewpoints regarding an issue. Single perspectives on an issue or topic are typically of less use to students because there is greater potential of bias.

- *Citations and references.* An author's ability to provide accurate and complete citations and references for the information that she extracts from other resources is a good indicator of the quality of information contained within his or her work. If quotes, statistics, and other excerpts have inaccurate citations or incomplete references, then you should examine the information with keen scrutiny.

- *Original source.* If you want to use a quote or specific fact from an earlier publication that is referenced in your current resources, you should always go back to the original source (that is, the referenced article or book) to verify that the current author's interpretation of the quote or fact is consistent with that of the original author. When original source documents are not available, then you should cite those resources appropriately (for example, "Stevenson, 1966 as cited in Voung, 2003").

> **STUDENT-TO-STUDENT TIP**
>
> To help ensure the validity of information, I would suggest selecting reliable material found on organizational websites or from online journals. Another tip I would suggest is to check and see if the author's name and credentials are listed, as well as the date of publication.

- *Support.* Quality information is rarely presented without corroboration. Authors should provide adequate support from additional journals, books, and other resources that substantiate their position and/or facts.

Information Usefulness

Lastly, you will want to evaluate potential resources for information based on their usefulness to your specific course assignment or activity. The unfortunate reality of research is that very few of the potential resources that you will review when searching for useful information will be of assistance in completing your college <u>coursework</u>. To help reduce the amount of time and energy that you spend reviewing resources that will not be useful in your assignment or activity, you will want to develop strategies for quickly assessing the potential utility of resources such as <u>webpages</u>, journal articles, books, and online databases.

- *Relate to goals.* Whether it is a <u>webpage</u> or academic journal articles, you will want to determine if (and how) each potential source of information relates to the goals of your course assignment or activity. Spending time to locate and read through sources of information that are not useful to your <u>coursework</u> is not a strategy for success in college.

ACTIVITY 3-1   Did This Section Click?

Evaluate an online news article from one of today's <u>websites</u> (for example, http://www.nytimes.com/college/students/, http://www.cnn.com, http://www.wsj.com), using the following table. Place a check mark next to each criterion as you review the resource. You should also copy this table and use it to evaluate online resources that you plan to use in papers and other assignments in your college courses.

RELIABILITY	QUALITY	USEFULNESS
☐ Contact information included	☐ Avoids broad generalizations	☐ Relates to your goals
☐ Satisfactory author credentials	☐ Up-to-date resources and references	☐ Relates to your writing or research outline
☐ Publication has a respectable reputation	☐ Consistency of facts	
☐ Sponsoring organization(s) of the author and/or publication are identified	☐ Appropriate grammar and spelling	☐ Appropriate or similar audience
☐ Blind peer–review process	☐ From an online database	☐ Appropriate level of detail for your goals
☐ Contacted author provided additional information	☐ Bias or one-sided perspectives	
	☐ Comprehensive review	
	☐ Citations and references are accurate and complete	
	☐ Resource is original source	
	☐ Support or corroboration of facts	

- *Outline before writing or researching.* One of the best ways to know what information will be the most useful in your <u>coursework</u> is to outline your assignments or activities before you start to write about or research a topic. While outlining your assignment or activity, you should be able to identify the types of information that will be most useful when you construct the submission. For example, when outlining an essay on the influence of affirmative action programs on the admissions policies of colleges, you would identify several locations in the paper where supporting statistical facts would be useful. Then in your search for useful resources, you would know what types of statistical facts would later be useful when you compose your essay.

- *Audience level.* Typically, sources of information that are written for an audience that is either below or above your level of expertise do not turn out to be the ideal resources for college <u>coursework</u>. Just as a high school chemistry book will not likely provide you with the information that you require for college courses, an engineer's guide to chemical reactions may provide you with information that is beyond your current level of understanding and that is of little use as well.

- *Level of detail.* Depending on the characteristics of your course assignments or activities, the level of detail that you are looking for in resources will help you narrow your search for useful resources. If you are required to write a one-page position paper on a current event topic, searching through statistical databases for obscure relationships and supporting data is not likely to be an effective use of your time.

Tips for Avoiding Plagiarism and Copyright Violations

The <u>Internet</u> and other e-learning technologies have brought unprecedented access to written, audio, and video resources that can be used to enrich your education. Many of these online resources are, however, the property of the creators and must only be used within the acceptable limits of copyright and intellectual-property laws. While the ethics of sharing music and video files is often debated on college campuses, the rules for using the words, ideas, music, and other forms of expression created by others are clear.

Verify Your Understanding of Plagiarism, Copyright, and Intellectual-Property Rights It is your responsibility to have accurate and up-to-date knowledge of both the laws and college policies regarding plagiarism and copyright. From submitting a term paper you purchased online to quoting an author without proper citations, defining the boundaries of what is and is not plagiarism is a skill that you will have to develop as a student.

- *Copyright* is the legal right granted to an author, composer, playwright, publisher, or distributor to exclusive publication, production,

TRY SOMETHING **NEW**

Web Tool: **http://www.zotero.org**

Finding valuable and usable information online that you can incorporate into your term papers or other college assignments is just one step toward applying necessary consideration of plagiarism policy and copyright law. Another important step is to properly cite and reference the source of the information; include date, author, title, and other details. As a consequence, organizing all of the potential resources you collect for your coursework become essential to your success—and this is where Zotero comes in. Zotero lets you capture and save all of the essential reference information for resources you find online, including websites, new articles, journal articles found through your library's research databases, and others. Zotero also works with your word processing software (such as Microsoft Word) to insert the appropriate citation and reference information when you decide to use information from an identified resource. Zotero, with its many other functions, is a powerful and free web tool for organizing your reference resources.

sale, or distribution of a literary, musical, dramatic, or artistic work. These works do not have to include the copyright symbol (©) to be protected under the law.

- *Plagiarism* is taking someone's words or ideas as if they were your own. This includes such violations as submitting someone else's paper or presentation as your own work, not providing adequate citations and references for the ideas of others, or misquoting the words of an author.

- *Intellectual property* is the intangible property that is the result of creativity. This includes both tangible (for example, a printed paper or purchased DVD) and intangible (for example, online or electronic copy of a paper, song, or movie) forms of that creativity.[3]

At the *E-learning Companion* Premium Website, you will find several online quizzes that will test your knowledge and understanding of plagiarism, copyright, and intellectual property. Completing these quizzes and reviewing the provided feedback will help guide you in the appropriate use of the resources in your college courses.

Review Your College's Code of Academic Integrity   As a college student, you have agreed to abide by the code of academic integrity (or honor code) of your school. Both the code and the related policies are available in most student handbooks and on college websites. This code applies to both the work that you submit to instructors as well as other publications, speeches, presentations, and other communications that you make as a student. You will want to review your college's code of academic integrity (as well as the related policies and penalties for violation) during your first semester and whenever you have questions.

Ask Questions Before Submitting   If you have any questions regarding your use of quotes, references, music files, pictures, or any work originally created by another person, you should ask your instructor (or your college's

Avoiding Plagiarism – Examples

Original Material: Cognitive learning involves mental processes we cannot directly observe—processes like thinking, information processing, problem solving, and mental imaging. Psychologists who study cognitive learning maintain that humans and other animals are, at least to a certain extent, capable of new behaviors without actually having had the chance to perform them or being reinforced for them.

Reference: Nevid, J. (2009). Psychology: Concepts and Applications (3rd Edition). New York: Wadsworth, Cengage Learning.

EXAMPLES OF PLAGIARISM	EXAMPLES OF CORRECT USAGE
No Citation for Quote: Cognitive learning maintains that humans, and other animals, are "capable of new behaviors without actually having had the opportunity to perform them or being reinforced for them." Cognitive learning involves mental processes, such as problem solving, that cannot be directly observed.	*Correct:* Researchers of cognitive learning "maintain that humans and other animals are, at least to a certain extent, capable of new behaviors without actually having had the chance to perform them or being reinforced for them" (Nevid, 2009, p. 199).
Only Rearranged Words: Processes like information processes, mental imaging, problem solving, and thinking are examples of cognitive learning since they involve mental processes we cannot directly observe.	*Correct:* Nevid (2009) states that, "cognitive learning involves mental processes we cannot directly observe—processes like thinking, information processing, problem solving, and mental imaging" (p. 199).
Paraphrasing Without Citation: Cognitive learning, which focuses on mental processes that we cannot observe directly, is studied by psychologists who believe that humans and animals can learn new behaviors without actually having the chance to practice or get reinforcements for them.	*Correct:* Nevid (2009) suggests that psychologists studying cognitive learning believe that humans and animals can learn new behaviors without practicing or getting reinforcements. Consequently they focus their studies on mental processes that cannot be observed directly.
No Quotation: According to Nevid, the author of our textbook, psychologists who study cognitive learning maintain that humans and other animals are, at least to a certain extent, capable of new behaviors without actually having had the chance to perform them or being reinforced for them.	*Correct:* According to Nevid (2009), the author of our textbook, "psychologists who study cognitive learning maintain that humans and other animals are, at least to a certain extent, capable of new behaviors without actually having had the chance to perform them or being reinforced for them" (p. 199).

Additional examples available at: http://www.indiana.edu/~istd/ examples.html

office of academic integrity) to review your assignment before submitting it. If a draft, prior to submission to an instructor, contains any violations, then you can correct those errors without penalty. When a paper, presentation, or other assignment has been submitted to your instructor, however, then violations may be cause for disciplinary action.

⊕ *If It Is Not Your Idea, Don't Use It Without a Citation and Reference* When you want to build upon the ideas or words of others, you must give them credit for their work. At the place (or places) where you capitalize on their ideas, provide a proper citation and then include the full reference for their work at the end of the paper. There are several formats for both citations and references, and your instructor will typically include which format you are expected to use in his syllabus (or the assignment description). At the E-Learning Companion

⊕ Can I Use This? Worksheet

Instructions – Complete a copy of this worksheet for each online resource you use in your paper.

Title:

Complete Website Address:

Date Retrieved:

Author(s):

Website Owner:

   [*If not evident, go to http://www.internic.net/whois.html*]

Volume, Issue, Page Numbers:

Is the copyright holder identified?   Yes   No

If Yes, who owns the copyright (e.g., magazine, journal, book publisher, or Website)?

What did you use from this resource?

   Quote(s) and their page numbers

   Paraphrased concept(s) and their page numbers

   Generalized concept(s)

Did you use more than 10% of the original ideas expressed by the author(s)?   Yes   No

If Yes, did you contact the copyright holder to gain rights to use this work?   Yes   No

Did you use an image, graphic, or illustration from this resource?   Yes   No

If Yes, did you contact the copyright holder to gain rights to use this work?   Yes   No

What percentage of your work was based on this resource?

   Less than 10%

   10–25%

   More than 25% (not recommended)

What original source articles, books, reports, Websites, or other resources referenced by the author did you use to verify this resource?

Premium <u>Website</u> you will find several <u>websites</u> that provide useful guides for formatting both citations and references in your college courses.

When in Doubt, Don't Use It What constitutes a violation of plagiarism and copyright is not always a black-and-white decision. If you find yourself in a gray area where it is unclear if your use of work created by another is proper, it is always better to err on the side of caution.

Paraphrasing Can be Plagiarism Even if you move the words around and/or change the paragraph structure, you can still be plagiarizing another author when you use their idea or concept in your paper. Plagiarism involves more than just the words. You can use their ideas to support your ideas, but in the end the ideas, words, and other materials that you submit in your college courses must be your own.

⊕ *Protect Intellectual Property* Just as you would not want other students submitting your term paper under their names, you will want to protect the intellectual property rights of others. You should review your college's rules and policies regarding the sharing or distribution of intellectual property (for example, music, videos, pictures, and papers), as well as applicable federal and state laws. Whenever these laws, rules, and policies do not provide clear direction, you will have an ethical choice to make. There are a variety of online resources available at the E-Learning Companion Premium <u>Website</u> to help you make an informed decision.

Tips for Online Security and Privacy

The Internet offers as many advantages to you as a student as it does to criminals and others who want to take advantage of the information available online. Your online habits are, nevertheless, the most effective deterrent of crimes such as credit card scams and identify theft. Manage your private information prudently and you should be able avoid security problems without limiting your use of online technologies.

Change Your Passwords Frequently For <u>email</u> accounts, bank <u>websites</u>, and other online tools that have access to your private information (for example, phone number, birthday, credit card, address, pictures), change your passwords every six to nine months. Many <u>websites</u> will remind you that it is time to change your password, but others will not and then it is up to you.

Use a Variety of Passwords Changing passwords frequently can make it difficult to remember which password is associated with which <u>website</u> or <u>email</u> account. It is often helpful to have four or five passwords that you simply rotate through, every six to nine months, for each account. For your primary college <u>email</u> account, however, do not use the same password that you use for other <u>website</u> or <u>email</u> accounts. This account should have a unique password just for it.

Be Careful with Posting Pictures Online Posting pictures online can be a great way to keep in touch with friends, but pictures posted to the Internet are not private. Even in social networking sites such as Facebook, online pictures can easily be copied and shared with others. Consequently, never post pictures online that you would not want your family or future employer to see.

Think Twice Before Sharing Personal Information From photo sharing sites to travel agencies, many <u>websites</u> will request your private information. Often there is no problem with sharing this information (such as when you make online purchases through reputable businesses), but you must be cautious in sharing personal information. Do not post personal information (such as age, date of birth, address, or phone number) to any <u>websites</u> unless there is some policy guaranteeing the security of your information; and never share it with strangers in chat rooms, social networks, or even online dating <u>websites</u>.

Watch Out for <u>Email</u> Scams Many (many) scams will come to your <u>email</u>. Often these will be disguised as legitimate business offers or friends seeking financial help. Your bank, for example, will never send you an <u>email</u> asking for private information or your password. Nevertheless, these <u>email</u> scams will often create <u>email</u>s and <u>websites</u> that look official (for example, including the bank logo) and request your private information; do not follow the links in these <u>email</u>s. Another popular <u>email</u> scam involves money orders; never cash a money order for anyone in order to send them the money—this is a scam.

Look for HTTPS When Paying Online When making online purchases, retailers use a secure Internet service known as HTTPS—thus the URL for the payment <u>website</u> will begin with https:// (rather than http://). As an alternative, may online stores also accept PayPal (http://www.paypal.com), which is a secure way to make purchases online either through your credit card or your bank account.

Keep Your Virus Protection Software Up to Date Virus protection software is only effective in protecting your computer and private information when it is update frequently. Look for alerts that tell you when new updates are available for your virus protection software.

Timesaving Technology Tips

In completing your online assignments and activities, you will want to take advantage of the many timesaving features that are common in today's <u>software</u> applications. Although using these functions will take some practice, you can use your time more efficiently by using just a few of the following timesaving features.

Make Use of Keyboard Shortcuts Keyboard shortcuts (or hot keys) are combinations of the keys that you can use to accomplish specialized functions. By using the keyboard shortcuts rather than taking the time to complete each step with the computer's mouse, you can efficiently do everything from copying-and-pasting to switching between your <u>email</u> and your online

TABLE 3-1   Right-Click Functions for Computers with Microsoft Software

SOFTWARE APPLICATION	SAMPLE FUNCTIONS AVAILABLE WITH RIGHT-CLICK
Microsoft Windows **desktop**	Arrange Icons, Line Up Icons, Refresh, Paste, Rename, New Folder, New Shortcut, New File, Properties
Microsoft Word	Cut, Copy, Paste, Font, Paragraph, Bullets and Numbering, Synonyms, Hyperlinks, Table Features, Translations, as well as Spelling Check and Grammar Check recommendations for indicated text
Microsoft Internet Explorer	Back, Forward, Save Image, Save Background, Set Wallpaper, Select All, Paste, Create Shortcut, Add to Favorites, View HTML Source, Print, Refresh, Properties

course materials. Take a few minutes to review some of the common keyboard shortcuts (see Table QR-1 in the Quick Reference section of this book) and then practice them the next time you are working at your computer.

For example:

Ctrl+ c	Copy (most Windows applications)	
Ctrl+ v	Paste (most Windows applications)	
Ctrl+ z	Undoes the last action (most Windows applications)	

You can also customize keyboard shortcuts for functions that you commonly repeat that may not be standard for the Microsoft Windows operating system. Additionally, many of these same keyboard shortcuts are functional on Macintosh computers as well.

Exploit the Right-Click   The typical computer mouse will have one or more buttons that can be pressed by your fingers as you move the mouse (as well as the pointer on the screen). Most of us are most familiar with the left mouse button because it is used to select software applications, open files, and do a variety of other functions with either single- or double-clicks. The right mouse button is, however, a useful timesaving tool that can be used effectively with little practice. Table 3-1 provides a list of sample functions that are available when you press the right mouse button in several software applications (for an Apple computer, hold down Control when clicking).

Tips for Accessibility

For all students, both those with disabilities and those without, creating a functional computer environment is essential for success in online coursework. From tools for turning text into speech to improving the contrast of colors on your computer screen, a variety of tools can be used to improve the accessibility of information on your computer. You should take a few minutes before the semester begins to explore the accessibility options available on your computer; using these tools may enhance the efficiency of your studies when you are spending long hours at the computer completing your coursework.

Capitalize on the Tools of the Operating System   The Windows Control Panel (accessed by clicking on the Start button and then selecting the Settings menu) can be used to increase the accessibility of information in your computer. These features are not only useful for those with learning or physical disabilities but also very helpful for anyone spending long hours at the computer completing online coursework.

ACCESSIBILITY OPTIONS

- Add visual notifications for sounds produced by the Windows operating system (for example, a visual alert that accompanies the sound associated with closing an application).

- Select high-contrast screen colors.

- Turn off the mouse and use only the keyboard.

- Select alternative input devices other than the keyboard and mouse.

DISPLAY OPTIONS

- Set the appearance to have high-contrast colors for application **windows**, menus, and other features.

- Use the settings tab to enlarge or reduce the size of images displayed on the monitor.

- Select the use of larger **icons** on the **desktop**.

KEYBOARD OPTIONS

- Increase or decrease the sensitivity of the keyboard.

MOUSE OPTIONS

- Select the mouse to be oriented for left- or right-handed use.

- Vary the speed of double-clicks with the mouse.

- Increase the size of the pointer image that is controlled by the mouse.

- Increase or decrease the speed of the pointer as it travels across the screen.

- Add a trail to the pointer image to increase visibility.

Advance Your Use of Software Applications   Individual software applications also typically have a variety of resources that can be used to expand accessibility.

WEB BROWSERS

- Web browsers (such as Microsoft Internet Explorer and Netscape Navigator) allow you to enlarge or reduce the text font size for webpages that you select to view. You can typically make these adjustments from the View menu.

- Text-to-speech is also available to assist those who are visually impaired. These <u>software</u> applications typically work with most <u>Web browser</u> applications.

- The Tab key can be used to advance through options (such as text **fields** in an online survey) available on many <u>webpage</u>s.

- If provided by the <u>webpage</u> developer, <u>Web browsers</u> can be set to provide text descriptions of online images.

WORD PROCESSING

- Text-based tips can be viewed to provide descriptions of <u>icon</u> <u>menu</u> options.

- To increase the visibility of text when using a <u>word processing software</u> application, you can improve the visibility of the document by increasing the font size or the zoom. Increasing the font size will increase the size of each letter (or character) in the document both on the screen as well as when the document is printed. Increasing the zoom (for example, from 75 to 120%) will improve the visibility only while the document is on the computer screen.

- Text-to-speech is also available to assist those who are visually impaired. These <u>software</u> applications typically work with most <u>word processing</u> applications including Microsoft Word and Corel WordPerfect.

- Sounds can be added for many <u>menu</u> options.

MAGNIFIER APPLICATION

- The typical installation of Microsoft Windows will include the Magnifier application (accessed by clicking on the Start button and then selecting the Programs <u>menu</u> and the Accessories and Accessibility sub<u>menus</u>). The Magnifier application allows you to enlarge any portion of the Windows screen for greater visibility.

ADDITIONAL INFORMATION

- Microsoft also provides a variety of assistive technologies, tips, and tools that are available online at

  http://www.microsoft.com/enable/default.htm

  Likewise, Macintosh provides an assortment of accessibility features, tips, and resources available at

  http://www.apple.com/disability/easyaccess.html

  These include guides for specific physical disabilities, information on using a keyboard with one hand or finger, and other resources that can improve the accessibility of computer resources.

ACTIVITY 3-2   Did This Section Click?

As a review, answer the following questions by marking the correct response.

1. Which key would you press in conjunction with the control (**Ctrl**) key to copy information that is highlighted?
   a. The "x" key
   b. The "c" key
   c. The "v" key

2. Which key would you press to move from one **field** to another (for example, name to address, or phone number to fax number) in a data form available on the World Wide Web?
   a. The Shift key
   b. The Tab key
   c. The Alt key

3. Which of the following functions is *not* available when you right-click in Microsoft Word?
   a. Change the font size, color, format, and so on
   b. Copy-and-paste
   c. Print

Tips for Managing Your Files

Keeping track of the many files that you will create throughout college will be an overwhelming burden if you don't set a strategy for staying organized from the first semester.

 Create a Folder Structure   Before you add any new files to your computer, you will want to develop a strategy for organizing the many files that will be created over the semester. To do this, you will want to construct a hierarchy of file <u>folders</u> in which you can store your many files. Putting a little thought into the structure of these <u>folders</u> before you begin classes can save you lots of time later in the semester.

A strategy that many students find useful is to first create a <u>folder</u> for each semester they are in college. Then within the appropriate semester, they create another level of <u>folders</u>, one <u>folder</u> for each course they are taking. All files related to the individual course will then have a specific location where they should be saved. In a similar manner, for courses with a large number of assignments or activities, a third level of <u>folders</u> may be used to organize files by assignment or activity.

Whatever <u>folder</u> structure that you select for organizing your files, you should go about creating the empty file <u>folders</u> at

STUDENT-TO-STUDENT TIP

Each online class generates a lot of files, so to keep track of them, I create a <u>folder</u> for each new class, and within that class <u>folder</u>, I create a <u>folder</u> for major assignments and then save corresponding files into those <u>folders</u>.

the beginning of each semester. This way, the <u>folder</u> structure will be in place, and you will be able to quickly identify which files should be saved in which <u>folders</u> throughout the semester.

Develop a File-Naming Strategy   When you create a new file (whether it is Microsoft Word document, a PowerPoint presentation, or a MP3 music file), you should have a naming strategy that will help you identify the files later on. Useful naming strategies will include essential information for identifying the contents of the file, including course name or number, assignment name or number, date of the file, or other information that will be useful when you later search for a desired file. In most **operating systems**, however, you cannot include the following characters in a <u>file name</u>:

  " " ' ' | \ / [ ] , ? * < >

By developing a file-naming strategy early on in your college experience, you will be less likely to lose valuable information, distribute the wrong files to classmates, or submit erroneous files to your professors for grading (see Table 3-2).

Don't Change the File Extensions   The <u>file name</u> that you give to your documents provides only part of the information necessary for you to access the file. Added to the end of each <u>file name</u> is a three- or four-character extension (after the last period) that identifies the computer application that should be used to open (or run) the selected file (see Table 3-3). For example, the end of a Microsoft Word file will typically have the extension .doc to indicate that the file can be opened with Microsoft Word or another application that supports Microsoft Word files.

The inclusion of the extension in the <u>file name</u> is essential in managing your files. Without the accurate extension, the computer cannot automatically open the file using the appropriate <u>software</u> application, thus causing the computer to request that you select the fitting application to open the file (which you may or may not remember later in the semester). Because most <u>software</u> applications will automatically include a default file extension, you should not change or delete the file extension on files that you create or rename.

TABLE 3-2 Examples of Effective Naming Strategies

INEFFECTIVE FILE NAMES	EFFECTIVE FILE NAMES
History1.doc	HIS101-assign1-draft3.doc
Termpaper.doc	10-12-09 EDU101 term paper.doc
Johns presentation.ppt	Assign2 John Reynolds.ppt
Music mix.mp3	Alternative Mix 4-10-11.mp3

TABLE 3-3   Common File Extensions

FILE EXTENSION	COMMON USE OF FILE	COMMONLY ASSOCIATED SOFTWARE
.doc (.wpd)	Word processing file	Microsoft Word (Corel WordPerfect)
.pdf (portable document file)	Document-sharing file	Adobe Acrobat PDF Reader or Adobe Acrobat PDF Distiller
.txt, .text (ASCII or Simple Text format), .rtf (rich text format)	Word processing file	Most any text or word processing software for Macintosh or Windows operating systems
.bmp, .gif, .jpg, .jpeg, .tif, .tiff	Graphics file	Most any graphics viewer including Microsoft Internet Explorer, Word, and Microsoft PowerPoint
.mov, .qt	Audio and video formats	Apple QuickTime
.mpg, .mpeg, .avi	Audio and video formats	Most any audio or video software including Microsoft Media Player and RealNetworks Player
.ra, .ram	Audio and video formats	Real Audio Player
.wav, .wave, .au, .aac	Audio file	Most any audio software including Microsoft Media Player, RealNetworks Player, and iTunes (iPods play .aac)
.ppt	Slideshow presentation	Microsoft PowerPoint (or the free Microsoft PowerPoint Viewer)
.exe	Executable file (starts a software application)	Windows operating system
.zip	File compression	WinZip. StuffIt, and PKZip software
.htm, .html (hypertext markup language)	Interactive files available on the World Wide Web	Microsoft Internet Explorer and Netscape Navigator

File extensions will also provide you with essential information when other students or instructors share files with you from their computer. By reading the file extension you will be able to identify whether or not you have suitable software for opening a file. For example, if your professor emails you a copy of the course syllabus in a file named

"Geo 101-3 syllabus.pdf," you would be able to determine that the <u>Adobe Acrobat PDF software</u> application was required for viewing the contents of that file.

Use the Tools for Finding Files   Microsoft Windows offers three primary tools for finding files after you have saved them to your computer's hard drive: Find Files or Folders, Windows Explorer, and My Computer. When you make use of each tool will depend on your file structure and how much you remember in locating the desired file.

> *My Computer.* This tool for accessing the file structure is most use-ful when you have a good idea about where the desired file is lo-cated. It will allow you to quickly move through file <u>folders</u> (in a single or in multiple <u>windows</u>) until you have located the file. My Computer does not, however, illustrate the <u>folders</u> structure in the viewable <u>window</u>. My Computer is accessible from the Windows <u>desktop</u>.

> *Windows Explorer.* This tool for finding files is useful when you are less sure of the location of a desired file. Windows Explorer allows you to navigate the contents of file <u>folders</u> quickly in a single <u>window</u> format that simultaneously shows both the hierar-chy of the <u>folder</u> structure as well as the contents of individual <u>folders</u>. Windows Explorer is accessible from the Start button <u>menus</u>.

> *Find Files or Folders.* The Find Files or Folders feature is accessi-ble from the Start button in Microsoft Windows and facilitates the search for files or <u>folders</u> when you do not know how to locate a desired file. The Find Files or Folders option allows you to select the hard drive (such as your C: drive), floppy disk, CD, or DVD in which you would like to begin the search. From here you can also narrow the search to a particular <u>folder</u> (that is, **file directory**).

The Find Files or Folders application will then search for the de-sired file based on the search parameters that you provide. For example, if you know that the file should have the course number included in its name, then you could search for "Bio 101," and the Find application would locate all files whose name includes "Bio 101" with the specified <u>folder</u> (<u>file directory</u>). You can also search for files by their file extension. For example, if you know that the desired file is a Microsoft PowerPoint presentation that should be located in the <u>folder</u> that contains all of the files from the fall of your first year in college, then you could search for all Power-Point files within that <u>folder</u> by using the **asterisk** to represent the name of any file (for example, *.ppt) and followed by a period and the file extension. Other search examples could include *.doc for any Microsoft Word document or *.ram for any Real Audio Player file.

ACTIVITY 3-3   Did This Section Click?

🌐 As a review, mark the correct word or phrase that completes the following statements.

1. The file extension for a file that is available on the <u>World Wide Web</u> and viewable using a <u>Web browser</u> is
   a. .exe.
   b. .ppt.
   c. .html.

2. The Find Files or Folders function is accessed by first
   a. clicking on the My Computer <u>icon</u>.
   b. clicking on the Start button.
   c. using a right-click.

3. In most <u>operating system</u>s, this character can be included in the name of file
   a. \
   b. -
   c. *

Back Up Your Files Every Week   To keep up with the organization and management of your files, you will want to <u>back up</u> your course files on a floppy disk, recordable CD or DVD, or other data storage device each week throughout the semester. Though memory failures such as hard drives freezing or CD-ROMs losing their data are less common with today's technologies, you do not want to risk losing the valuable files that you are creating in completing your college <u>coursework</u>. Take a few minutes each week to <u>back up</u> your course files to a recordable CD or DVD (or to another back-up system like a shared <u>server</u>, secondary hard drive, or even a floppy disk).

Tips for Using Apps

<u>Apps</u> are <u>software</u> programs that run on a **smart phone**, such as an iPhone, G1, Windows Mobile or BlackBerry (and more recently, apps are also available for the Apple iPod). These add-on software applications are typically free or inexpensive, and offer numerous tools that you can use to support your college success.

Download Educational <u>Apps</u>   From specially designed assignment calendars to customizable flash cards, there are numerous <u>apps</u> that can make success in your courses a little easier. <u>Educational portal</u>s, like BlackBoard, also offer <u>apps</u> to access your online courses.

Try New <u>Apps</u>   New <u>apps</u> come out every day; give many of them a try to see which work best for you. Apps are generally free or inexpensive, and many of those that cost money offer *lite* or *trial* versions that you can test out for free.

Use Integrative Apps   Many of the apps for smart phones integrate with other websites, such as apps that let you access your Google Calendars, Skype, or Facebook from your smart phone. These apps integrate many of the most useful websites into easy-to-use tools on your phone.

Use Apps to Stay Organized   Calendars, dictionaries, and note pads are all useful apps for keeping organized and having class information available when you want it.

Look for Study Aids   From SparkNotes, CliffNotes, and audiobooks to the periodic table and test preparation guides, there are many apps that can be useful study aids for every subject from sociology to Greek history. Look for useful apps that can help you succeed in your college courses.

Tips for Using the World Wide Web

Know Some of the Web Basics   The World Wide Web offers an assortment of resources that will be essential to your college education. From accessing course materials that professors make available in educational portals to conducting library research from home, the World Wide Web will provide you the critical information for being successful while giving you access to that information 24 hours a day. However, you will often find that you can access information faster if you use the World Wide Web in the morning before 11:00 A.M. or after 10:00 P.M. because the number of users is typically lower during those hours.

The basic function of the World Wide Web is to provide the connection between millions of computers that share information. Individuals or organizations that want to offer information on the World Wide Web simply make the information available on a specialized computer called a server, which is then linked to the network of computers around the world. Distinct files can then be added to the server and made available to all of those who are connected to this worldwide network; these files are what we call webpages. (When multiple pages are linked together through hypertext, they are called websites.)

TRY SOMETHING NEW

Web Tool: **http://www.delicious.com**

From Amazon.com to Zotero.org, you likely have numerous websites that you enjoy, find useful, share with friends, or simply save as a reminder to return to it later. In the past you may have saved these websites as bookmarks (or favorites) on your personal computer, making them difficult to share with others or find again when you are on someone else's computer – such as a roommate's, work, or lab computer. To free yourself, and more important, your favorite websites, give Delicious a try. Delicious offers a user-friendly tool for storing and sharing your favorite websites. Rather than using traditional file structures, Delicious uses tags (or key words) to keep your bookmarks organized and easily share relevant bookmarks with others. You may, for example, want to share your favorite chemistry website with other students in your class, and Delicious makes this easy, fast, and flexible.

Given that there are millions of webpages available everyday on the World Wide Web, **URLs** (uniform resource locators) are used to provide an address for webpages so that users of the network can locate desired files. The URL has four primary components that provide computers with the network address for desired files:

Protocol. The protocol provides the computer with a set of rules for exchanging information across the World Wide Web. The hypertext transfer protocol (**HTTP**) and file transfer protocol (FTP) will likely be the ones that you use most often as a student. As their names suggest, the first is for the transfer of webpages (which are typically hypertext files with the extension .html or .htm), and the latter is for the transfer of files from one computer to another.

Web server. The Web server name provides the computer with information regarding the location of the computer that **hosts** the desired webpage. Though you will typically use a textual description for the desired Web server (such as http://www.youruniversity.edu), this will actually be converted into a numeric Internet address that is used to determine the location of the Web server using a **domain name system** (DNS). When an individual or organization purchases the rights to use a URL name (such as http://www.youruniversity.edu), the name is registered with an organization that assigns a numeric address to the URL name.

Directory. When your computer has identified the address of the **Web server** that contains the files that you desire, you will frequently then provide additional information that identifies the folder location of the specific file you want to view. The same organizational structure used in your personal computer, files stored in folders, is also used in Web servers. The file directory location indicates the folder location of the desired file.

File. The file name and extension provide the computer with specific information regarding the name and type of file that is stored in the file directory on the Web server. Most commonly, the files that you view on the World Wide Web are hypertext markup language (HTML or HTM) files. If you do not know the specific file that you want to access when you enter a Web server and file directory, then by default the file that will be accessed is index.html.

Use Your Institution's Educational Portal Educational portals are a specialized type of Internet portal used by colleges and universities to provide a variety of resources (such as synchronous chat rooms, discussion boards, email, and technical support) through a single website that can be easily accessed by students and instructors. Some of the most common educational portals at colleges and universities are WebCT, Blackboard, Angel, and eCollege.

You should be familiar with the variety of resources that can be accessed through your institution's <u>educational portal</u> before you are required to use it in one of your courses.

Tips for Downloading

Download Additional Tools and Resources That May Be Useful   <u>Downloading software</u> applications from the <u>World Wide Web</u> can add useful tools and resources to your computer. From adding <u>software</u> that will compress files so they take up less space on your computer to accessing tools for improving the search capabilities of your <u>Web browser</u>, you should become familiar with the procedures for <u>downloading</u> and installing <u>software</u> from the <u>World Wide Web</u>. This will allow you to expand your use of the computer as a tool for learning.

There are five primary types of <u>software</u> that you are likely to <u>download</u> from the <u>World Wide Web</u> as a student:

- *Updates.* Companies often provide files that you can <u>download</u> and install in your computer to improve the performance of <u>software</u> that you have already purchased.

- *Plug-Ins (or add-ons).* These <u>software</u> applications are directly tied to <u>Web browsers</u> and once installed they will automatically activate themselves when required.

- *Apps.* Small <u>software</u> applications that run on <u>smart phones</u> or iPods, expanding the capabilities to include such tools as dictionaries, course assignment trackers, and shared calendars.

- *Trials.* Because potential clients often want the opportunity to try out <u>software</u> that they may later purchase, many <u>software</u> developers offer 30-, 60-, and even 90-day trials of their <u>software</u> that you can <u>download</u> for free.

- *Shareware.* Individual <u>software</u> developers commonly make their <u>software</u> applications available on the <u>World Wide Web</u> for anyone to <u>download</u> and install. Shareware developers commonly request a small payment ($5 to $20) for their product, but no mandatory fee is charged.

- *Freeware.* Individual <u>software</u> developers may also make their <u>software</u> applications available to the public without charge (or expectation of payment).

When you have selected and clicked on the link to a file that you would like to <u>download</u>, the <u>Web browser</u> will take you through the necessary steps for moving the file from the <u>Web server</u> to your personal computer. You should be sure to note the file <u>folder</u> in which you are <u>downloading</u> the desired file to your computer. This is important because after the file has been <u>downloaded</u>, you will then have to identify the location of the file on your computer in order to install or open it.

If you are <u>downloading</u> a file that contains a <u>software</u> application (that is, with a file extension of .exe), then you will want to double-click on the file

TABLE 3-4   Free Software Applications That You Can Download

SOFTWARE APPLICATION	USE	AVAILABLE FOR DOWNLOAD FROM
Adobe Acrobat Reader	Allows you to view PDF files	www.adobe.com
WinZip	Allows you to compress (or decompress) large files	www.winzip.com
Skype	Allows you to do audio or video calls with other Skype users, as well as make to inexpensive international phone calls.	www.skype.com
Ad-Aware	Protects your computer against a variety of security threats.	www.lavasoft.com
AVG	Free antivirus software to protect your computer and information.	www.avg.com
QuickTime	Allows you to view audio and video files that are created in the Apple QuickTime format	www.apple.com
RealOne Player	Allows you to view audio and video files that are created in the RealPlayer format	www.realnetworks.com
Shockwave Player	Allows you to view online animations created in the Shockwave format	www.macromedia.com
Flash Player	Allows you to view online animations created in the Flash format	www.macromedia.com

to start the installation process. The installation file will guide you through the necessary steps to install the software application in your computer.

Table 3-4 lists several practical tools and resources that you may want to download and install from the World Wide Web at no cost.

Tips for Searching the World Wide Web

Have A Strategy for Searching the Web   To find more of what you want on the World Wide Web, you will want to develop multiple strategies that can be used in searching for information. Depending on what information that you want to find, the detail of the information that you require, and how much you already know about the topic, you will want to use distinctive search strategies to locate useful information most efficiently.

- Be specific in your search. For example, if you are looking for information regarding the history of the Seminole Indians during the Civil War, you will likely find more information that is of value to your coursework if you search for "Seminole Indians Civil War History" rather than simply "Seminole Indians."

- Many **search engines** allow you to limit your search to websites that provide specific types of information or files (such as news, shopping, pictures, and audio). Use these features to reduce your search time; buttons provided on the search engine webpage can access them.

- Use the plus (+) and/or minus (–) signs to include or exclude terms from your search. For example, if you are looking for information on the members of the U.S. Congress in 1970, you would want to search for "congress + members + 1970." Likewise, if you wanted to search specifically for those members of Congress in 1970 that were not in Congress in 1975, you would want to search for "congress + members +1970 – 1975."

- If you wanted to locate information on the World Wide Web that is a phrase (such as "MTV music awards"), then you would use quotation marks to indicate that only instances where the multiple terms are used in a specific order should be identified.

- Boolean search commands (such as "and", "or", and "not") can be used with most search engines to provide additional information for the search. For example, if you were looking for information on the European Axis powers during World War II, then you would want to search for "War and Germany or Italy not Japan".

- When searching for information that you know is contained on a specific Web server (such as www.nasa.gov), you can limit your search only to those files found on the specific Web server by using "site:" or "host:." For example, if you were looking for information on NASA programs regarding Jupiter, then you would want to search for "site:www.nasa.gov + Jupiter." (AltaVista.com uses "host:" whereas Bing.com, Google.com, and Yahoo.com use "site:.")

- You can also use the "site:" or "host:" commands to limit your search to a specific type of Web server (such as .edu for educational institutions or .com for private organizations). For example, if you wanted to restrict your search for information on Jupiter to only sites maintained by government agencies, you would search for "Jupiter + host:gov."

- Many search engines also have additional software that you can download to improve your search capabilities as plug-ins for your Web browser. These software applications typically add search features to your Web browser that permit you to conduct searches limited to the pages within the website that you are viewing without having to leave the website.

- Don't be fooled into believing that if a webpage comes up at the top of the list it is necessarily the most useful one for finding the information that you desire. Most <u>search engine</u>s provide placement within search results based on advertising revenue provided by <u>webpage</u> owners. For example, if you wanted to market a product, you could pay many <u>search engine</u>s to show your <u>webpage</u> near the top of the list when people search for similar products.

- If you have found a <u>webpage</u> that provides useful information and you believe that additional information may be contained elsewhere on the <u>website</u> (that is, <u>Web server</u>), then you can *back search* by removing first the <u>file name</u> from the <u>URL</u> and then (if necessary) elements of the directory (see the <u>URL</u> figure on page 53). The process of back searching will provide you access to other files available within the same <u>file directory</u> as the file you initially found in your search. For example, if you were searching for information on strategies for using <u>search engine</u>s, you may locate the <u>webpage</u>

STUDENT-TO-STUDENT TIP

<u>Search engine</u>s are powerful tools, but relying simply on the basic search for advanced searches is not very useful. Each <u>search engine</u> has its own set of rules, so it is a good idea to actually read the online directions for using and getting the most out of the <u>search engine</u>'s capabilities.

http://searchenginewatch.com/reports/seindex.html

If you would like more information on <u>search engine</u>s, you would not have to conduct another search but could back search by removing the <u>file name</u> and extension (seindex.html) from the <u>URL</u> and pressing Enter. This would leave you with

http://searchenginewatch.com/reports

Tips for Choosing a Search Engine

Know Which Search Engines to Use   There are three primary types of <u>search engine</u>s that you can use, depending on your search requirements. You will want to practice using each type of <u>search engine</u> so that you can later evaluate which ones will be the most effective and efficient tools for finding the information that you desire on the <u>World Wide Web</u>. Determine which is your personal favorite in each category and keep those <u>bookmarked</u> in your <u>Web browser</u>.

You can also use Noodle Quest to identify appropriate <u>search engine</u>s. Noodle Quest is a search strategy **wizard** that recommends <u>search engine</u>s based on your search requirements. You can access Noodle Quest at

http://www.noodletools.com/noodlequest/

Basic Keyword Searches

Keyword <u>search engine</u>s are the most commonly used. These <u>search engine</u>s review the keywords contained on millions of <u>webpage</u>s to provide you with a list of <u>webpage</u>s that may be useful in providing you with the information you desire. These <u>search engine</u>s are most valuable when you want to conduct a general search for information and have few leads as to where this information may be found on the <u>World Wide Web</u>. Disadvantages to keyword <u>search engine</u>s include the large number of useless <u>webpage</u>s that they provide in their search results.

Examples of <u>search engine</u>s of this variety include Altavista.com, Google.com, Bing.com, Directhit.com, Lycos.com, Excite.com, and Fast-search.com.

Web Directories

Web directories are the "Yellow Pages" of the <u>World Wide Web</u>. They can assist you in quickly identifying <u>webpage</u>s that may be useful resources by providing you access to millions of pages that have been classified into categories by topic. Web directories are most useful when you can categorize the information that you are searching for into broad categories (such as government agencies, history, and baseball) because they will commonly provide you with a larger percentage of useful <u>webpage</u>s than other types of <u>search engine</u>s.

Examples of <u>search engine</u>s of this variety include Yahoo.com, About.com, and Looksmart.com.

Metasearches

<u>Search engine</u>s that provide a metasearch use the resources of many other <u>search engine</u>s to provide you with a list of <u>webpage</u>s that are most likely to meet your search requirements. By using other <u>search engine</u>s to provide information, metasearches are most useful when you have had little success with your favorite <u>search engine</u>. Results from multiple <u>search engine</u>s can be used to locate resources that may not be found by any single search. Like with keyword searches, however, the percentage of useful <u>webpage</u>s may be low with meta<u>search engine</u>s.

Examples of <u>search engine</u>s of this variety include Dogpile.com, Meta-crawler.com, and Savvysearch.com.

Tips for Using Your Web Browser

Effectively using the many resources that are available on the <u>World Wide Web</u> requires that you learn to use the features and tools available in your <u>Web browser</u>. Below are several suggestions for taking advantage of these browser capabilities:

- ☐ <u>Download</u> the most recently available <u>plug-in</u>s or your <u>Web browser</u> before the semester begins. You do not want to find out that you do not have the latest release of a <u>plug-in</u> required for accessing course materials the day an online assignment is due.

AltaVista.com Tips[4]

☐ You can enter up to 200 characters (15 to 20 words) into this search box.

☐ To reduce the number of documents retrieved by your search, try combining multiple terms with the search operators. Here's an example: + "mountain climbing" + photos – tours finds pages containing the phrase *mountain climbing* and the word *photos*, but not the word *tours*.

Dogpile.com Tips

☐ If your search uses the NOT operator, note that when your search is forwarded to search indexes that don't support its use, the operator and the word that follows will be removed from the search statement.

☐ Dogpile will also use the NEAR operator for indexes that support it (AltaVista, InfoSeek). Entering the search "cat NEAR dog" will match documents where these words are in close proximity to each other. For search engines that do not support NEAR, Dogpile will substitute the AND operator.

Google.com Tips

☐ Google is not case sensitive. All searches are processed as lowercase.

☐ Google doesn't perform word stemming. A search for "cat" will not retrieve documents containing the word *cats*.

☐ Google ignores common words (for example, "and" and "is,") and single characters and digits in its searches. To force Google to include a common word, single character, or digit in a search, precede it with a + sign.

Yahoo.com Tips

☐ Documents matching more of the search terms appear before those matching fewer.

☐ Matches to words in the Yahoo! category tree are sorted higher than matches in Web documents.

☐ If there are multiple matches within the Yahoo! category tree, a higher placement is given to the broader, less specific category.

☐ Matches to words in the titles of webpages will appear before matches to words in the body text of webpages.

☐ Creating bookmarks (or *favorites*) for webpages that you find useful can help you find the resources you want, when you want them. It is also useful to create folders within the bookmarks directory for keeping valuable webpages organized.

☐ When you locate your college's <u>educational portal</u> on the <u>World Wide Web</u> (or other course <u>websites</u> that you plan to use often), you should create a **shortcut** to the page that appears as an <u>icon</u> on your computer's <u>desktop</u>. By clicking on this <u>shortcut,</u> the computer will automatically open a <u>Web browser</u> and locate the specific page you have selected.

☐ When you have selected a link to another <u>webpage</u> that you would like to view, you can open that link in a new <u>Web browser</u> <u>window</u> by selecting the Open in New Window option when you right-click on the link. As a result, you will not have to click on the Back button to return to the initial <u>webpage</u>. This is also useful if you want to conduct multiple searches for the same information using more than one <u>search engine</u>.

☐ When printing <u>webpages</u> that are contained within a frame (that is, a smaller <u>window</u> appears within a larger <u>window</u> that commonly contains <u>menu</u> options), you can print the contents of the frame without printing the entire page. By right-clicking on the area of the <u>webpage</u> that you want to print, you can select the print option and only print the contents of that <u>window</u>.

☐ When you post information to a <u>webpage</u> (such as on a <u>discussion board</u>), the information that you post may not automatically appear on the screen. If this is the case, then you should click on the Refresh (or Reload) button on the <u>Web browser</u>'s **menu bar** to retrieve an updated copy of the <u>webpage</u>.

☐ <u>Web browsers</u> typically read <u>webpages</u> that are written in <u>HTML</u>. These files should have file extensions of either .html or .htm in order to be

ACTIVITY 3-4   **Did This Section Click?**

🌐 As a review, match the following word with the correct definition.

1. ___ Google.com

a. An example of a <u>search engine</u> that uses a directory to search for information on the <u>World Wide Web</u>

2. ___ and

b. An example of a <u>search engine</u> that uses keywords to search for information on the <u>World Wide Web</u>

3. ___ site:

c. A Boolean search command that can be used with most <u>search engines</u> to provide additional information for the search

4. ___ Yahoo.com

d. Can be used to limit a search of the <u>World Wide Web</u> to a specific phrase

5. ___ quotation marks

e. Can be used to limit a search of the <u>World Wide Web</u> to only those <u>webpages</u> found on a specific <u>Web server</u>

viewed properly. If you have entered a <u>URL</u> with one of the two file extensions (for example, .html) and the file does not open, you should try entering the same <u>URL</u> with the alternative file extension (in this case, .htm).

☐ **Cookies** are typically small files that some <u>webpages</u> will automatically <u>download</u> to your computer in order to remember information about you (such as shopping preferences, mailing address, and credit card information). By adjusting the *security control features* of your <u>Web browser,</u> you can open or deny <u>webpages</u> access for storing <u>cookies</u> on your computer. <u>Cookies</u> can be good or bad depending on their use and your desired level of privacy. You should decide what level of privacy fits best with your use of the <u>World Wide Web</u> and review the Help <u>menu</u> of your <u>Web browser</u> for directions on setting the appropriate level of security.

Tips for Using Email

While you have likely developed many useful strategies for using <u>email</u>, the following list of tips can provide you with some additional technical skills for making the best use of the many features that most <u>email</u> <u>software</u> applications and Web-based <u>email</u> systems offer for students.

☐ Most colleges and universities will provide students with access to individual student <u>email</u> accounts through the <u>World Wide Web</u> (commonly referred to as *webmail* and often included in <u>educational portals</u>). Using these online systems to manage your <u>email</u> gives you access to your <u>email</u> from any computer linked to the <u>World Wide Web</u> and with many of the same features as <u>email</u> programs that are not Web-based. However, you can only access these features when you are connected to the <u>Internet</u>.

As an alternative, you may want to <u>download</u> and install an <u>email</u> application (such as Microsoft Outlook or Qualcomm Eudora) to your personal computer for managing your <u>email</u>. These <u>software</u> applications allow you to view, create, and edit <u>email</u> messages even when your computer is not linked to the <u>Internet</u>. They also offer many features for organizing and managing the numerous <u>emails</u> you will receive as a college student (for example, a common feature of <u>email</u> <u>software</u> applications allows you to conduct keyword searches through past <u>emails</u> that you have either sent or received).

☐ Use the <u>email</u> account provided by your college or university for all of your <u>coursework</u>. The college or university is responsible for maintaining your access to only that account. If you are using a private <u>email</u> account through another service and it stops functioning properly, professors are less likely to be lenient in accepting late assignments. Most often if the college or university <u>email</u> system fails to function properly, instructors will take delays resulting from the failure into account because it is a system maintained by the institution.

HOW TO
21

HOW TO
28

HOW TO
35

HOW TO
42

☐ In college courses, you will frequently be required to attach files (such as Microsoft Word documents or <u>Adobe Acrobat PDF</u> files) to <u>emails</u> that you are sending to your professor or fellow students. Practice attaching files to your <u>emails</u> prior to the start of classes to verify that this feature works with your current <u>email</u> <u>software</u> (for example, send yourself an <u>email</u> with an attached file).

☐ Many <u>Web portals</u> and <u>email</u> <u>software</u> applications require that you first identify the file that you want to include as an <u>attachment</u>, often done by clicking on a Browse button and then attaching the file in a second step by clicking on the Attach button.

☐ When you receive an <u>email</u> with a file attached, *be cautious*. Files that are attached to <u>email</u> may contain computer viruses. If you do not know the sender of the <u>email</u> or if you are not expecting an attached file from an instructor or classmate, do not immediately open it. Take the time to <u>email</u> the sender to verify that she did intend for you to receive the file and that the file does not contain a computer virus. It is worth the extra time to be cautious because a computer virus can wipe away months of your work in just a few minutes.

☐ Whether it is an <u>email</u> <u>software</u> application that you have installed on your computer or a Web-based <u>email</u> system, you will want to create an *address book* that organizes the <u>email</u> addresses of your many classmates and instructors. Using the address book will save you time and can help avoid potential problems that occur (such as missing periods or reversed letters) when you type in <u>email</u> addresses. When creating your address book, it is recommended that you **cut-and-paste** <u>email</u> addresses from previous <u>emails</u> into the book rather than manually typing in each address; this will again save you time and avoid potential errors in spelling and punctuation.

☐ Most <u>email</u> <u>software</u> applications and Web-based <u>email</u> systems allow you to create a **signature** that will appear at the end of each <u>email</u> message you send. This can be useful since you do not want to send <u>email</u> messages without important contact information for the recipient to use when replying to your message. Your **signature** file should be concise and only provide essential information for contacting you in reply to the <u>email</u> message (for example, do not include long quotes, jokes, or other extraneous text messages with your <u>signature</u>).

☐ To be successful in college, you will want to remain organized, and this includes managing your numerous <u>email</u> messages. Do not plan to store all your <u>email</u> messages in your <u>email</u> Inbox. By creating <u>folders</u> (much like you would on your computer hard drive), you can organize your <u>emails</u> based on a structure that you determine to be effective. Typically, having <u>email</u> <u>folders</u> for each college course is recommended since it will allow you to quickly access the <u>email</u> messages related to course assignments and activities without a prolonged search.

☐   Email is not always the most appropriate tool for communicating with your instructor or fellow students. Before sending an email, you should review the message to verify that using technology is fitting for the message's context. For example, if you would like to request an extension to an assignment deadline due to an illness in your family, this may not be an appropriate conversation to have through email. Requesting a convenient time for a phone conversation or scheduling a discussion during an instructor's office hours is often more appropriate for conversations related to grades, complex questions, or personal matters.

☐   When you want to share a URL (website address) with your fellow students or instructor, you should insert the URL between a "less-than" character (<) and a "greater-than" character (>). This technique will clearly indicate for the recipient what marks the beginning and the end of a URL. For example,

<http://www.cengage.com/success/Watkins/ELearning3e>

In addition, as with email addresses, you will want to **cut-and-paste** URL information into the message rather than typing in each character. This will reduce the likelihood of mistakes in spelling or punctuation.

Tips for Using Microsoft Word

Like many of today's software applications, Microsoft Word has far too many useful features to be listed in this companion. The following list of tips for using Word highlights a few of the more useful functions for students completing online course assignments and activities.

☐   You will want to set Word to automatically save any document that you are working on every 3 to 5 minutes. By setting this in the Options menu, you will ensure that recent changes to your document are saved even if power is lost to the computer or other technology failures trouble you. To set the time interval for automatic saving of your document, go to the Options menu located under the Tools menu in Word.

☐   The first time you save a Word document, you will be asked to name the file and select the folder location where the file will be stored. You may also select the file format in which you wish the file to be saved if you prefer an alternative to the default, which is the version of Word you have installed (for example, Microsoft Word 2003 or XP). Often you will want to **back save** files to earlier versions of Word because your classmates or instructors may not use the most recently released version that you have.

☐   When searching for specific words or phrases within a Word document, you can use the find feature (Ctrl + f) to quickly locate all instances when the word or phrase are used in the document. You can even select to have the word or phrase replaced with an alternative each time it is identified.

- If you have created a Word document that extends onto the following page by just a few lines, you can use Word's Shrink-to-Fit feature to automatically format the document so that no text is left at the top of the last page. The Shrink-to-Fit feature can be accessed through the Print Preview option.

- When working with other students in the development of a Word document, you can activate the Track Changes feature through the Tools <u>menu</u>. This feature monitors the additions, deletions, and comments of each student who edits the document, allowing others to later accept or reject their changes.

- In Word you can format a word (such as making it **bold,** <u>underlined</u>, or *italic*) by moving the cursor anywhere inside the word and selecting the desired format. You do not have to highlight the entire word by dragging your mouse pointer over the word in order to change the format.

- You can construct creative tables in Word by using the Table AutoFormat feature found in the Table <u>menu</u>. Table AutoFormat provides a long list of table-formatting options that, when selected, are automatically applied in your document.

- If you are searching for just the right word and your cursor is any-where inside the word you can access Word's Thesaurus by holding down Shift + F7 on your keyboard.

- In Word's File <u>menu,</u> you can quickly open files that you have recently created or edited in the past. In the Options feature found in the Tools <u>menu</u>, you can select the number of recently used files that are view-able, up to nine.

- By using the right-click function of your mouse, you can quickly correct spelling and grammatical errors identified by Word. Word indicates spelling and grammatical errors by red or green wavy underlines, respectively; simply right-click on the underlined text to select a suggested revision.

- Word's ruler can be used to create consistent indents, tabs, and margins for any document. This is far more efficient than using the Tab key and can be accessed through the View <u>menu</u>.

- All Word documents that you create should include page numbers. By selecting Page Numbers from the Insert <u>menu,</u> you can quickly add page numbers to your documents. If page numbering is not sequential in the document that you are creating, then you can use section breaks to vary page numbering (See Word's Help <u>menu</u> for more information on using section breaks).

- Additional information regarding the document can be added to the top or bottom of each page by using a **header** or **footer.** Inserting titles, chapter names, and dates can be useful when you are creating many Word documents for a course. You can add <u>header</u> and <u>footer</u> information through the View <u>menu</u>.

☐ Word will automatically count the number of words in any document. You can access this information through the Tools <u>menu</u>.

☐ Comments can be added to Word documents that will appear for others who may review the file. Adding such comments can be useful when you are reviewing the work of other students or having others review your work before submitting it to the instructor because these comments can be hidden later on.

> **STUDENT-TO-STUDENT TIP**
>
> I copy-and-paste class readings into Microsoft Word and use the highlighter and comment functions to make notes in my online reading. I also copy my citation information into Word before I start to read an article or other information so that I can easily take the highlighted information and have the citation ready.

☐ Word can insert footnotes and endnotes into the document to add additional information that may be useful to the reader but is not necessary within the main text. Word numbers and organizes both footnotes and endnotes, making this an easy feature to add to your college <u>coursework</u>.

Tips for Using E-Books

E-books, or electronic books, offer a viable alternative to many traditional textbooks. From stand-alone devices (such as the Amazon Kindle, Samsung Papyrus, iRex iLiad, or Sony Reader) to interactive books that are available as <u>websites</u>, e-books frequently offer useful tools and interactive elements that improve your reading comprehension. While the availability of your college textbooks in an e-book format will greatly depend on the texts selected by your instructors, if you are given the opportunity and decide to purchase the e-book version of your textbook then there are a few valuable tips that can help improve your study skills.

☐ E-books are a relatively new technology and you may find challenges in applying your most useful study strategies and note-taking techniques when reading from e-books. Consequently, if you are new to using e-books then you may want to become more familiar with the technology by purchasing an e-book for pleasure reading—such as a novel—before trying to use an e-book for one of your college courses.

☐ Before purchasing an e-book reader (such as an Amazon Kindle or Sony Reader) discuss the use of e-books with your instructors to determine which brand will offer the greatest number of college textbooks for your courses in the e-book format. Many e-books will only be compatible with one brand of e-book reader.

☐ Practice using the features of your e-book before the semester begins. For example, if your e-book reader or online text offers search functions or note-taking capabilities then you will want to be familiar with how those work before you start to read for class assignments.

☐ It is just as important with an e-book as it is with a traditional paper book to read in the appropriate study environment. Take time to create a positive study environment before you begin to read. (See Chapter 2.)

☐ While e-book readers can offer a great deal of flexibility as to where and when you read for your college courses, these devices run on batteries and they are of no value when the batteries run out. There-fore you will want to charge your e-book reader every few days to ensure that the battery is fully charged when you ready to study.

☐ Work to apply the same note-taking and study strategies that you have found to be most beneficial to your college studies when using an e-book. Just because the paper is being replaced with an electronic screen does not mean that you have to start from scratch in develop-ing good study habits. For example, if you typically use the SQ3R (see Quick Reference Guide) process to improve your reading comprehension, then you should continue to apply the same tech-nique when using an e-book.

Tips for Technology Support

Before starting online coursework, becoming familiar with the online sup-port services offered to you as a student can be beneficial. From technology support provided by the institution offering the course to support provided by manufacturers of hardware and software, you will want to be familiar with available support services since problems always arise at the worst times when you are taking any course.

Online Technology Assistance

Your college or university will typically offer a variety of technology sup-port services for students. For students taking courses that require online coursework, these services will be of great value because, at some point during your college education, you will likely have many questions regard-ing technology. With a little planning and time spent getting to know the support services available to you as a student, inevitable problems with technology won't keep you from success.

Starting on the first day of classes, you should take the time to explore your school's website to determine what resources are available to you. Often, technology support services will be di-vided among various operations within the institution. One support group will provide assistance when the school's Internet portal does not respond, while another group will help out when your email account stops sending messages.

STUDENT-TO-STUDENT TIP

The worst situation that you can be in is wanting advice or assistance and not knowing where or how to get it. I found that by understanding the student support system most of the issues that I had could be resolved in very short order.

www.cengage.com/success/Watkins/ELearning3e

We recommend that students maintain a list (on the inside back cover of this book) with contact information and service hours for the technology support units that provide support for each technology that you may use in completing online course requirements. This list should include support units for the school's <u>Internet</u> portal (for example, Blackboard and WebCT), <u>email</u> accounts, on-campus computer labs, and <u>Internet</u> connections that you may have available in your dorm. Having this information handy will be useful at some point, and getting timely assistance can make the difference between success and failure.

Manufacturer (Hardware or Software) Customer Support

If you do purchase a computer or other technology (for example, digital camera and scanner) to meet the requirements of a college course, then the support services available from the manufacturing company will often provide you limited services 24 hours a day. These can be invaluable when your <u>operating system</u> freezes up at midnight while you are preparing for your class presentation the next day or when your <u>Internet</u> connection fails while you are searching the college's online library for resources. Often the support services provided by the manufacturer will also provide you with troubleshooting guidelines for errors that may not be linked directly to their products, so don't be afraid to ask them a variety of questions.

Like with the technology support services provided by the college, keeping a list (including contact information with phone numbers and <u>email</u> addresses, as well as hours of operation) for the services available

---

ACTIVITY 3-5   Did This Section Click?

As a review, match the following word, phrase, or acronym with the correct definition.

1. ___ <u>shortcut</u>

2. ___ address book

3. ___ <u>bookmarks</u>

4. ___ shift + F7

5. ___ <u>Ctrl</u> + f

a. Keyboard shortcut for access of Microsoft Word's Thesaurus

b. A feature in <u>email</u> <u>software</u> applications to organize <u>email</u> addresses

c. An <u>icon</u> that can be created on your computer <u>desktop</u> to provide quick access to a specific file, <u>folder</u>, or <u>webpage</u>

d. Keyboard shortcut for Microsoft Word to quickly locate specific words or phrases used within a document

e. A link in a <u>Web browser</u> to provide quick access to specific <u>webpages</u> available on the <u>World Wide Web</u>

to you from the manufacturer is a good idea. The last thing you want to worry about at midnight before a class presentation is going through a year's worth of old receipts trying to find the toll-free number for your laptop.

Developing a Technology Contingency Plan

Computers and other online technologies will inevitably fail to work from time to time during your college experience. Unfortunately, these failures will most commonly happen when you can least afford it, such as when an assignment is due the next day. However, knowing that these failures will happen is to your advantage. Creating a technology contingency plan is an essential skill for students who are going to be successful in college. Contingency plans merely outline what resources you have available if (and when) the technology that you normally use fails to function properly. Here are a few tips for outlining your technology contingency plans.

> **STUDENT-TO-STUDENT TIP**
>
> Make sure that you have at least limited access to one additional computer with an Internet connection in case the computer that you primarily use malfunctions. Find out if your local library has computers for public use, or if you could use the computer lab at a local high school, community college, YMCA, or other education facility, just in case.

☐ Identify alternative on-campus computer labs that you could use at any time throughout the semester. Most college and university campuses will have a limited number of computer labs that are open 24 hours a day. If necessary, you may have to make arrangements at the beginning of the semester for access to the lab and its resources.

☐ Since going to campus is not always an option, identify classmates who you can contact if you lose access to your computer or the World Wide Web. They can provide you with updated information on assignments as well as contact instructors to let them know of the technology problems.

☐ Install antivirus and anti-spyware software on your computer and keep them up-to-date. These programs (like the free versions of AVG and Avira) can provide essential protection from viruses, Trojan horses, malware, and spyware—all of which can cause major problems for your computer. If do you get a virus, one option that frequently helps is to install a program to fix the problems caused by viruses, such as the free MalwareBytes' Anti-Malware software, while using your antivirus software to remove the virus.

☐ Establish a secondary email account that can be used in case the email account provided by your college is temporarily out of service. There are

ACTIVITY 3-6 **Are You Prepared?**

🌐 Given that problems with technology typically occur when you can least afford to be slowed down in your studies, it is essential for your success in college that you are prepared with all the essential information for solving a problem quickly. Take a few minutes now to complete the Important Contact Information page on the inside back cover of this book. Your college's <u>website</u> should provide you with the contact information for technology support services, on-campus computer labs, and library services. For contact information from your <u>Internet</u> service provider and computer manufacturer, you should review their <u>websites</u> and/or other documentation that they provided at the time of purchase.

By keeping this information with you whenever you are completing online <u>coursework</u>, you will have the necessary contact information for getting help quickly and getting back to your studies when technology problems do occur.

free <u>email</u> accounts provided by a variety of <u>websites</u> (such as http://www.mail.com, http://mail.yahoo.com, and http://www.hotmail.com).

☐ Have the contact information for your professor (including office phone and fax numbers) written down in case you can't access your computer or the <u>World Wide Web</u> during a technology failure.

☐ Have the contact information for the technology support services written down on the inside back cover of this book in case you can't access your computer or the <u>World Wide Web</u> during a technology failure.

☐ <u>Back up</u> your course files every week. As a result, even in the event that you cannot access your computer, you will continue to have access to the course files that you require.

☐ If power failures are common in your home, you may want to invest in a power backup system that supplies your computer with energy through a battery when the power goes out.

Summary

Taking advantage of the many tools and resources that are available to you when you are using the computer and <u>Internet</u> to complete your course assignments and activities requires that you become familiar with the functions of a variety of <u>software</u> applications, including your <u>operating system</u> and <u>word processing software</u>, as well as your <u>Web browser</u>. By learning more about the available options, you will be able to improve both the efficiency and quality of your studies in college. Periodically review the technology tips provided in this chapter and throughout the book because you will likely forget to use these techniques and strategies as your college courses start to demand more of your time.

Chapter 3 Exercise

To begin the exercise, you will want to access your Web-based course materials (that is, <u>educational portal</u>), using a <u>Web browser</u> (such as Netscape Navigator or Microsoft Internet Explorer). In addition, you will want to open a new document in a <u>word processing</u> program (for example, Microsoft Word).

Though each <u>Web portal</u> (or <u>educational portal</u>) used for online <u>coursework</u> will likely be a little different, the following steps should provide you with an activity that you can complete within most Web-based course programs. If the buttons and links described in the activity are slightly different from those within the <u>educational portal</u> you use for online <u>coursework</u>, be flexible and try a few until you click on one that seems to provide the functionality described in the activity. If you have any problems identifying appropriate button links or completing any of the steps below, be sure to use the Help option provided within the Web-based course <u>software</u> program.

STEP 1: Using the <u>Web browser</u> <u>software</u>, locate two <u>search engine</u>s, one that uses basic keywords (for example, http://www.google.com or http://www.altavista.com) and a second that uses Web directory format (for example, http://www.about.com or http://www.yahoo.com).

STEP 2: Using both of the <u>search engine</u>s that you have selected, complete a search to identify at least three <u>websites</u> that provide useful tips for improving your writing skills (for example, search for "college writing skills").

STEP 3: Based on the information included on the three <u>websites</u> that you have identified through your search, select five writing skills tips that you believe will be useful in improving your writing skills in college.

STEP 4: Using your <u>word processing</u> <u>software</u>, create a list of the five tips that you identified for improving your writing skills. Save this document to your computer's hard disk with the title "Writing Skills" and place it in a <u>folder</u> where you will be able to find it later.

STEP 5: Log into the <u>email</u> account provided by your college (for example, myname@mycollege.edu). Use the college's <u>Web portal</u> or the <u>email</u> <u>software</u> to access your <u>email</u> account.

STEP 6: Create a new message and include your <u>email</u> address in the recipient <u>field</u> (that is, myname@mycollege.edu).

STEP 7: Using the <u>email</u> <u>attachment</u> feature, attach the "Writing Skills" file that you created in step 4. Depending on the <u>email</u> <u>software</u> that you use to access your <u>email</u>, you may have to "browse" the list of files that you have stored on your computer's hard disk drive in order to locate the "Writing Skills" file that you saved. When you have located and selected the file, you will typically click on OK to attach the file to your <u>email</u>.

HOW TO
20

HOW TO
27

HOW TO
34

HOW TO
41

HOW TO
2

HOW TO
4

HOW TO
21

HOW TO
28

HOW TO
35

HOW TO
42

STEP 8: Send the <u>email</u>, along with the <u>attachment</u>, to yourself. When you receive the <u>email</u>, open the attached "Writing Skills" file to verify that it arrived without any changes to the content.

Did You Stay Focused?

After completing this chapter, you should be able to do the following. If there are tasks below that you cannot do, take a few minutes to review the chapter, focusing on those areas that you may have missed the first time through.

☐ I can *manage* my use of copyrighted materials as well as other intellectual property.

☐ I can use keyboard shortcuts in order to save time.

☐ I can use the right-click features to more efficiently access <u>software</u> features.

☐ I have the skills to *manage* the files on my computer.

☐ I have *created* a checklist for evaluating information found on the <u>World Wide Web</u>.

☐ I can select an appropriate <u>search engine</u> to find what I want on the <u>World Wide Web</u>.

☐ I am able to take advantage of features included in my <u>Web browser,</u> <u>email,</u> and Microsoft Word <u>software</u>.

☐ I have *created* a contact information list of technical support options.

☐ I have *created* a technology contingency plan.

☐ I have completed the chapter activities.

Additional Resources

🌐 Additional resources on topics covered in this chapter are available at the Premium <u>Website</u> for the *E-Learning Companion*.[5]

Notes

1. See http://www.virtualsalt.com/evalu8it.htm.
2. See http://www.radford.edu/~thompson/obias.html or http://www.runet. edu/~thompson/obias.html.
3. All three definitions are based on http://dictionary.reference.com/definitions (as of June 20, 2006).
4. Tips were previously available at http://www.findspot.com.
5. Free online books for many <u>operating system</u>s and <u>software</u> applications are available at http://inpics.net/.

4 Time Management Strategies

Managing your time as a college student is essentially your responsibility. From making arrangements to arrive to your classes on time each week to ensuring that personal com-

STAY FOCUSED

By the end of this chapter, you will be able to
- *Evaluate* your time management skills and preparations.
- *Manage* your time more effectively.

mitments do not interfere with your academic success, staying organized and managing your time is a task that only you can supervise. Fortunately, a diverse assortment of technologies can assist you in managing your time more effectively. At the same time, many of the tried-and-true strategies for managing your time remain effective even when your courses require online participation.

Success Strategy One: Don't Procrastinate

Sounds simple doesn't it? Unfortunately, avoiding procrastination is rarely as easily accomplished as it is said. Overcoming the temptations that lead to procrastination will be an essential component to your success in college. One useful technique to steer clear of procrastination is to break your course assignments into smaller chunks that you can accomplish prior to the due date for the entire assignment.

To illustrate this concept, imagine that your chemistry professor requires that you know the molecular structure of elements defined in the periodic table. You know that merely memorizing the elements of the table the weekend before the exam will not be enough to ensure your success. Therefore, you decide to divide the periodic table so that you have a week to study the molecular composition of the elements in each row. By sticking to this timeline, you can evade the temptations of procrastination and still find plenty of time throughout the semester to focus on your other courses.

www.cengage.com/success/Watkins/ELearning3e

STUDENT-TO-STUDENT TIP

The best advice that I can give to you is to keep up with your assignments. You can get your work done at the last minute, but it will be a lot less stressful and you will be able to process the information more effectively if you keep up. Do not procrastinate!

The same principle can be applied to any of your course activities or assignments. If you are required to make a presentation to the class at the end of the semester, set interim deadlines for yourself including a deadline for selecting a topic, finishing your research, writing a first draft of the slides and handouts that you will use, and giving a practice presentation to your friends for feedback. By breaking down any assignment into smaller assignments that you can do more easily, you can avoid procrastination.

Another useful technique to help avoid procrastination is to tell a variety of people about both the deadlines that you have set for yourself as well as those set by the professor. Ask roommates, sorority sisters, lab partners, and others to remind you of your commitments or to ask you about your progress. Don't limit this to your roommate or best friends, ask the other students in your class to keep in touch with you as well. They can send you emails or contact you using instant messaging to inquire about your progress. This not only keeps you on task but also helps keep them on task as well. After all, peer pressure doesn't have to be seen only as a negative tool. You can use it to your advantage as well.

STUDENT-TO-STUDENT TIP

Treat each assignment as a project. Plan for *every* component, allowing plenty of time for review and revision.

Success Strategy Two: Don't Wait for Perfection

It has been said that "anything worth doing is worth doing poorly . . . at least at first."

Upon first reading the above quote, you may not find it to be all that insightful, nor of much use in being successful in your online coursework. Yet while the implications of the quote may be subtle, the value of the perspective it brings is priceless. In trying to live up to the expectations and pressures of college, too often you will want to strive for the perfect term paper, the flawless class presentation, or even the ideal procedures for calculating a formula. Although each is a laudable goal, the reality is that the amount of time and energy put into attempting to achieve perfection is rarely the best approach to being successful.

Managing your time requires that you negotiate a balance that makes it possible for you to do high-quality work that will accomplish your goals while attaining similar goals in your other college courses, work obligations, and personal commitments. With only 24 hours in the day and more to do than simply fixate on any one assignment, finding this balance will require that you turn in many assignments and activities that are not perfect but good enough to receive the grade you desire.

Continuing to revise and revisit the same assignment until it reaches a level of perfection isn't practical for students who want to be successful. Find a balance for yourself, where you can accomplish all your goals without sacrificing one in attempting to achieve perfection in another.

Success Strategy Three: Combine Activities

Most all of us, from time to time, will overcommit to too many projects, activities, courses, and so forth. As you take on more responsibilities, through personal and professional commitments, the pressures to get more done in less time will only continue to grow. One of the best survival techniques to apply is finding out how to meet the requirements of several obligations through the same activity. For example, if you are required to write a term paper for your English course and you also have to fulfill university requirements for volunteer work in the community, try to find a way to combine these two activities so that you can do your research for the term paper while assisting a local social services agency in doing its work.

ACTIVITY 4-1   **Combine Your Activities**

🌐 In the following table, write five course-related activities or assignments that you will be completing over the next 2 weeks (such as writing a reaction paper to a chapter in your sociology text book, studying for an exam in biology, or searching online for information regarding an upcoming term paper in history). When you have identified five upcoming course activities or assignments, connect the activity or assignment with another task that you will also be working on this semester. You should attempt to determine at least three activities from this list that you can combine with other activities during the semester.

Time Management

COURSE ACTIVITY OR ASSIGNMENT	TO BE COMBINED WITH
Example: Library research for a English paper due next week	Example: Research for class presentation in my communications course
1.	
2.	
3.	
4.	
5.	

Success Strategy Four: Don't Expect Your Instructor to Always be Online

Do not wait until the day before an assignment is due to <u>email</u> your instructor with questions concerning the assignment requirements or asking for feedback on your first draft. Professors are typically busy with much more than just teaching courses; being online to answer your questions is not something they do 24 hours a day.

 You should plan your time wisely, so here are a few tips:

- <u>Email</u> questions as soon as possible after an assignment is given.

- Schedule at least 48 hours in advance to meet online with your instructor.

- Include with your <u>email</u> any draft documents and other files that may be useful for your instructor to review in answering your question.

- Keep a copy of any <u>email</u> correspondence that you have with your instructor and fellow students; documenting the conversation can be useful later on.

- Don't wait until the last minute to start your assignments; inevitably you will have questions, so plan accordingly.

Success Strategy Five: Keep to a Schedule

For the majority of courses that you will take in college, the pace of assignments, tests, group projects, and other <u>coursework</u> will increase throughout the semester. As a result, the only way that you can keep up and be successful is to be organized. Writing down all your assignments and other commitments will be essential for staying on task and not falling behind.

Keep the schedules for your various academic, work, and personal commitments all in one place. Whether you use an online calendar (such as Google Calendar), **personal digital assistant**, <u>smart phone</u>, or paper calendar on your desk, write down everything that you are supposed to do as soon as you commit to doing it. By having all your commitments in one calendar, you can effectively manage your time and ensure that you are not obligated to be in two places at the same time.

Based on your consolidated calendar of commitments, each day write down a daily to-do list. Your daily list will help you to plan your time effectively and avoid procrastination.

> **STUDENT-TO-STUDENT TIP**
>
> Set aside a time each day to work, read, write, and post. Keep it the same time and stick to it. Before long, that work time simply becomes part of the fabric of your life. I actually discovered free time by keeping myself on a schedule.

Success Strategy Six: Use Your Free Time Wisely

Though you will often feel like there just isn't enough time in the day to get all of your school responsibilities done, you can recapture some of that time by using your free time wisely. Maybe it is 15 minutes between classes or 5 minutes waiting for group members to show up for a class project meeting; in either situation (or any of the thousands of other situations in which each of us finds ourselves), there is typically some free time each day that we cannot afford to waste.

To use this time effectively, you have to be prepared. Carry note cards with you so that you are always prepared to review key definitions or formulas when you have a few minutes without other things to do; keep your calendar with you when you are riding the bus so that you can update your daily to-do list; bring a textbook with you when you go to a doctor's appointment; or keep a pen and paper handy so that you can take down some notes for an upcoming assignment as you wait for the bus. Your time is a valued commodity, and you shouldn't let any of it go to waste when you have so much to do.

TRY SOMETHING NEW

Web Tool: **http://calendar.google.com**

Are you tired of trying to keep all of your class assignments, team meetings, work projects, and social activities organized? Do you frequently forget to attend important meetings? Give Google Calendar a try. Google Calendar supports multiple calendars (such as a distinct calendar for each of your courses) that can be viewed separated or together, color coded, or even shared independently with others. The calendar can also be synced with some cell phones or it can send reminders to your cell phone using text messages. Start using it today and see how its many features can help you improve your time management.

Success Strategy Seven: Learn to Say No

In the book *The One Minute Manager Meets the Monkey,* the author explores how many of us fail to be successful in our work when we take on the responsibilities of others.[1] Monkeys, within the context of the book, are the challenges and responsibilities that each of us carries on our backs every day. For you, your monkeys may include course assignments, responsibilities to your fraternity or sorority, a commitment to the marching band or drama club, family obligations, and the like. And everyone you know will also carry numerous monkeys on their backs as well.

These monkeys can, however, limit your success in college when people start passing their monkeys off to you. For example, though you may be up late studying for a quiz, your roommate may decide to pass one of her monkeys on to you. Maybe it is her responsibility to make signs advertising the new positions available at the college radio station, but she also wants

ACTIVITY 4-2   Find Your Free Time

⊕ For a typical week during the semester, complete the following table by estimating the number of hours you spend doing each of the activities.

Finding Your Free Time

	MON.	TUES.	WEDS.	THURS.	FRI.	SAT.	SUN.
[Completing homework]							
[Reading for school]							
[Working on the computer for coursework]							
[In class]							
[Traveling to and from school or work]							
[Waiting between classes]							
[Cooking and eating]							
[Watching television]							
[Playing video games]							
[Leisure activities (sports, movies, parties, and so on)]							
[Community service]							
[Family activities]							
[Checking email or surfing websites]							
[Club or association activities]							

to go to the movies with friends tonight. So she may try to pass this monkey along to you by asking if you could do her a big favor.

We all know people who are continually asking others to take a monkey off their back. And sometimes we do want to offer them our support. But most often we each have enough monkeys of our own to keep ourselves busy.

Don't get burdened with other people's monkeys. They will only slow you down on your way to success. By saying no, you can escape the additional weight of carrying other people's monkeys along with your own.

Success Strategy Eight: Make Use of Technology

In recent years, there have been many technological advancements that can help you better manage your time. Successful students take advantage of these new technologies and use them effectively (and efficiently) to stay organized, to make use of their time, to communicate with fellow students and instructors, and to cope with competing demands for their time. In the pages that follow is a short list of technologies (many of these are defined in more detail in the next chapter) and a description of how you can use them to help manage your time. You can likely think of other tools and their uses, and you should use those as well to become a successful student.

Personal Digital Assistant (PDA) or Smart Phone

Personal digital assistants (such as Palm, Apple iPod, or PocketPC) and smart phones (such as Apple iPhone or BlackBerry) are common devices typically used for scheduling events and keeping an electronic calendar that can be linked to your personal computer. PDAs and smart phones can also help you manage your time by giving you access to personal notes and other documents that you would otherwise have to carry with you on paper. Many of these devices allow you to create and read email messages and allow you to use the device to access the Internet from any location through cell phone services (See Chapter 3).

In addition, many online courses will have information from the course that you can download directly to a PDA or smart phone, providing you with access to course calendars, instructor lectures, and other information at any time. This feature allows you to use your free time to catch up on coursework, take notes for upcoming assignments, email fellow students about assignments, and even review past lectures when preparing for tests.

Online Calendars and Groupware

Keeping your own schedule is typically enough of a challenge, but when your courses require that you work with other students to complete group projects, then the additional task of coordinating the schedules of several people can be a real burden. To be successful, students today have got to use the technology available to them, and online calendars and **groupware** should not be overlooked. These online programs, often available free of charge, allow you to create group areas online where you can contribute to a common calendar for scheduling meetings and other events. You can also post files for others in the group to review and respond to, organize project-related tasks, and do many of the other project management–related tasks that must be accomplished in order for the group to be successful.

Though many of these services are available throughout the <u>Internet</u>, here are a few <u>websites</u>:

http://www.ning.com   http://www.calendars.net

http://groups.yahoo.com   http://calendar.yahoo.com

http://groups.google.com   http://calendar.google.com

http://www.facebook.com   http://www.huntcal.com

http://www.localendar.com

Email and Instant Messaging

Although <u>email</u>, <u>instant messaging</u>, and other online technologies that assist you in becoming a successful student will be discussed in more detail in the next chapter, it should be noted here that these tools can also be used to help you manage your time. From sending files to professors instead of taking the time to walk across campus to preparing for a mid-term exam with a partner who lives out of town, online technologies can save you time and ensure that you are using effective study techniques even when you are outside the classroom or library.

Cell Phones and <u>Smart Phones</u>

While most colleges and universities don't permit the use of cell phones in the classroom, your cell phone or <u>smart phone</u> (such as iPhone, BlackBerry, or G1) can still be a useful tool in managing your time. With your cell phone, for example, you can keep in touch with members of your study group even when you are not in your dorm room, change meeting times, let them know about the new reference you found in the library, or even participate in a three-way call instead of meeting after class. With your <u>smart phone</u> you can further expand the capabilities of your phone to include <u>email</u>, course calendars, online books, customizable flashcards, and other tools to improve your college studies (see Chapter 3).

The flexibility and freedom of cell phones and <u>smart phone</u>s can be a tool for your success, though they can also lead to your failure if you allow them to be a distraction from your studies. Text messages, games, <u>surfing</u> the Web, and even just talking with friends can all divert your attention if you do not manage your time wisely.

Success Strategy Nine: Manage the Time That You Spend Online

It is easy for most of us to spend hours at our computer looking up information online, <u>chatting</u> with friends, sending <u>email</u>s to our family, or just browsing random <u>websites</u>. Because you do not want the time that you spend online to interfere with your other academic and social commitments, you should work to manage your online activities. From keeping a log of how much time you spend online each day to limiting the number of times you update your <u>blog</u> each week, you should develop a plan for ensuring that your computer remains a valuable resource in your education rather than a detriment to your college success.

Success Strategy Ten: Know Your Studying Prime Times

Finding the hours when you can gain the most from your studies is essential for managing your time. If you can complete a required assignment in just

---

ACTIVITY 4-3 **Prime Times**

🌐 To help determine what time of day is your studying prime time, answer the following questions.

1. When the alarm goes off in the morning, do you
   a. throw the clock against the wall?
   b. immediately get out of bed?
   c. hit snooze at least three times?

2. An hour after you get out of bed, are you
   a. somewhat asleep and little dazed?
   b. unmotivated to get things done?
   c. wide awake and ready to get the day started?

3. Around noon, are you
   a. so focused on your work that you have to be reminded of lunch?
   b. not able to concentrate because you are hungry?
   c. daydreaming about what you are going to do that evening?

4. At midafternoon, are you
   a. still dazed from your lunch?
   b. focused on your work?
   c. wondering what is happening on television soap operas?

5. At dinner time, are you
   a. not able to concentrate because you are hungry?
   b. distracted by activities with family and friends?
   c. able to concentrate on what you are reading?

6. In the early evening hours, are you
   a. distracted by television or activities with friends?
   b. able to concentrate on what you read on the <u>Internet</u>?
   c. too tired to keep your eyes open?

7. Around midnight, are you
   a. energetic and able to focus on what you are reading?
   b. sleepy and your eyes keep drifting shut?
   c. busy flipping through all of the channels on television?

8. Write one to two sentences summarizing when you can study most effectively:

   _____

2 hours of studying in the early afternoon rather than 4 hours of studying late at night, then why would you want to procrastinate? Not only do you want to manage your time so that you can effectively manage your way to success, but you also want to consider the efficiency of your studies.

A word of caution, however: don't fool yourself into believing that your personal prime time for studying is at the odd hours that surround the times of your other personal activities. Though many college students might say that they can study effectively at 1:00 A.M., the truth is that for most of us the peak hours for staying focused on our work and effectively learning new skills is during the day or early evening. So you must be honest with yourself … your success in college depends on it.

Summary

Though there are only 24 hours in each day, by applying time management strategies you can get more done each day than you likely believe possible. Managing time, instead of letting time manage you, is an essential skill for being successful in college. Technology offers us many tools and resources for managing our time, but building those into your daily and weekly study habits does take some practice. Adopt the time management strategies provided in this chapter over the next several weeks; using these to improve the effectiveness and efficiency of your time will not only improve your productivity at college but will also give you more free time to spend with friends and family.

Chapter 4 Exercise

Creating a family calendar can be a useful activity that gives you the opportunity to explore the features available through any online calendar while developing a practical tool for your family. To begin the exercise, you will want to access the World Wide Web, using a Web browser. After completing the exercise, take a few minutes to consider how you can effectively use online tools to facilitate group meetings throughout your college experience.

STEP 1: Locate the calendar tool of your college's educational portal or select one of the online calendar sites listed previously in this chapter. If you select a calendar tool outside your college's educational portal, follow the unique instructions for registering a new account with the online calendar site. Because these companies may add you to email lists for advertising purposes you may not want to use your primary email account. Many students find it useful to establish a secondary email account through a free service (for example, http://www.hotmail.com, http://mail.yahoo.com, or http://www.mail.com) that you can use when you would like to divert possible advertising emails.

STEP 2: When you have registered for the calendar service that you selected, create a new calendar. Include in the calendar your birthday and the birthdays of your parents, spouse, children, and/or siblings.

STEP 3: Add to the calendar the assignments for at least one of the courses that you are currently enrolled in. If available through the online calendar service that you selected, include an <u>email</u> reminder for the next assignment that will be due for at least one of the courses that you are currently enrolled in.

STEP 4: Make your calendar available to at least one friend, family member, or another student in the class. This feature is available with most online calendars, though you may have to provide the person with information regarding the calendar site so that they can also register for an account.

Did You Stay Focused?

After completing this chapter, you should be able to do the following. If there are skills that you cannot do, take a few minutes to review the chapter, focusing on those areas that you may have missed the first time through.

- ☐ I can *manage* my activities to save time.
- ☐ I know that every assignment and activity doesn't have to be perfect for me to turn it in.
- ☐ I am able to say no to friends and family when I have to get my <u>coursework</u> done.
- ☐ I have several strategies for avoiding procrastination.
- ☐ I know to contact my instructors early because I realize that they will not be online at all times.
- ☐ I *evaluate* my daily schedule and to-do list for priorities.
- ☐ I use technology to *manage* my time.
- ☐ I *manage* the amount of time I spend online.
- ☐ I *evaluated* my studying prime times.
- ☐ I have completed the chapter activities.

Additional Resources

🌐 Additional resources on topics covered in this chapter are available at the Premium Website for the *E-Learning Companion.*

Note
1. Blanchard, 1989.

5 Developing Positive Online Relationships

STAY FOCUSED

By the end of this chapter, you will be able to

- *Communicate* more effectively with your instructors.
- Use online tools to *communicate* with classmates.
- *Integrate* the use of online communications (for example, <u>chats</u>, <u>email</u>, and <u>instant messaging</u>) with your other college study skills.

The social life of an online student can be an active and stimulating one, but it doesn't happen without some directed effort. From reviewing draft term papers for other students to social <u>chats</u> about which instructors to take and which to avoid, the online communities that can be developed through online technologies both parallel and support many of those that you are likely more familiar with from the conventional classroom. In the past, we have seen students become close friends with online classmates and at the same time seen students struggle in their online <u>coursework</u> because they could not build the social structures that were necessary for their success.

The extent to which an online social life is necessary for your success in online <u>coursework</u> somewhat depends on your learning and studying preferences. Some students prefer to discuss ideas before starting to put anything on paper, while others don't even want to have draft manuscripts reviewed by fellow students. But to some extent, most students do better when they are involved with other students, whether it is an on-campus social life or an online social life.

The opportunity to get friendly feedback on using the correct formula in chemistry before submitting it to the instructor can be the difference between an outstanding grade and merely a passing grade. Although an online study group the week before an exam may not be ideal for your studying style, it can better ensure that you are adequately prepared for whatever questions that the instructor may ask. Yet, beyond the value of study groups and peer feedback, the relationships that students can develop with other students transform what could be a lonely, or isolating, course experience into one that is interesting, motivating, and even enjoyable.

Most often, you can not rely on your instructor to push your online relationships forward. The talents of the instructor to develop activities and assignments that engage students as a learning community will vary and can only go so far. It remains up to the individual student to devise a plan and follow through with that plan, to create a supportive network of fellow students that will make for an attention-grabbing and noteworthy learning experience.

> **STUDENT-TO-STUDENT TIP**
>
> Be bold and ask questions. Give positive comments and praise in the class work. There is sometimes more of an opportunity for this in the online environment than in a face-to-face learning situation. Some people tend to be more constrained when face-to-face.

Online Relationships

The skills for developing positive online relationships are not necessarily unique to the online environment. Often, you will want to adapt the same skills for creating a positive relationship that you use when you are in the classroom, the library, the student lounge, or anywhere else. Sometimes you will want to adopt new skills. However, most of us don't normally recognize the skills that we are applying when building relationships with other students or our professors (for example, eye contact, body language, and first impressions). Therefore, we have to pay extra attention to these skills when we are attempting to develop useful online relationships. The limited types of communications available to you when using online technologies, typically <u>synchronous</u> or **asynchronous** text communications, only further require that you examine how you can go about building positive relationships with other students online.

> **TRY SOMETHING NEW**
>
> Web Tool: **http://www.doodle.com**
>
> All of us are busy and therefore scheduling times for team meetings, study groups, or other activities is often challenging. On Mondays, for example, one study partner may have a biology class in the evening and on Wednesdays another study partner may have to work all day, making it difficult to find a time that works for everyone in the group to prepare for an upcoming exam. Rather than sending numerous emails trying find to a time, give Doodle a try. Doodle provides a free service that quickly and easily surveys team members, classmates, and friends to identify which day and time works best for everyone. In just a couple of minutes you can eliminate many of your scheduling nightmares.

Making a Good First Impression Online

Online relationships with your fellow students will be very similar to those that you will have in the conventional classroom. And just like in the traditional classroom, first impressions can make all of the difference online as well. To establish good working relationships with your classmates, even the wording of your <u>email</u>s is of critical importance in developing a good first impression that can pave the path for your success.

Here are a few steps that you can use to ensure that you make the right first impression in your online communications:

☐ *Take a few extra minutes* in your initial <u>email</u>s to your fellow students to make sure that they are grammatically correct and that the spelling is checked.

☐ Take time to *personalize* your <u>email</u>s to your fellow students. Just as in the classroom when you may ask them first how their day has been before asking to borrow their notes on a previous lecture, you should do the same online. Making a good first impression typically requires a personal touch.

☐ Provide fellow students with your *contact information* (that is, the <u>email</u> account you want them to use, your <u>instant messaging</u> name, or

E-Learning Experiences

A few years ago, I was teaching a course delivered completely online with students from around the world, many of whom were in their last semester of their master's degree. And like in any class, online or on-campus, I had some students who were active participants in every discussion and others who preferred to primarily listen and only interject when necessary. Two students in the class were both the former, active participants in every discussion and very involved in a team project in which they happened to be paired together. Levonnie was a spirited elementary school teacher who lived in southern Georgia, and Emily was just establishing her own consulting company in Las Vegas to develop online training courses for real estate agents. As you can imagine, both had an assortment of exciting stories to share with each new discussion topic, from stories of life growing up in rural Georgia to the exhilarating chronicles of life in "Sin City."

During the semester, Levonnie and Emily became close friends, and both spoke impatiently about finally meeting each other for cocktails after graduation at the end of the semester. Unfortunately, at the last minute Emily wasn't able to attend graduation due to a health problem in the family. Even if the story ended there, the support and friendship that Levonnie and Emily built that semester would be an excellent example of how online relationships can develop and how those support networks can be used to ensure that everyone is successful in their online <u>coursework</u>. But the story doesn't end there. Weeks after graduation, I got an <u>email</u> that Levonnie and Emily were headed to New York City for a "girl's weekend out" and to finally meet in person, building on a friendship and supportive relationship that they developed initially online.

The development of an active social life within online <u>coursework</u> does, however, require some purposeful effort. I am confident that neither Levonnie nor Emily would have been as successful in my course if they had not developed a relationship beyond the all-too-common short <u>email</u>s asking when the next assignment was due. Nor would they have had the opportunity to create within the online course a comfortable environment where they, and other students, felt that they could learn among friends.

even your phone number if you want them to call you). Being able to contact other students is a first step in developing positive relations.

☐ Take into account that when you are talking with a fellow student online (either through <u>email</u>, <u>chat</u>, or <u>instant messaging</u>) that the *nonverbal* clues that you may rely on for building a successful relationship in person may not be available. Later in this chapter, we provide more information on how nonverbal communication skills can be transferred to online discussions.

☐ Include specific information regarding *what should happen next* (for example, when you will contact them again, a proposal for the next steps to be taken, or questions you would like for them to answer). It is often best to propose what you believe should happen next and then ask for feedback to make sure that your proposed schedule is workable in their schedule.

> **STUDENT-TO-STUDENT TIP**
>
> Do not take yourself or any course too seriously! You can't learn if you are not having fun. Keep an open mind! Learn from the vast experiences and knowledge that everyone brings to the table.

Effective Online Communications Tips

Communicating effectively is hard enough when you are in the same room with a person. But when the distances that separate you from other students are measured not only in the thousands of miles but by the cultural differences as well, effective communication in an online course can be a real challenge. Gaining the skills to communicate effectively online with a diverse group of fellow students will be a key to your success.

In the pages that follow are five strategies that you can use to be more effective in your online communications.

Spell Check and Grammar Check Everything Related to Your Coursework

Although your typical <u>email</u>s to friends and family may be informal and misspelled words may be common, when establishing good relationships with your classmates, make sure that you spell check and grammar check all correspondence. Misspelled words or incorrect grammar may give the wrong impression about your abilities as a student, the priority the course has for you, your attention to detail, or other characteristics that would keep fellow students from wanting to work with you throughout the course.

Fortunately, most <u>educational portal</u>s (for example, Blackboard) and <u>email</u> applications (for example, Microsoft Outlook and Qualcomm Eudora) will have spell check and grammar check options. If your <u>email</u> service doesn't have these features, then you should first write your message in a <u>word processing</u> program (for example, Microsoft Word) using the <u>word</u>

processing program's Spell Check and Grammar Check features. Afterwards you can copy-and-paste the checked and corrected message into your <u>email</u>.

Compensate for Not Having Nonverbal Communications

QR Online communications are predominantly text-based conversations. And while there are advantages to communicating largely through written text

---

ACTIVITY 5-1   First Impressions Case Study

🌐 *Situation:* Today is your first day of class in the Introduction to Early American Literature 101 course at your college or university. Though you are somewhat disappointed that the instructor is a doctoral student and not a full-time faculty member, the reading list for the course does seem appealing to you. The course assignments, however, will require that you work with a student partner in developing a critique on a novel of your choice from the genre, as well as a presentation at the end of the semester for other students in the class. When the instructor assigns partners, however, you find out that your partner, Samuel, lives an hour away from campus and that his work schedule will keep him from meeting with you on campus for the project. After your short discussion at the end of class, you decide to work on the project together using online technologies like <u>email</u> and <u>instant messaging</u>.

Activity: On a piece of paper (or on a computer), write an initial <u>email</u> to your partner for the project. In the <u>email</u>, lay the groundwork that will lead to later success. Do this before reading on.

Feedback: Below is an example of what your first <u>email</u> may include when attempting to make a positive first impression. There is no "perfect" initial <u>email</u>, but this example contains many elements of a successful first impression. Review your initial <u>email</u> for similar characteristics with this example.

> Samuel,
>
> After our brief meeting in class yesterday, I am excited about the opportunity to work with you on the course project for Early American Literature 101. Though this is only my second literature course at the university, my experiences last semester in critiquing British literature should be helpful as we move ahead on our project.
>
> I know that your commute to campus is long, and I agree that we can use <u>email</u> and <u>instant messaging</u> for most of our conversations regarding the project. My <u>instant messaging</u> contact information and my phone number are listed below. Also, if you could <u>email</u> me your contact information, I would appreciate it.
>
> By next Monday, I will send you a list of possible novels that we could consider for the project. If you could create a list of your own, that would be useful for comparison.
>
> I hope that you have a good weekend, and I will be back in touch with you on Monday.
>
> Thanks,
>
> Natasha
>
> Natasha@mycollege.edu

(for example, you can reflect on an <u>email</u> before sending it), the lack of non-verbal communication techniques can make online communications very frustrating. Researchers estimate that about 55% of what is communicated is actually passed on through nonverbal communications (for example, eye contact and body language).[1] Making up for the lack of nonverbal communication strategies is therefore an essential element for your success. Try using **emoticons** and acronyms (for example, LOL for laughing out loud) to express your ideas and words (see the Quick Reference Guide for additional examples). These replacements for nonverbal communications can help you accurately convey a message, though they are not appropriate for all communications. Just as you would not wink or use slang terms during a job interview, likewise you will not want to use these communication tools in the wrong context. Among friends and classmates, for example, you can use <u>emoticons</u> and acronyms to express yourself, but when writing your instructor or a financial aid officer you should strive for a more professional communication.

> **STUDENT-TO-STUDENT TIP**
>
> Without the nonverbal clues that we receive in face-to-face interactions, it's difficult to gauge tone in <u>emails</u> and postings. Learn to put your personality as well as your intentions into words in order to create a better and clearer relationship.

Avoid Miscommunications

Whenever you are communicating online, you will want to actively look out for and avoid possible miscommunications with other students or the instructor. However, when using online communications tools for your college courses, there will be times when miscommunications occur. Typically, in conventional conversations, you most often naturally pick up on clues of miscommunication (for example, a questioning gesture with a person's eyebrows), but in online discussion, you will most likely have to work at searching out clues of possible miscommunications. This is true whether you are sending messages or receiving messages because both actions offer a variety of opportunities for miscommunications.

Avoid Writing in All Capital Letters

When expressing emotions in online conversations, it has become common for people to use all CAPITALIZED letters when they want to shout or express other argumentative positions. Writing in all CAPITAL letters is often referred to as "flaming" and is considered unacceptable in most academic- or school-related conversation.

You should avoid using all CAPITALIZED words in your <u>emails</u> whenever possible; shouting or other confrontational

> **STUDENT-TO-STUDENT TIP**
>
> Using <u>emoticons</u> or just clearly stating your intentions improves rapport and creates a foundation upon which to build relationships. Simply typing "hee hee!" portrays a friendly gesture, and the receiver knows to accept the material in a lighthearted way.

ACTIVITY 5-2   **Did This Section Click?**

 After reviewing the examples in the Quick Reference Guide, match the following emoticons or acronyms with the correct definition.

1. :-/ or :-\   a. Expresses laughter in an email or chat

2. :e or :-e   b. Expresses shock or screaming in an email or chat

3. :@ or :-@   c. Expresses disappointment in an email or chat

4. ROF   d. Expresses boredom or tiredness in an email or chat

5. <Y>   e. Indicates undecided, confused, or skeptical in an email or chat

communications rarely accomplish any goals and typically shut down future opportunities for success. If you are frustrated or have other emotions that you would like to share with others, try using the less aggressive tools like emoticons and acronyms.

Be Sure Not to Reply to Everyone on the Listserve

Listserves, as described in Chapter 6, are common tools used for communicating with a large number of students in a course. For example, your instructor may use a listserve of all students in the course to send out email messages announcing reading requirements for an upcoming test; this saves him the effort of sending the email to each student individually. To send an email to a listserve, you simply address the To: area of the email with the listserve instead of an individual recipient (for example, Spanish101Section2@state.edu).

When replying to an email message that you received from a listserve, you will want to make sure that the To: area of the reply message doesn't go back to everyone signed up on the listserve. If you use the Reply All option of your email software application, that is exactly what will happen, and everyone in your course will receive the email that you intended only for the instructor. Take the time before sending a reply to a listserve message, or any message, to double-check the fields that indicate who the recipients of the email should be; it is well worth the extra few seconds to avoid potential miscommunications.

Staying Organized Online

Although remaining organized with your online coursework is essential for your success in any class, keeping track of your academic and social relationships with other students is also critical. Sending a message to the wrong classmate can be not only embarrassing but also damaging to your relationships with many other students. (Don't think that gossip is limited to the boundaries of the dorm.) Losing your copy of a group assignment can also lead to awkward relationships with your fellow students.

Here are several strategies for staying organized with your online coursework:

☐ Maintain a separate <u>folder</u> within your <u>email</u> account for each course. Keep all the <u>email</u>s that you exchange with the instructor and other students in this one place so that you can always come back to them later.

☐ Create a <u>folder</u> for each of your courses in the <u>file directory</u> of file <u>folder</u>s on your computer. Copies of all drafts and final documents related to course requirements should be kept in this <u>folder</u> for safekeeping. Even if other students are responsible for portions of a group project, keep your own copies of all files; if you want, you can always delete them after the course is complete.

☐ Be careful not to send <u>email</u>s to the wrong students. Check, and double-check, to make sure that your <u>email</u>'s To:, Cc:, and Bcc: <u>field</u>s include only the addresses to which you want the <u>email</u> sent. (Cc: stands for carbon copy and adds recipients to the <u>email</u>; Bcc: stand for blind carbon copy and also adds recipients to the <u>email</u> although other recipients will not see that they have been included as recipients of the <u>email</u>.)

☐ Separate <u>email</u> accounts may be useful to keep course-related <u>email</u> separate from other personal or work-related <u>email</u>s (for example, personal, school, and work). Many colleges and universities will give you an <u>email</u> account while you are a student, and a host of other free online <u>email</u> services (for example, http://www.hotmail. com, http:// mail.yahoo.com, and http://www.mail.com) is also available to help you keep your many online communications organized.

☐ Include the date that you created the file in the name of the file. For example, if you are creating a file that will be the first draft of a history assignment on the Revolutionary War, then include in the title the date of the draft (for example, "4-23-11 history assignment.doc"). This will help you, and any other students you may have to share files with in group assignments, quickly know which file is the latest and which should be submitted for grading.

☐ When submitting files to your course instructor,

TRY SOMETHING NEW

Web Tool: **http://docs.google.com**

Keeping documents and files organized when working with others, such as on a team project, can be challenge. The next time you are working with other students on a project give Google Documents a try. Google Documents allows you to create and share text, spreadsheet, and presentation files online. Once created (or uploaded), files are edited with similar tools as other <u>software</u> programs (such as Microsoft Word or PowerPoint), but the files can edited by more than one student at the same time, giving you the opportunity for real-time collaboration. Likewise, this free web tool also tracks versions of the files so you can review edits made yesterday or last week. When complete, files can be downloaded in a variety of <u>format</u>s, including the Microsoft Word or Adobe PDF formats.

double-check to make sure that you are submitting the file in the right format and in the correct manner. Course assignments will typically specify the file format requested by the instructor (for example, Microsoft Word or Adobe Acrobat PDF). Often, professors will want you to email some assignments to their email accounts, while requesting that you upload other assignments to specific folders with an educational portal (for example, WebCT or BlackBoard). Take a few extra minutes to check the required file format and method for submitting each assignment; on your road to success, you don't want to lose points for files that didn't end up in the correct place for grading.

Adding a Personal Touch

Because most of us enjoy and perform better in a course when we have a mixture of academic and social relationships with our fellow students, it is often essential that you personalize your relationships with other students. This isn't to say that you have to divulge personal information about yourself, nor do you have to build lifelong friendships, but you should attempt to create an environment where other students don't feel that you are merely using them to increase the odds of your success in the course. By adding a personal touch to your online communications, you can make great strides in developing the type of social relationships that are the most useful for your success and theirs.

Following are four steps for personalizing your online communications:

☐ We are often tempted to save time and send the same email to everyone in the class, yet sending individual emails to each student (that is, with their name at the top) can show that you are taking the time to write them specifically. It may sound like an unimportant and small detail, but you would be surprised how many students feel isolated from others in their courses. When time is tight, however, you can cut-and-paste (or copy-and-paste) the same core message into each email and then customize each email with a few unique and distinctive sentences for each recipient.

☐ If you do have to send a mass mailing to many students in your course, then use the Bcc: (blind carbon copy) field to add recipients to the email. This will send the email to each individual, while not indicating that other students are also receiving the exact same email. In many email applications, you can include all recipients in the Bcc: field without having to include any individuals as To: or Cc: recipients.

☐ Add a unique question or comment to individual emails to let each student know that you are keeping in touch with them (for example, "How are things at your fraternity?" "Did you do well on the last quiz we studied for?" "Are you still planning to take Astronomy 200 next semester?"). Each individualized question or comment can help build a stronger relationship.

☐ Resist sending every <u>email</u> joke or chain letter that you receive to others in your class. A quick joke every now and then is fun, but repeated messages that start with "forwarded" or "FWD:" can be a turnoff.

Attachment Etiquette

Attaching files to an <u>email</u> or submitting files to online <u>discussion boards</u> can be an effective tool for communicating with other students as well as the instructor. But the last thing you want to do is frustrate others with files that they cannot find (or open) for one reason or another. Here are two simple suggestions for avoiding disaster when sharing files.

Don't Change the Extension Included at the End of the File Name If you are using the Windows <u>operating system</u>, files are named with two elements, the title and the extension. The extension follows the last period in the name and is typically three letters long (for example, .doc for Word files, .pdf for <u>Adobe Acrobat PDF</u> files, .htm for files that can be read by <u>Internet</u> browsers). These extensions are critical because they indicate to the computer which <u>software</u> application to use to open the file. Thus, if you alter or remove the extension, the computer does not know which <u>software</u> application to use in opening the file.

Extensions are automatically created when you save a file, but if you later change the name on the file, the extension can be lost. Therefore, be careful whenever you change the name of a file to ensure that you do not erase the extension.

Include in the Email Message or Discussion Board Posting the Name of the File and Software Application Used to Create the Attached File For example, if you are sending a classmate a draft of a chemistry assignment that was written in Microsoft Word (the XP version), then you would want to include in the <u>email</u> "The attached file, 10-4-12 chemistry assignment .doc, is a Word 2007 file. Please let me know if you have any problems opening the file." If a classmate has any trouble finding or opening the file, she now has adequate information for solving the problem.

TRY SOMETHING NEW

Web Tool: **http://www.twitter.com**

Have you ever been running late for class and wanted to let a classmate know so they can take notes for you? Or have you ever thought about calling a classmate late at night while studying but worried that they might be in bed? Twitter, a real-time short (140 character) messaging service lets you send updates, or read the updates of others, known as *tweets*. Tweets can go to <u>email</u> accounts or cell phones, letting people stay connected throughout the day. If, for example, you are late to class and you send a tweet that goes out to five or six classmates letting them know that you will be late, then numerous people are available to take notes or let the instructor know that you are on the way.

Getting to Know Your Instructor

Even when you are not in the classroom, you can develop a very positive relationship with your instructor and doing so is well worth the time and effort. Professors, whether online or in the classroom, are by and large passionate about the courses they teach and spend a good amount of their time each day communicating with students and others about their interests. Don't be shy about communicating with your instructor when you have questions or want an alternative perspective on a topic. After all, your instructor is the most valuable resource you have for being successful in college.

> **STUDENT-TO-STUDENT TIP**
>
> Communication is important in any relationship and even more in the online environment. Communication with the instructor in the online environment is a way for the instructor to "feel" your presence and a way for you, the student, to share in the learning experience and gain a sense of community in the class.

Don't Wait Until the End   Waiting for the last weeks of a course to make initial contact with your professor isn't likely going to do you much good. Starting the first weeks of class, be sure to take the time to get to know your instructor. Ask questions about homework assignments that may be confusing or request additional information on a topic covered in the lecture; regardless of the purpose of the contact, it is good for the instructor to know you by name well before the midterm exam.

 Use a Professional Communications Style   Email and other online conversations with your instructors should be treated as professional communications. By applying similar standards of courtesy and respect as you would to communications with an employer, you can typically improve the online relationship you have with your instructors. You should be polite in your communications, refer to your instructors by their titles (for example, professor or doctor) rather than their first names, use complete sentences and paragraphs, provide necessary contact information, and thank them for their time and effort.

Find Areas of Common Interest to Start the Conversation   Instructors are generally more than happy to develop mentoring relationships with their students; their goal is to help you be successful as well. They are typically very interested in the subject they are teaching and enjoy sharing their passion for the subject with others who are interested. It is often valuable to review your instructors' biographies on the college's website to find out more about their interests and to discover interests that you may have in common. You can use this information later to start conversations with them.

Ask for Feedback Throughout the Course   Many students find that receiving feedback throughout a course is useful for ensuring their success. Don't wait for the mid-term exam to find out if you are on target for success; ask about weekly quiz grades, exam scores, or participation points throughout the semester to make sure that you are doing what is required to be successful.

Creating a Supportive Online Learning Community

In most college courses, success will come with much less effort if you take the time to develop a learning community in which you can freely share ideas, obtain peer feedback, and together discover what it takes to be successful. Developing a supportive learning community typically doesn't happen, however, without time and energy from you and other students.

Isolation is typically the most common obstacle to success in online coursework. Without a supportive community of other students, it can be challenging to keep your motivation, find the feedback you have to be successful, and generally enjoy the learning experience. Building an online learning community requires that someone take a leadership role in organizing the community. Often, the instructor will do this by assigning students to study groups or organizing "office hours" or other times when students can meet together online to discuss course-related topics.

If these elements are not built into your course experience, then with a little effort you can build an online community yourself. Take the first step by emailing one or two other students to let them know that you would like to work with them throughout the semester; reviewing papers for each other, asking questions of each other about lecture materials, and so forth. These do not have to be formal events, but having a "study buddy" for online coursework can be very useful.

Support Functions of an Online Community

An online community can provide you with many resources that will be of value throughout the semester. Five of the primary functions for an online community are described below.

Motivation Life will interfere with your studies without regard, obstructing your path toward success. Staying motivated throughout a 3- or 4-month semester is a challenge even for the best students. Maintaining your motivation and keeping a positive attitude about your studies is essential, and having a few supportive friends online who can help you through those tough times can be valuable (see Chapter 7).

> **STUDENT-TO-STUDENT TIP**
>
> Be assertive and "kindly critical." Learn to suggest alternatives and compromises when you disagree with a group member. Instead of blatantly saying, "You're wrong," give the other person several suggestions to choose from regarding an alternative plan of action.

Peer Feedback   Peer feedback is likely the most helpful yet underutilized tool available to students who want to be successful. Waiting for your instructor's grade as the first feedback you get on your work isn't a strategy that will lead to your success. Get as much feedback as you can before submitting any assignment. Classmates, roommates, sorority sisters and fraternity brothers, friends from the marching band, or anyone else can often provide you with some initial feedback on your assignments.

It is worth the extra time and effort to have someone else review your work. From grammatical errors to inverted numbers in a formula, having an extra person or two look over your work can help avoid minor (as well as serious) mistakes that could reduce your grade. With email and other online technologies, you can quickly share draft files without even leaving home. But don't wait until the last minute to build the online relationships that can be helpful in getting peer feedback; build your online support community from the first day of class.

> **STUDENT-TO-STUDENT TIP**
>
> When permitted, it is helpful to discuss your answers with someone else (either online or otherwise) before submitting your assignments. Often, you will find that some part of your response does not come across in writing or have the emphasis you wish.

Technical Support   Your college's technical support services may not always be the best place for you to go when you have questions or technology problems. Often your family, friends, coworkers, and online classmates can provide you with much of the technical assistance that you may require. Many of the people around you will have experience with technology, and often times they will have struggled with similar technology questions and problems at some point as well. Do not be afraid to ask questions or request help from those around you; with technology there truly are no dumb questions.

> **STUDENT-TO-STUDENT TIP**
>
> Take a survey of your family, friends, and coworkers to see what skills, abilities, and areas of knowledge they have. The fact that my husband is a programmer and could help me with technical difficulties was an enormous advantage.

Study Groups   Study groups can be active online communities. From sharing notes to asking each other review questions using instant messaging, online technologies can help any study group function. For example, in preparing for exams at the end of each semester, trying to schedule a time for a study group to meet on campus can be difficult to say the least. But you can use email, chat, and instant messaging to reduce (or eliminate) the amount of time you have to meet together, allowing each study group member to add flexibility to their schedule.

Enjoyment   Getting to know your fellow students online can also be exciting and fun. You may be surprised by how many interesting people you can meet, especially when they all don't have to be sitting with you in the same classroom for the conversation to get started. Students from around the world may end up being part of your course, or maybe just students from another major that you wouldn't likely see on campus. No matter the case, try to make some friends, share some interesting stories, and enjoy your learning experience.

ACTIVITY 5-3   Did This Section Click?

🌐 As a review, read the following statements and then circle T (true) or F (false) for each one.

1. T F   You should always include your name and contact information in an <u>email</u> to a classmate or instructor.

2. T F   You can develop many positive friendships with other students without having to meet them in the classroom.

3. T F   Checking for spelling and grammar errors in <u>email</u> messages related to your <u>coursework</u> is *not* necessary.

4. T F   When you get funny <u>email</u> jokes, you should share them with all the other students in the class to build friendly relationships.

5. T F   You should take time before the midterm exam each semester to make initial contact with your professor.

Summary

Developing an online social life can help sustain your motivation throughout the semester by giving you the opportunity to communicate with others about what is happening in the course. College courses typically present a variety of obstacles for students, and being able to discuss complex problems or formulas with other students (or even with your professor) can provide you with the necessary information and confidence to ensure your success. Take the time to get to know your online classmates and instructors; it will not only benefit your academic success but also can help you enjoy your college courses all the more.

Chapter 5 Exercise

To begin the exercise, you will want to access the <u>World Wide Web</u>, using a <u>Web browser</u> (such as Netscape Navigator or Microsoft Internet Explorer). In addition, you will want to open a new document in a <u>word processing</u> program.

STEP 1: Select an upcoming assignment or activity for the course that you are taking and identify a student in that course who you have not met before. You can likely find a list of students in the class in the course's <u>educational portal</u> or <u>webpage</u>. (If not, you can ask the instructor for a list of student <u>email</u> addresses in order to create an online study group.)

STEP 2: In a <u>word processing</u> document, write a three-sentence introduction of yourself that you could send to the classmate you selected. Include your name, the course you are in with the class-mate, and why you are motivated to be successful in the course.

STEP 3: For the assignment or activity that you have selected, identify three to five major tasks that must be accomplished in order for you to be successful (for example, select an appropriate topic for a research paper, understand the relationship of two mathematical formulas, or learn to read the periodic table).

STEP 4: In the word processing document, list the tasks that must be accomplished for the assignment or activity, as well as an explanation of at least one way that studying with another person would be use-ful in being successful in each task. For example, "Because the assign-ment requires that we identify an appropriate topic for our research, it would be useful for me to have someone review my list of possible topics to determine if any would work for the assignment."

STEP 5: For each task and rationale for studying with a partner, identify an online technology (see Chapter 6) that may be useful in communicating online with the classmate. For example, you might identify the use of email to share word processing documents or instant messaging to share descriptions of how mathematical formulas relate to one another.

STEP 6: In the word processing document, combine your introduction (step 2) with the rationale for working with other students on each of the required tasks (steps 4) and the proposed online communica-tions tools that could be used (step 5). Though you do not have to email this message to your classmate at this time, you should keep the word processing file as a model for the time when you do want to form an online study group.

For example,

Alexia,

Hello, my name is Mehadi, and I am a student with you in Span-ish101. My major is Political Science, and because I have to get at least a B in this course, I would like to form an online study group to ensure that we can all be successful.

As you know, assignment 2 is due in 3 weeks, and to be successful in that assignment, we have to complete the following tasks. For each task, I have included ideas about how we can have an online study group that will provide each of us with practice and feedback.

First, we are to identify . . .

Please let me know if you would like to join the online study group.

Thanks,

Mehadi

Mehadi@mycollege.edu

Did You Stay Focused?

After completing this chapter, you should be able to do the following. If there are tasks below that you cannot do, take a few minutes to review the chapter, focusing on those areas that you may have missed the first time through.

☐ I can *communicate* a good first impression online.

☐ I can use separate <u>folders</u> and <u>emails</u> accounts to stay organized with my online relationships.

☐ I use spell check and grammar check on all correspondence with other students and my instructors.

☐ I add information regarding the name and file type for any files I attach to <u>emails</u> or <u>discussion board</u> postings.

☐ I have *integrated* the use of <u>email</u>, <u>chats</u>, and other online tools into my study habits for all of my college courses.

☐ I have *communicated* online with my instructor.

☐ I compensate for the lack of nonverbal communication strategies available online by using <u>emoticons</u> and acronyms.

☐ I add a personal touch to every message that I send to help build online relationships.

☐ I actively look out for and avoid possible miscommunications in my online communications.

☐ I have completed the chapter activities.

Additional Resources

🌐 Additional resources on topics covered in this chapter are available at the Premium Website for the *E-Learning Companion*.

Note
1. http://www.hspeople.com/archives/HSCareers/CareerPlanning/021102.asp.

6 E-Learning Vocabulary

STAY FOCUSED

By the end of this chapter, you will be able to

- *Define* the key vocabulary of online learning.
- *Determine* if you have adequate *access* to the tools necessary for online success.
- *Evaluate* your knowledge of e-learning terms and technologies.

Either as a supplement to traditional on-campus courses or as part of entirely online courses, online **e-learning** is today an essential ingredient in an education for students at all stages of their academic and professional careers. No longer are students limited by the boundaries of geography and time that once characterized the traditional college classroom. Educational technologies (such as the computer, World Wide Web, and audio/video conferencing) have transformed colleges, universities, libraries, and other training centers from 9:00 to 5:00 organizations (with some limited evening and weekend opportunities) into institutions that have the opportunity to serve your ever-growing educational requirements 24 hours a day, 7 days a week, 365 days a year.

The first step to success in online college coursework is therefore being prepared to take advantage of the learning opportunities supported by the technology. From retrieving your email, to viewing video lectures on your computer, to being prepared to meet the technology requirements, you have to know the basic terminology of online coursework. In this chapter, we will discuss many of the frequently used words and phrases that you are likely to find when you enter the online classroom. Beginning with words like "email" and "instant messaging," building your e-learning vocabulary will help you understand the online requirements of your college courses and be the first step on your journey to success.

Understanding the Basic Lingo

The basic lingo (or terminology) of online coursework is woven into the fabric of our daily conversations. From website addresses included in lemonade commercials to discussions of the wireless networks in many college dorms, today most students are more familiar with the technology lingo than those students entering college just a few years before them. Yet many terms, which you may be less familiar with, are frequently used in relation to online coursework.

To be successful in online coursework, you will want to be familiar with terminology that your instructor may use in defining assignments or discussing online supplements to course materials.

This chapter provides an abridged dictionary of common technology terms and is supplemented by additional e-learning vocabulary contained in the glossary.

What follows is a short list of terms commonly used in describing the technologies of online coursework.[1]

Web Portal

DEFINITION: A Web portal is a website considered as an entry point to other websites. Web portals commonly provide links to a variety of online tools, resources, and links. Many colleges and other educational institutions will use Web portals (also called educational portals or course management systems) that include online tools like grade books, real-time chat, discussion boards, online whiteboards, and other course resources and links.

TYPICAL USES IN ONLINE COURSEWORK: College courses will utilize Web portals to provide students with easy access to multiple resources through a single website. Angel, BlackBoard, eCollege, WebCT, Moodle, and other Web portals are commonly used educational portals at many institutions.[2] These services also provide the structure in which instructors can create course materials, interact with students, grade tests, and even maintain an up-to-date grade book. These websites commonly require that students use a password for access, and they typically include links to tools including real-time chats, discussion boards, and email, as well as access to lectures and assignments. For students, these online software applications can provide one-stop access to most resources required in completing online coursework.

Real-Time Chat

DEFINITION: Real-time chat (Internet rely chat, or IRC) is a network of Internet servers through which individual users can hold real-time online conversations. Instant messaging is a type of real-time chat.

TYPICAL USES IN ONLINE COURSEWORK: <u>Chat</u>s are commonly used when an instructor wants to encourage <u>synchronous</u> (at the same time) discussions. These discussions can be between individual students and the instructor, groups of students, or even the entire class. <u>Real-time chat</u>s do, however, require that all participants be linked to the <u>Internet</u> at the same time. Areas within <u>educational portal</u>s that are designated for <u>real-time chat</u>s are typically called <u>chat</u> rooms, and most educational <u>Web portal</u>s will offer features including whiteboards for sharing graphics, multiple <u>chat</u> rooms for side discussions among student groups, and even whisper functions that allow students to <u>chat</u> with just one other individual within a larger group <u>chat</u>.

Discussion Board

DEFINITION: A <u>discussion board</u> (bulletin board system, or BBS) is an electronic communication system that allows users to leave messages and to review messages, as well as upload or <u>download software</u>.

TYPICAL USES IN ONLINE COURSEWORK: <u>Discussion board</u>s are likely to be one of the most frequently used tools for online interactions that you will have with other students and instructors. Like the name implies, students and the instructor can leave messages for others to view on a virtual bulletin board. These messages can be viewed at different times by different members of the learning community and are thus considered a form of <u>asynchronous</u> course communication. Like with <u>real-time chat</u>s, most <u>educational portal</u>s will include <u>discussion board</u>s within the online classroom. Common features in many portals include **thread**ed discussions (where you can visually see which messages are replies to other messages), file <u>attachment</u>s, restricted access to messages defined by the instructor, and the ability to link to <u>webpage</u>s outside of the portal.

Email

DEFINITION: <u>Email</u> is a feature that lets a computer user send a text message to someone at another computer using the <u>Internet</u>. <u>Email</u>, or electronic mail, can duplicate most of the features of paper mail, such as storing messages in "in boxes" and "out boxes," forwarding messages, providing delivery receipts, and sending multiple copies.

TYPICAL USES IN ONLINE COURSEWORK: As with <u>Internet</u> <u>chat</u>s and bulletin boards, instructors commonly use <u>email</u> to communicate with students (students also use it to interact with other students and the instructor). Instructors will frequently use <u>email</u> to make announcements regarding course assignments, to discuss individual grades with students, and to manage other course-related activities.

Email Attachments

DEFINITION: An email attachment is a file of any file format (such as, a word processing document or picture) that is attached to an email. The contents of an attachment usually do not appear within the body of the email message but can be accessed by email recipients by clicking on an appropriate icon.

TYPICAL USES IN ONLINE COURSEWORK: From term papers to doctoral dissertations, email attachments are regularly used to send larger

TRY SOMETHING NEW

Web Tool: **Google's Mail Goggles**

Just seconds after clicking on the send button for an email or text message have you ever had the sinking feelings of regret? Though, as of yet, no Web Tool can keep us from all of our mistakes, if you use Google Mail (a free email service available at http://mail.google.com) you do have an option that will at least make you think twice before sending late-night emails that may regret the next morning. If you enable the Google's Mail Goggles option (within the labs area of the settings menu) you will be required to answer a series of mathematical problems before you can send an email. You choose the days and times when the feature is activated and the web tool will do its best to keep you from sending messages that you may later regret.

files (for example, text files that are more than a few pages long or that include graphics). In completing assignments, instructors will often request that related files be emailed to them as attachments. These files can be in most any file format (for example, Microsoft Word, Adobe Acrobat PDF, and Microsoft Excel), and as a courtesy you should include the file name and file format in the text of the email accompanying the attachment. Depending on the software that you use to access your email, the process for attaching a file to the email may differ.

Blog (and Vlog)

DEFINITION: Short for "Web log," a blog is a website that displays personal journal entries by one or more individuals in chronological (or reverse chronological) order and usually has links to readers' comments on specific postings.[3] Blogs are typically editable webpages that do not require individuals to know specialized coding (that is, HTML) to post their journal entries. A vlog, short for "video blog," is a specialized type of online journal in which the journal author(s) incorporate video clips (often in addition to text and other content) into their entries.

TYPICAL USES IN ONLINE COURSEWORK: Recently, both college students and instructors have found interesting and valuable ways to use blogs (and/or vlogs) to enhance and expand the learning experience. From course assignments that require students to maintain a blog describing their learning throughout a course to the creation of vlog lessons that can supplement classroom lectures, the use of journal-like technologies can provide creative and useful learning experiences.

Wiki

DEFINITION: A wiki is collaborative website whose content can be edited by anyone who has access to it.[4] Wikis are typically editable webpages that do not require the contributors to know specialized coding (that is, HTML) to post their entries or edits.

TYPICAL USES IN ONLINE COURSEWORK: A wiki provides an editable webpage that both instructors and students can contribute to and update throughout a course. College instructors will often use a wiki when course materials are frequently updated and student involvement in the development of the course is desired. Because any student can add to, delete, or edit information contained on the wiki, it can offer many unique opportunities for students to interact with other students and/or the instructor.

Instant Messaging

DEFINITION: Instant messaging is a type of real-time communication that enables you to conduct a private chat with one or more other users. Typically, the instant messaging software will allow you to create a list of individuals that you want to have private chats with and alert you whenever somebody on your list is online. You can then initiate a chat session with that particular individual or multiple individuals.

TYPICAL USES IN ONLINE COURSEWORK: Instant messaging offers students taking online courses synchronous (real-time, or simultaneous) communications with other students and/or the professor. From asking quick questions of the instructor to working in collaborative teams on a project, instant messaging services (like Microsoft Messenger, ICQ, Yahoo Messenger, AOL Messenger, and many others) can provide you with a communications resource that can facilitate many of the discussions that you will want to have while taking an online course. Most instant messaging programs will also allow you to include attachments with your messages. Traditionally, each user

> **STUDENT-TO-STUDENT TIP**
>
> When working on group projects, instant messaging saved me time and frustration because I could always know when other group members were online and working.

had to use the same <u>instant messaging</u> <u>software</u> in order to communicate, but in newer releases of <u>software</u>, several companies now offer <u>instant messaging</u> <u>software</u> that can communicate through multiple <u>instant</u> <u>messaging</u> programs (for example, you could instant message with classmates that use AOL Messenger as well as classmates that use Microsoft Messenger).

Videoconference

DEFINITION: A videoconference is a meeting or conversation conducted between two or more participants at different sites by using computer networks to transmit video and audio files.

TYPICAL USES IN ONLINE COURSEWORK: Sometimes used as the primary means for communication in some long-distance education courses, videoconferences are most typically limited to only those instructional activities that require synchronous (at the same time) two-way interactions among participants, due to the expenses involved. Instructors will often use videoconferences for guest speakers or to provide unique opportunities for students in multiple locations to interact regarding a specific topic. Videoconferences use satellites or high-speed computer networks to link to two (or more) sites so that participants can communicate both verbally and visually with each other in a <u>synchronous</u> format. Typically, videoconference equipment utilizes television technology that is supplemented with computer technology.

Desktop videoconferencing is also available for participants to exchange both audio and video information through their personal computers. The quality of audio and video using desktop videoconferencing equipment depends on the speed of <u>Internet</u> access available at each computer engaged in the conference and the computer itself.

Streaming Audio and Video

DEFINITION: Streaming audio and video is a technique for transferring data from one computer to another such that it can be processed as a steady and continuous stream. Streaming technologies are becoming increasingly important with the growth of the <u>Internet</u> because most users do not have fast enough access to <u>download</u> large multimedia files quickly. With streaming audio and video, your <u>Web browser</u> can start displaying the audio or video data before the entire file has been received.

TYPICAL USES IN ONLINE COURSEWORK: Instructors often use audio or video segments to supplement classroom instruction or to provide complete lectures to long-distance students. Like other forms of video or audio (for example, DVDs, videotapes, and compact discs), students may watch or listen to the instructor at any time they wish.

Given file size and cost limitations, streaming audio and video are most commonly used when the instructor wishes to convey a large amount of course content, in the same format, to all students in the course (rather than individualized instruction for particular students).

Listserve

DEFINITION: A <u>listserve</u> is a mailing list manager used for the distribution of <u>email</u> among the list's members.

TYPICAL USES IN ONLINE COURSEWORK: Today's college instructors typically use <u>listserves</u> when they want to communicate the same message to all students in a course or when they want to facilitate discussions that can include multiple students outside of the classroom. Most <u>listserves</u> require a subscription or registration before sending or receiving messages with other members of the <u>listserve</u>. Often, however, instructors will subscribe all students in a class to a course <u>listserve</u> to facilitate communications. Although <u>listserves</u> do not allow instructors or students to limit the recipient list for broadcast <u>emails</u>, they can be effectively used to facilitate online <u>coursework</u> (especially when students have limited access to the <u>Internet</u> and their <u>email</u>).

Podcast

DEFINITION: A <u>podcast</u> is a type of audio file that is shared using the <u>Internet</u> and played using a personal computer, Apple iPod or iPhone, or other MP3 player. Unlike other <u>download</u>ed or streaming audio files, <u>podcast</u>s enable users to subscribe to a collection of audio files

---

ACTIVITY 6-1   Did This Section Click?

As a review, answer the following questions by circling T (true) or F (false) for each statement.

1. T F   A <u>listserve</u> uses <u>email</u> to communicate the same message to many members of a group.

2. T F   <u>Instant messaging</u> allows you to communicate online using similar techniques to those that you would use on a <u>discussion board</u>.

3. T F   You must use a separate <u>software</u> application to send <u>attachment</u>s with an <u>email</u>.

4. T F   <u>Educational portal</u>s provide a single <u>website</u> that students can use to link to many online resources.

5. T F   A <u>discussion board</u> offers a form of <u>synchronous</u> conversation for students.

that can be routinely updated and automatically <u>download</u>ed to their computer or audio player.

TYPICAL USES IN ONLINE COURSEWORK: College instructors use podcasts to offer lectures, supplemental course content, or even the answers to frequently asked questions in a portable audio format that can be used by students either with their personal computer, Apple iPod or iPhone, or an MP3 player. The flexibility of the podcast allows an instructor to regularly update audio materials and inform students of recent releases while providing students with course materials that can be used at times and locations that are convenient for them.

Checking Technology Requirements

Many of the courses that you will take as part of your college education will require the use of some form of computer technology. From finding books in the college library to continuing discussions of class topics well after the on-campus lectures, technology today is interwoven into the curriculum of most courses. Some <u>coursework</u> may require that you have access to video-conferencing equipment, whereas others may require specific <u>software</u> applications. In all cases, though, when classes begin each semester, you should explore the course requirements to make sure that you have adequate access to all the necessary resources to be successful.

It is also often useful, when possible, for you to contact the course instructor prior to starting classes to review the technology requirements. During this introductory conversation (either using <u>email</u> or the telephone), you will want to determine not only what technology resources are required for the course (such as <u>Internet</u> access, <u>email</u>, and <u>word processing</u>) but also the extent of previous online experiences the instructor recommends for students. Depending on your access to technology, you may also want to ask the instructor about the technologies available through the institution rather than purchasing them yourself for personal use.

For most college students, financial considerations are part of course enrollment decisions each semester. Additional hardware or <u>software</u> requirements should also be considered as part of the cost associated with a course. However, there are alternatives to purchasing the hardware or <u>software</u> for your personal use. Many students unfortunately do not take full advantage of the computer technologies (including <u>Internet</u> access) commonly available in college or public libraries. Many local recreation centers and public schools also offer free (or low-cost) access to <u>Internet</u> or other technologies that you may require. These, and other alternative resources, can be used to reduce the costs of technology requirements.

Not all minimal hardware requirements will apply to all courses offered under an umbrella organization (a community college, university, or corporation). For example, while broadband access (for example, DSL or cable **modem** connection) may be required for courses that use <u>synchronous</u> video

Important technology questions to ask your instructor:

- What online technologies will be used in the course (for example, the Internet, email, online discussion boards, and online library databases)?
- What minimum computer specifications are recommended for students in the course (such as current versions of software applications)?
- How much experience should students have with online technologies in order to be successful in the course?
- Do the college's computer labs have the necessary software?

and audio chat software (for example, Microsoft Netmeeting), the course that you are interested in may only require dial-up modem access if the instructor uses only asynchronous discussions (such as discussion boards) for course communications. Therefore, it is important to examine the hardware requirements of both the individual course that you are considering as well as the requirements of the institution offering the course.

Additional hardware that may be required for online coursework could include desktop video systems, digital cameras, scanners, access to videoconferencing equipment, and other technologies. Whatever the technologies that you will be required to use, you should become familiar with the requirements as early in the semester as possible. This will give you time to identify alternative resources if you do not own or wish to purchase the required technologies, and it will give you time to try them out once or twice before your course assignments are due.

Familiarizing Yourself with Required Hardware

The hardware requirements necessary for online coursework should be examined in detail as soon as they are available. Typically, they will be specified in a syllabus or other information provided by the instructor during the first week of classes. Also, don't hesitate to contact the instructor prior to the first day of class to identify what hardware may be required for success in the course. To verify that you have met the specifications, spend whatever free time that you have before the course begins to get familiar with the required hardware to ensure that it works correctly.

A few terms related to computer hardware that you should be familiar with in determining if the technology you have available meets the minimal requirements are listed next.

CPU (Central Processing Unit)

DEFINITION: The CPU is the part of a computer that interprets and executes instructions (that is, it is the "brain" of the computer). Sometimes referred to as the processor or chip, the CPU is where most calculations take place. In terms of computing power, the <u>CPU</u> is not the only critical element of a computer system, though it is likely the most important element.

WHAT IS IMPORTANT AND WHY: Additional information on the <u>CPU</u> is available at the Premium Website for the *E-Learning Companion.*

Hard Disk Drive

DEFINITION: A hard disk drive is a rigid metal disk (called a platter) fixed within a disk drive and used for storing computer data even when the computer is turned off. Hard disks provide considerably more storage space and quicker access than most other data-storage devices.

WHAT IS IMPORTANT AND WHY: Additional information on the hard disk drive is available at the Premium Website for the *E-Learning Companion.*

RAM (Random Access Memory)

DEFINITION: All data does not require storage on the hard disk drive for later use. Storing data that is required for only a short time, while the computer is making calculations, is done using random access memory (RAM). RAM allows the <u>CPU</u> to access the data it requires without having to go through other data first, making RAM faster than memory that offers sequential access (such as a hard disk drive or CD-ROM). When a computer is turned on, the information from the start up is immediately loaded in RAM. New or changed data will be stored in RAM until it can be written to a hard disk or other storage device. Data stored in RAM is lost, however, every time the computer is turned off or loses power.

WHAT IS IMPORTANT AND WHY: Additional information on RAM is available at the Premium Website for the *E-Learning Companion.*

Modem or Network Interface Card

DEFINITION: A dial-up <u>modem</u> is a device or program that enables a computer to transmit data over telephone lines and allows access to the <u>Internet</u> and <u>World Wide Web</u>. A dial-up <u>modem</u> converts data from digital signals to analog signal and vice versa so that computers can communicate over telephone lines, which transmit analog waves. Newer <u>modem</u>s can also provide similar service through cable television lines or high-speed <u>Internet</u> access through fiber-optic phone lines.

A network interface card, often abbreviated as NIC, is a device that allows your computer to be connected directly (that is, without using phone lines) to a network of multiple computers that are linked together, and then the entire network can be linked to the Internet and World Wide Web. Most NICs are designed for a particular type of network, protocol, and media, although some can serve multiple networks.

When a computer network doesn't use wires to connect to computers it is called wireless (or wifi). A wireless router is commonly connected to a modem in order to transform the signal from one transmitted by wires to a wireless signal. For a computer to access the wireless network, a built-in wireless antenna or an external wireless NIC (sometimes called an airport card) is used to communicate with the modem.

WHAT IS IMPORTANT AND WHY: The speed, range, and stability of your access to the Internet and World Wide Web depends on the relationship between each of these components, therefore it is important to verify with your college or local Internet service provider that you have the appropriate equipment to gain access to your online course materials.

Internet and World Wide Web

DEFINITION: The Internet is a massive network that connects millions of computers together globally, forming a network in which any computer can communicate with any other computer as long as they are both connected to the Internet. Information that travels over the Internet does so via a variety of languages known as protocols.

ACTIVITY 6-2   Did This Section Click?

As a review, mark the phrase that correctly completes each of the following statements.

1. Data stored in random access memory (RAM)
   a. is erased when the computer is turned on.
   b. is erased when the computer is turned off.
   c. can only be erased by the user.

2. The hard disk stores information on a
   a. plastic disk called a plate.
   b. metal disk called a platter.
   c. length of plastic tape.

3. A modem converts
   a. analog data into digital data.
   b. digital data into analog data.
   c. analog data into digital data and digital data into analog data.

The <u>World Wide Web</u>, or simply web, is a way of accessing information over the medium of the <u>Internet</u>. It is an information-sharing model that is built on top of the <u>Internet</u>. The web uses the hypertext transfer protocol (or <u>HTTP</u>), only one of the languages spoken over the <u>Internet</u>, to transmit data. Web documents using <u>HTTP</u> can contain graphics, sounds, text, and video.[5]

🌐 **WHAT IS IMPORTANT AND WHY:** Additional information on the World Wide Web is available at the Premium Website for the *E-Learning Companion.*

Familiarizing Yourself with Required Software

Determining if you have the <u>software</u> required for online <u>coursework</u> can be as confusing as the hardware. You should take the time prior to enrolling in an online course to resolve what <u>software</u>, if any, is required. Many courses use only <u>Internet</u>-based <u>software</u> that is purchased, administered, and maintained by the institution offering the course (see <u>educational portals</u> defined previously), but other <u>software</u> may be required to complete course requisites. For example, many instructors will only accept research papers and other documents in Microsoft Word or <u>Adobe Acrobat PDF</u> formats.

> **STUDENT-TO-STUDENT TIP**
>
> Prepare yourself technically by conducting all computer-related checks prior to the course start date; technical problems can set you up for failure and impact motivation.

No matter what <u>software</u> is required, you will want to be familiar with the functionality of the <u>software</u> prior to starting the course. There are many similarities in how you can access analogous features in different <u>software</u> programs; as a result, learning to use the functions of your <u>software</u> is not as challenging as it may seem at first. With a healthy amount of curiosity and some patience, you should be able to quickly learn how to use most of the <u>software</u> features required in your college courses.

> **STUDENT-TO-STUDENT TIP**
>
> Become familiar with the <u>software</u> that you are going to use for the online educational experience and with what it can do. Test the various areas. Practice with the <u>software</u>'s tools every opportunity you get, until your use of the tools is intuitive.

Operating Systems (Macintosh and Windows)

DESCRIPTION: An <u>operating system</u> is the foundational <u>software</u> installed on a computer that negotiates the basic functions between the hardware (such as hard disk drive, <u>modem</u>, and CD-ROM,) and the <u>software</u> (such as Microsoft Word, <u>Adobe Acrobat PDF</u> Reader, and

Netscape Navigator). Modern <u>operating systems</u> also offer a variety of features that can be used to organize files, search for files, edit basic text, repair damaged files, and so forth.

The two leading <u>operating systems</u> for personal computers are the Macintosh <u>operating system</u> and the Microsoft Windows <u>operating system</u>.

The Macintosh <u>operating system</u> (OS) is installed on a popular model of computer made by Apple Computer. The Macintosh OS was the first to feature a graphical user interface (GUI) that utilizes <u>windows</u>, <u>icons</u>, and a mouse to make it relatively easy for novices to use without learning a complex set of text commands.

As a result of the GUI <u>operating system</u>, all applications that run on a Macintosh computer have a similar user interface. Once a user has become familiar with one application, he or she can learn new applications relatively easily. The success of the Macintosh OS led to the widespread use of graphics-based applications and <u>operating systems</u>. The Windows <u>operating system</u> interface copies many features from the Macintosh OS.

Like the Macintosh OS, Microsoft Windows provides a graphical user interface that allows users to easily learn a variety of <u>software</u> applications. Although Windows was released after the Macintosh OS, to gain market share Microsoft permitted other companies to develop <u>software</u> applications that would run within the Windows <u>operating system</u> while Macintosh maintained proprietary control over the Macintosh OS, allowing few <u>software</u> applications to be created by other companies. The greater number of <u>software</u> applications available for the Windows <u>operating system</u> has made it the most used <u>operating system</u> in the world. By some estimates, nearly 90% of all personal computers in the world utilize a Windows <u>operating system</u>.

 WHAT IS IMPORTANT AND WHY: Additional information on <u>operating systems</u> is available at the Premium Website for *E-Learning Companion.*

Microsoft Office Suite

DESCRIPTION: Microsoft Office Suite is a collection of Microsoft's primary <u>software</u> applications for computers running either Microsoft Windows or the Macintosh OS. Depending on the package, it includes some combination of Word, Excel, PowerPoint, Access, and Schedule, along with a host of <u>Internet</u> and other related utilities. The applications share common functions, such as spell checking and graphing, and objects can be dragged and dropped between applications.[6]

 TYPICAL USES IN ONLINE COURSEWORK: The Microsoft Office suite provides a variety of <u>software</u> applications in one package.[7] Although competing companies offer <u>software</u> with similar functionality, to ensure compatibility, many colleges and universities (as well as individual instructors) require that course-related materials be submitted in the <u>file format</u>s associated with the products included in the Microsoft Office Suite. This isn't to say that you can't use alternative <u>software</u> to create the files, but the copy of the file submitted to the instructor will most often have to be saved in Microsoft Office format.[8]

Within the Microsoft Office Suite, the <u>software</u> program that you will most likely use is Microsoft Word. Using this <u>word processing</u> <u>software</u>, you can create documents that include text, images, graphics, tables, and other features. Most editions of the Microsoft Office Suite also include Microsoft PowerPoint, which facilitates the creation of graphical images that can be used as slides in a presentation or as handouts for class discussions. Like with Microsoft Word, PowerPoint files can be saved in a <u>HTML</u> <u>file format</u> for publishing to the <u>World Wide Web</u>. Other <u>software</u> included in most editions of the Microsoft Office Suite can be used for creating databases (Microsoft Access), organizing data (Microsoft Excel), and completing the requirements of many of your course assignments. Even if you have experience with one or more of the programs available in the Microsoft Office Suite, you will want to review the technology tips provided in Chapter 2 and complete How To Tutorials 5 and 6, as well as examine the online tutorials available through links provided at the Premium Website for *E-Learning Companion.* 🌐

> ## STUDENT-TO-STUDENT TIP
>
> Get to know the various functions of the <u>software</u> you will be using and "test drive" it every chance that you get until the features are second nature.

Web Browser

DESCRIPTION: A <u>Web browser</u> is a <u>software</u> application used to locate and display <u>webpages</u>. The three most popular browsers are Netscape Navigator, Mozilla Firefox, and Microsoft Internet Explorer. Each is a graphical browser, which means that it can display graphics as well as text. In addition, most modern browsers can present multimedia information, including sound and video, though they require <u>plug-in</u>s for some formats.[9]

TYPICAL USES IN ONLINE COURSEWORK: Throughout your college education you will most likely use <u>Web browsers</u> for at least one assignment in each course. From finding resources required for a term paper to participating in a group project hosted in the college's <u>Web portal</u>, you will want to be familiar with the functionality of the <u>Web browser</u> that you decide to use. The <u>Web</u> <u>browser</u> <u>software</u> will provide you with a variety of resources for expanding your educational experience, including the ability to save <u>bookmarks</u> so that you can quickly come back to your favorite <u>websites</u> again and view <u>webpages</u> even when you are not connected to the <u>Internet</u>.

Choosing a <u>Web browser</u> is not necessarily a critical decision. Newer versions of each <u>software</u> programs have few differences in functionality for the average user. Our primary recommendation to students is, however, to select one browser and stay with it. By using one <u>Web browser</u> for your online <u>coursework</u>, you can customize the <u>software</u> so that it is easy to find the <u>websites</u> that you use most (using the Favorites function in Internet Explorer or Bookmarks in Netscape Navigator). Organizing these favorite <u>websites</u> in <u>folders</u> that allow you to easily find information when you require it can save you time. Finding these <u>folders</u> can be a challenge if you have some <u>websites</u> noted in one program and additional sites identified in another. In addition, by staying with the same <u>Web browser</u>, you will not discover the night before a term paper is due that your <u>Web browser</u> requires additional <u>software</u> (for example, a <u>plug-in</u>) for accessing the files you want to use.

For a comparison of <u>Web browser</u> versions, accessibility features, and vulnerabilities, you can visit a <u>wiki</u> that is frequently updated at

http://en.wikipedia.org/wiki/Comparison_of_web_browsers

Plug-In (Add-In)

DESCRIPTION: A <u>plug-in</u> is an accessory program designed to be used in conjunction with an existing application (especially common with <u>Web browsers</u>) to extend its capabilities or provide additional functions.

TYPICAL USES IN ONLINE COURSEWORK: Most colleges use a variety of <u>software</u> applications to <u>host</u> the many resources that are used in completing online <u>coursework</u>. From <u>real-time chats</u> to streaming video, often the <u>software</u> used to create and distribute information to students will require additional <u>software</u> that is not included with a <u>Web browser</u> or other <u>software</u> applications. When necessary, you should be able to <u>download</u> and install required <u>plug-ins</u> (typically for free) to ensure that you have access to all <u>software</u> functions necessary for your success in online <u>coursework</u>. Examples of <u>plug-ins</u> that are commonly required to access online resources include Macromedia Flash Player, Apple QuickTime, and Adobe Acrobat PDF Reader. (See Table 3-4 for a list of <u>plug-ins</u> and other <u>software</u> applications that are available for free.)

Antivirus Software

DESCRIPTION: <u>Antivirus software</u> is a utility that checks <u>emails</u>, memory, and disks for computer viruses and removes those that it finds. Because new viruses arise and corrupt, periodically update the <u>antivirus software</u>'s virus definitions on your computer. Some programs will now do this automatically over the <u>Internet</u>.

TYPICAL USES IN ONLINE COURSEWORK: Throughout your college experience, you will be receiving numerous <u>email</u>s, as well as <u>downloading</u> many files from course <u>websites</u> and other sources, which may contain virus applications that can destroy data stored in or disrupt the performance of your computer. Installing an <u>antivirus software</u> application (such as McAfee Antivirus and Norton Antivirus) and keeping the virus definitions file up-to-date can protect you from these potential threats by scanning each file that enters your computer for known computer viruses. Many colleges provide <u>antivirus software</u> to students at no charge, and many others require that students purchase <u>antivirus software</u>.

Adobe Acrobat PDF (Reader and Writer)

DESCRIPTION: <u>Adobe Acrobat PDF</u> is document-exchange <u>software</u> that allows documents created on one platform to be displayed and printed exactly the same on another, no matter which fonts are installed in the computer. The fonts are embedded within the Acrobat document, which is known as a PDF (portable document format) file, thus eliminating the requirement that the target machine contain the same fonts.[10]

TYPICAL USES IN ONLINE COURSEWORK: As discussed earlier, instructors are commonly concerned with the compatibility of files from differing <u>software</u> programs. When twenty-five students submit essay answers to online exam questions, those submitted in <u>file format</u>s that the instructor cannot access can lose points (if for no reason other than the negative feelings on the part of the instructor who has to install <u>software</u> to convert a file from one format to another). <u>Adobe Acrobat PDF</u> attempts to facilitate the sharing of files by moving documents into a standardized <u>file format</u> (PDF) that can be viewed and printed using <u>software</u> made available to users for free by the company.

Many institutions and individual instructors therefore require that files submitted to them be in the PDF format. The <u>Adobe Acrobat PDF</u> Reader[11] can then be used to view and print the documents submitted by students without any worries concerning <u>file format</u>s.

However, to create a document in the PDF format, you must have access to (or purchase) the Adobe Writer that facilitates the creation of PDF documents.[12] When the Adobe Acrobat Writer <u>software</u> (also called Adobe Acrobat Distiller) is installed, you can then create PDF files from

> **STUDENT-TO-STUDENT TIP**
>
> To understand the concept of an <u>Adobe Acrobat PDF</u> file, think of it as a photograph of a document. You cannot edit the file, but you may attach comments to the text. The comments appear as "sticky notes" on the file.

many other <u>software</u> programs through the print function (for example, using Microsoft Word, Microsoft PowerPoint, and Corel WordPerfect).

File Transfer Protocol

DESCRIPTION: A file transfer protocol (FTP) is used to transfer files over a network (such as the <u>Internet</u> and UNIX). For example, after developing the <u>HTML</u> pages for a <u>website</u> on a local machine, they are typically uploaded to the <u>Web server</u> using FTP.[13]

TYPICAL USES IN ONLINE COURSEWORK: A variety of <u>software</u> programs facilitate the transfer of files from one computer to another using FTP.[14] In addition to <u>software</u> programs that you can install for transferring files, most of the <u>Web portal</u>s that you will use in online <u>coursework</u> (for example, eCollege, Blackboard, and Angel) will have FTP <u>software</u> built into the Web-based applications. This will facilitate your moving files (such as term papers, pictures, and other course-related documents) from your computer to the course <u>website</u> for the instructor or other students to view (this is called "uploading") or moving files from the course <u>website</u> to your computer (this is called "<u>downloading</u>").

Typically, you will not be aware that an FTP program is being used when you want to upload (or post) files to the course <u>website</u>. These Web-based FTP options will be a common tool that you will use when submitting assignments to your professors or sharing files with fellow students through the college's <u>Web portal</u>.

FTP <u>software</u> that is not Web-based will be used primarily when you have created <u>webpages</u> of your own. To make these <u>webpages</u> accessible to others using the <u>World Wide Web</u>, you will want to move <u>webpages</u> or other documents from your computer to a <u>host</u> computer (or <u>server</u>). As you gain more experience in completing online <u>coursework</u>, you will likely want to install and become familiar with the operations of an FTP <u>software</u> program that is not Web-based because it provides additional flexibility for storing files on <u>server</u>s and accessing <u>Internet</u> resources.

Web Authoring <u>Software</u>

DESCRIPTION: Web authoring <u>software</u> (<u>HTML</u> editor) is a program that allows you to create <u>webpages</u> using similar tools and resources as you would use when developing a new document in a <u>word processing</u> program. It generates the required hypertext mark-up language (<u>HTML</u>) code for the pages and can switch back and forth (in varying degrees) between the page layout and the <u>HTML</u>.

ACTIVITY 6-3   **Did This Section Click?**

🌐 As a review, match the phrase, initialism, or acronym with the correct definition.

1. ___ GUI

2. ___ HTML

3. ___ Web browser

4. ___ PDF

5. ___ Operating system

a. A <u>software</u> application that allows you to view files available on the <u>World Wide Web</u>.

b. <u>Software</u> designed to control the hardware of a specific computer system in order to allow users and application programs to employ it easily.

c. The <u>file format</u> for files available on the <u>World Wide Web</u>.

d. An interface that uses <u>icons</u> to illustrate objects such as files, <u>folders</u>, and other computer resources.

e. The <u>file format</u> that allows files to be shared between users of computers with different <u>operating systems</u>.

TYPICAL USES IN ONLINE COURSEWORK: Some, but not all, courses may require that you submit your <u>coursework</u> through a <u>website</u>, outside of the <u>Web portal</u>, that you design, maintain, and control. If this is the case or if you just want to create a <u>website</u> for some other reason, then you will likely want to become familiar with Web authoring <u>software</u>. <u>Software</u> programs like Macromedia's Dreamweaver and Microsoft's Frontpage can be used to create a single <u>webpage</u> or a complete <u>website</u> (the Netscape Web browser also includes free <u>software</u> for creating basic <u>webpages</u> called Netscape Composer). These <u>software</u> programs (as well as many other programs offered by other <u>software</u> companies, some of which can be <u>download</u>ed for free) provide for the development of <u>webpages</u> using an interface that allows you to see the page as it will look on the <u>World Wide Web</u> at the same time that you are creating it (also called "what you see is what you get," or WYSIWYG technology). These programs make it much easier to create a <u>webpage</u> that has the look that you intended because they function much like a <u>word processing</u> program.

<u>Webpages</u> created with Web authoring <u>software</u> will have to be uploaded to a <u>server</u> using an FTP program (described previously) in order to be viewable to the public. <u>Server</u> availability is typically provided to students by colleges, so check with your college's technical support services before purchasing <u>server</u> space from another provider.

Summary

Success in online <u>coursework</u> requires at least a basic understanding of the terminology used in relation to computer hardware, <u>software</u>, and the <u>Internet</u>. In this chapter we examined many of the fundamental words and phrases that you are likely to hear when being assigned or completing online course assignments and activities. Reviewing these terms, as well as those defined in the glossary, periodically throughout your college experience can help prepare you for success in online <u>coursework</u>.

Chapter 6 Exercise

To begin the following exercise, you will want to access your Web-based course materials (that is, <u>educational portal</u>) using a <u>Web browser</u> (such as Netscape Navigator or Microsoft Internet Explorer).

HOW TO 20

STEP 1: Using the <u>Web browser</u>, access your course <u>website</u> using the login and password provided to you by the instructor or institution. When you have entered the Web-based course site, enter the area that includes the course syllabus. Within the course syllabus, identify the assignments that will be used to grade your performance in the course.

HOW TO 27

STEP 2: Highlight (by dragging your mouse over the text describing the assignments) and copy (by selecting copy from the Edit <u>menu</u> at the top of the screen) the text.

HOW TO 34

STEP 3: When you have copied the assignments, enter the area that includes the <u>discussion board</u>s for the course. Typically, within <u>discussion board</u>s, you will have links to a variety of topics for discussion that have been created by the instructor. For this activity, you may select any one of these areas by clicking on it.

HOW TO 41

HOW TO 24

STEP 4: Though each Web-based course program is slightly different, you should see a Post or Reply button. Click on that button, and a <u>window</u> should appear where you can post a message. Typically, your name and the date will automatically appear with the message, but you can create a title of your own. Title this message "Course Assignments." Then put the cursor in the message <u>window</u> by clicking in the space provided.

HOW TO 31

HOW TO 38

STEP 5: Paste the course assignments that you have copied into the message <u>window</u> (by selecting paste from the Edit <u>menu</u>). When you have done this, continue to step 6.

HOW TO 44

STEP 6: Select the Submit (Upload, OK, or similarly named) button from the message <u>window</u>. The message should then be included within the <u>discussion board</u> topic that you have selected.

Did You Stay Focused?

After completing this chapter, you should be able to do the following. If there are skills below that you cannot do, take a few minutes to review the chapter, focusing on those areas that you may have missed the first time through.

- ☐ I can *define* (and give an example) of an <u>Internet</u> portal that may be used for online <u>coursework</u>.

- ☐ I can *define* the different uses for <u>real-time chats</u>, bulletin boards, and <u>instant messaging</u> for online communication.

- ☐ I have checked to ensure that I have *access* to a computer with a <u>CPU</u> that meets the minimal requirements for the required online <u>coursework</u> <u>software</u>.

- ☐ I have checked to ensure that I have *access* to a computer with enough RAM memory to access online course materials.

- ☐ I have checked to ensure that I have *access* to a computer with adequate <u>Internet</u> bandwidth to access online course materials.

- ☐ I have *evaluated* my computer skills and knowledge.

- ☐ I have checked to ensure that I have *access* to the <u>software</u> required for completing online <u>coursework</u>.

- ☐ I have completed each of the chapter activities.

Additional Resources

🌐 Additional resources on topics covered in this chapter are available at the Premium Website for the *E-Learning Companion*.

Notes

1. Unless otherwise noted, definitions based on Kleinedler, 2001.
2. For additional information and links to these services, visit http://www.e-learningcentre.co.uk/eclipse/vendors/campusportals.htm.
3. *American Heritage® Dictionary of the English Language*, 4th edition. © 2006 Houghton Mifflin Company.
4. Ibid.
5. http://www.webopedia.com/.
6. From http://www.techweb.com/encyclopedia/.
7. Software suites from companies like Corel or Lotus also offer similar functionality, though they have a smaller number of users than Microsoft. A free software suite is also available at http://www.openoffice.org
8. If you use an alternative software program to the one included in the Microsoft Office Suite, ensure that you can save files into the Microsoft format before assignments are due in the course. See the Help <u>menu</u> for this information in most software programs.

9. From http://www.webopedia.com.
10. From http://www.techweb.com/encyclopedia/.
11. Available for free at http://www.adobe.com/.
12. Other software programs for creating PDF files are available, though compatibility can vary.
13. From http://www.techweb.com/encyclopedia/.
14. A variety of companies offer FTP software. Several are available for free through sites like http://www.shareware.com or http://www.tucows.com.

7 Maintaining Motivation in an Online Course

STAY FOCUSED

By the end of this chapter, you will be able to

- *Manage* all aspects of your life that impact on your e-learning success.
- *Integrate* your study skills from the traditional classroom with the e-learning skills that will help make you a successful online student.
- *Create* a positive environment that encourages your online success.

As we have discussed previously, the social network of an online student is one that must be developed intentionally through involvement with other students and the instructor. This social network, in most cases, also will serve as a foundation for the necessary motivation required to succeed in college. As distracting events occur, you will want to have a motivational support system on which you can rely. From fellow students who provide encouragement when your grades aren't as high as you had hoped to friends who won't push you to join the softball team when your studies must take priority, getting motivated and staying motivated requires the assistance of others.

In the end, however, your success in any college course is primarily your responsibility. Of course, there will be some instances when an inexperienced online instructor may not provide sufficient support for your success, but in the majority of cases, students who fail to succeed in college courses are not successful due to their own actions. In some cases, they are not prepared for the demanding study schedule of online course assignments and activities, while in other cases they do not spend the time during the first weeks of the course to establish adequate study habits for preparing for online exams. Likely the most common reason for lack of success in a college course is nevertheless a decrease in the student's motivation as the course continues through the semester.

For many of us, the opening excitement of initially learning more about a topic can generate some unrealistic expectations. We can often overestimate the time that we have available and even convince ourselves that we will be interested in all of the tedious facts that will be covered. Yet, when the reality of daily course requirements sets in (such as <u>discussion board</u>

127

postings and online readings that take place during our favorite television shows) is when our motivation is most challenged.

Adding to the threats to your motivation will be some of the unique characteristics of online <u>coursework</u>. Many of the conveniences offered through online <u>coursework</u> may also present many motivational challenges. Ask any of your friends or colleagues who have tried working exclusively out of their home office about the challenges of staying motivated when your office (or classroom) is only steps from your bed or television. Likewise, while taking and completing online assignments and activities, there will be many tempting distractions that aren't there while you are sitting in the classroom. Few conventional classrooms offer cable television, <u>instant messaging</u>, <u>email</u>, phone calls, and other distractions like those you will have while completing your assignments online.

> **STUDENT-TO-STUDENT TIP**
>
> Begin the semester with enthusiasm. Line up the sites that you want visit, the books and articles that you want to read, and the people who you want to contact before you begin. Then, jump into the course.

Strategies for getting motivated and staying motivated will require your attention throughout any college course, especially in courses that use online technologies. In this chapter, we discuss strategies for finding and keeping your motivation throughout the entire course. After all, motivation that lasts only through the first few weeks is never enough to ensure that you are successful.

Selecting Courses

As a student, it is most difficult to sustain your motivation throughout a semester when you enter a course with little or no motivation to be successful. It is possible that you will not be highly motivated for all of your courses in college. If you select courses in which your odds of success are low (see Chapter 1), then finding and maintaining your enthusiasm throughout the course will require additional attention and resources. Typically, your likelihood of success in a course is closely related to your motivation. Consequently, whenever possible, you should select courses where your motivation is greatest.

For example, if your academic interests tend to provide you with more motivation in the applied sciences, then taking a theoretical physics course as an elective is likely to be more of a challenge to your motivation that semester than taking a course in applied physics. You may not always be able to dictate what courses you take, but if you have been successful in taking courses that use online technologies and you are given the option to take one of multiple course selections that are taught online, then you should consider your motivation in the course when making your decision.

> **STUDENT-TO-STUDENT TIP**
>
> As with anything that you do, when you're engaged in activities that you value and enjoy, doing the research to learn and understand are very pleasant experiences. The time just seems to zip past, and the results reflect your level of enthusiasm.

Finding an Application

By enrolling in a course, you are hopefully motivated to be successful; however, that may be defined within the context of your experience. Initial motivation to enroll in a course is unfortunately not enough to keep you motivated throughout the course and ensure your success. Finding the motivation to maintain your learning skills and study habits will often require different strategies throughout a course. Grades may motivate you at times, but at other points (often in the same course) career or personal ambitions may be the better motivator.

Throughout any college course, you should try to link the topics that you are studying to their application outside the course context. Focusing on how the knowledge and skills that you learn from your biology class will be useful to you as an environmental engineer after college can encourage you to maintain your concentration when studying for an exam. Likewise, linking any course topic to other personal interests can be useful to maintain motivation. For example, though you may not be interested in a career in journalism, learning to communicate effectively through writing will likely be a useful skill even if you intend to practice sports psychology after you have graduated. Focusing on the impact that the course may have on your long-term goals may also help provide you with the enthusiasm necessary to be successful in English 101. Although the links may not always be as strong as the examples we have provided, trying to find a link can help sustain your motivation.

Keeping Your Goals in Mind

A mix of long- and short-term goals can provide a foundation for your motivation in college. Both your long- and short-term ambitions can be used throughout any college course to sustain your motivation because there will be times when graduating with honors doesn't have the same motivational impact as getting a better grade than your study partner.

- Link your long- and short-term goals to help ensure that using either as a source of motivation will keep you on the right path.

- Setting your goals in measurable terms will help you better assess where you are, where you want to be, and how you will know when you have arrived.

> **STUDENT-TO-STUDENT TIP**
>
> Motivation is important in traditional and online coursework. A student must develop skills to set his own goals and manage his own learning in the online learning environment.

- Because most of us quickly forget the details of our goals (for example, do you recall the New Year's resolution that you set last year?), putting your long- and short-term goals down in writing is an essential step in using them as a motivational strategy. When you write goals down, you are also more likely to stick with them until they are achieved.

- Keep a copy of the file with your goals on your computer's <u>desktop</u> or print out a copy that can be posted on the bulletin board next to your desk. No matter where you keep the goals, you should review them every few weeks to ensure that they remain fresh in your memory.

Developing Your Motivational Support System

You will want to develop a learning support system to lend a hand when finding the motivation to keep up with the course requirements becomes too much. Your support system may be made up of fellow students, coworkers, roommates, family, or just about anyone else who is willing to help you get and stay motivated in order to achieve success.

- At the beginning of each semester, identify at least two individuals you can rely on when your motivation slips. These should be responsible classmates, family members, or friends who will encourage you to maintain successful study habits. Be sure to let them know that you may come to them during the semester for motivational support; this will help ensure that they can provide you with useful assistance when (and if) the time comes.

- Peer feedback is a crucial element to motivation. In developing your motivational support, you should contact other students in your courses to exchange draft assignments and activities for review. By providing each other with supportive feedback, you are more likely not only to remain motivated but also often to attain greater academic achievement.

- Find a mentor who can help prepare and guide you throughout your college experience. Your mentor should not be your peer but an experienced student who has a record of being successful in college courses and who is willing to commit time to helping you be successful. Most often, you will want to select a mentor who has been

---

TRY SOMETHING NEW

Web Tool: **http://www.facebook.com**

From maintaining your social support system by keeping in touch with family and friends to organizing study groups, social networking web tools can provide a variety of useful resources to support your success in college. If you have not tried Facebook, or one of the other social networking web tools such as Ning.com or Myspace.com, then it is worth giving try this semester—with some caution. The purely social aspects of these web tools (for example, looking up friends from middle school) can definitely be a distraction from your studies. Nevertheless, the groups function and the ability to quickly <u>chat</u> online with classmates can offer enough benefits that it is worth giving it a try. The next time you start a study group, for instance, set up a Facebook group to share resources and keep in touch.

ACTIVITY 7-1   **Did This Section Click?**

🌐 As a review, read the following statements and then circle T (true) or F (false) for each one.

1. **T F**   By finding an application of course topics to your work or professional goals, you may improve your motivation.

2. **T F**   A mentor should be a peer with about the same amount of experience in college courses as you have.

3. **T F**   You are more likely to achieve goals that you have written down.

4. **T F**   Your friends and family should know about the study habits that you plan to use to be successful in your college courses.

5. **T F**   If you are motivated at the beginning of the semester, you will stay motivated until the end the semester.

---

successful in your major or a similar major because she will have experiences in the courses that you are taking.

- Motivation is a two-way street, and you can't expect others to always provide the encouragement. You will also be called upon throughout your college experience to help others make difficult decisions and maintain their motivation. Be encouraging and help them accomplish their goals as well.

Visualizing Your Success

Visualizing your success doesn't necessarily mean that you should close your eyes and picture yourself walking across the stage at graduation dressed in the valedictorian's gown. Though many students use literal visualization as an effective motivational strategy, you can simply focus your thoughts on many of the benefits of your pending success and still find the necessary inspiration to succeed. This type of visualization is more analogous to what most of us do when purchasing a lottery ticket for a multimillion-dollar prize. We daydream about the luxurious life that we will live after we have won that week's lottery drawing. In the same manner, we can daydream (that is, visualize) about our success in college.

Communicating with Your Instructor

Your instructors will typically be an excellent source of motivation. They will not only know you personally through the course but also will know your past performance, upcoming course requirements, and generally understand why the topics covered in the course should be of interest. All can be useful in improving your motivation throughout the semester.

- When you are struggling to sustain your motivation, <u>email</u> your professor and ask a few questions that may be helpful in revitalizing your motivation. For example, in a college algebra course, you could ask the instructor to suggest any books that would provide you with exercises and examples of college algebra within the context of your major, business management.

- If family or other personal illnesses result in reduced motivation during the semester, you should contact your instructor immediately. Instructors are often willing to make individual arrangements that may reduce your stress levels and improve your motivation. In addition, most colleges and universities offer a variety of support services (from counseling to tuition refunds) about which your instructor should have information.

Being an Active Participant

TRY SOMETHING NEW

Web Tool: **http://www.yousendit.com**

Attaching large files—such a group presentation with numerous pictures or graphics—to an email address can slow your computer to a crawl or lead to undelivered <u>email</u> due to storage limitations. YouSendIt offers a free alternative for sending large files to classmates or instructors. You can simply upload large files (up to 100MB for free) to the YouSendIt website and then insert the <u>email</u> addresses of your classmates or instructor. Your recipients will receive a message from YouSendIt letting them know that they can download the file anytime in the next week; it is that easy. Give YouSendIt a try the next time you are submitting a large assignment or sending numerous pictures to friends.

Likely, the most useful strategy for sustaining enthusiasm throughout the semester is to remain an active participant in the course. When you have fallen behind or lost touch with other students in the course, reviving the motivation that you had at the beginning is often difficult. Throughout the semester, remain involved in course discussions, group projects, and other activities because each will help you sustain your motivation. Asking questions, providing valuable comments, and organizing study groups are all techniques for maintaining your connection to the course.

Rewarding Yourself Throughout the Semester

Nothing is as rewarding or fun as celebrating our successes. So why wait for the end of the course to celebrate? Set intermediate goals throughout the course that will provide you with milestones that when accomplished

E-Learning Experiences

Throughout elementary school, I participated on a variety of Little League baseball teams, none of which ever managed to win more than a game or two per season. Because my teams didn't win often, my parents couldn't wait to celebrate until my team won a game (at the time, my favorite way to celebrate my successes was a trip to Dairy Queen for ice cream). If they had, I would still be waiting for my ice cream. Therefore, they found the little things to reward: I didn't strike out after the first three pitches, or I stopped the ball from going behind me in the outfield. Now for those on the winning teams, these wouldn't have seemed like events worth celebrating, but to me they would be the highlights of my baseball career. And though I didn't go on to participate in high school or college sports, one of the lessons I learned from those early experiences was to reward yourself whenever you can.

The same is true in college; you should celebrate even the smallest victories. Whether it is going out with friends after you finish the research for your term paper or having pizza when you get a B on your physics lab report, treating yourself to something special (ice cream, a movie, a night out with friends) will keep you on top of your tasks and avoid procrastination.

successfully are worth celebrating. If you receive an A on the mid-term exam, enjoy an evening at the movie that you have been waiting to see (with a big bag of popcorn, of course). Master the skills necessary for uploading new <u>website</u> graphics, and treat yourself to your favorite ice cream.

Developing Healthy Habits

The health of your body is very influential in your motivation to be successful in college. Maintaining healthy habits like a balanced diet, consistent exercise, and adequate rest are all essential ingredients to sustained motivation and a successful college experience. Consider for a moment how difficult it is to concentrate on your studies or keep a positive attitude about your courses when you have a cold or the flu.

- Review your eating habits every few weeks to determine if you are getting an adequate balance of nutritional foods. Stay away from eating too many fatty, sugary, or salty foods, and don't go on drastic diets that may not provide you with adequate nutrition.

- Exercise on a regular basis, especially around times when you are studying long hours (such as during end-of-the-semester exams).

- Manage your time to ensure that you are able to get sufficient amounts of sleep each night. At a minimum, you should get at least 6 hours of sleep each night, and it is often best to sleep for regular periods each night (for example, always going to sleep between 10:00 and 11:00 P.M. and waking between 7:30 and 8:30 A.M.).

ACTIVITY 7-2 **Did This Section Click?**

🌐 As a review, complete the following statements by marking the correct phrase.

1. When you are having a hard time staying motivated in a college course, you should not
   a. contact your instructor to get feedback and suggestions on your performance.
   b. put off doing any assignments or activities for the next week.
   c. talk to classmates about study strategies they are using to be successful.

2. To visualize your success in college courses, you should
   a. close your eyes tightly and meditate on quiz questions.
   b. play soft music in the background as you study.
   c. relax and think about accomplishing your goals.

3. To stay healthy and perform your best on your course assignments and activities, you should
   a. adopt a diet with no fat or sugar.
   b. exercise regularly.
   c. try to stay up all night studying once a week.

- Schedule routine visits to your doctor and dentist. Preventive medicine can keep you on track to success; after all, the last distraction you want from studying for your mid-term exam is a toothache or other medical emergency.

Summary

Finding and maintaining your motivation throughout the semester is essential for your success in college. By using the goals that you have set for yourself as a guide and adopting several strategies suggested in this chapter, you can improve your motivation as well as create a support system of friends and family who can offer encouragement when you struggle to stay motivated. No matter how excited you are about your college courses, at some point during your college experience, academic or other events are likely to test your motivation for success. By planning appropriately and developing useful motivational habits with your study skills, you can overcome these obstacles to success and achieve your goals.

Chapter 7 Exercise

To begin the exercise, you will want to access the World Wide Web, using a Web browser. In addition, you will want to open a new document in a word processing program.

STEP 1: Using the <u>Web browser</u>, access your course <u>website</u> (or <u>educational portal</u>) using the login and password provided to you by the instructor or institution. When you have entered the course <u>website</u> or portal, enter the area that includes the course syllabus. Within the course syllabus, identify the assignments and activities that will be used to grade your performance in the course.

STEP 2: Copy-and-paste the course assignments and activities from the syllabus into a new <u>word processing</u> document. After each course assignment, insert into the <u>word processing</u> document your goal for the assignment or activity (such as the grade that you want to receive on the assignment or activity).

STEP 3: For each assignment and activity, identify a potential reward to give yourself when you successfully accomplish your goal. The rewards don't have to be big, but they should be something that you would consider to be a treat for being successful.

STEP 4: For each assignment or activity, identify at least one positive use for the knowledge or skills that you are demonstrating. This can be a constructive use in another college course you are taking (or planning to take) or a valuable skill that you can (or will) apply in your profession.

STEP 5: Identify for the course at least two people (such as classmates, friends, or family) who will encourage you throughout the semester for the selected course.

STEP 6: Review the lists created in steps 3 to 5 whenever you struggle to stay motivated in the selected course.

Did You Stay Focused?

After completing this chapter, you should be able to do the following. If there are tasks that you cannot do, take a few minutes to review the chapter, focusing on those areas that you may have missed the first time through.

- ☐ I can *integrate* and apply what I learn online in my other courses and my work.
- ☐ I can *manage* both my long-term and short-term goals in planning for each semester.
- ☐ I have *created* a motivational support system that can encourage me.
- ☐ I can visualize my success.
- ☐ I am an active participant in my courses.
- ☐ I have *integrated* support from others into my plans for online success.
- ☐ I have adopted healthy eating, sleeping, and exercise habits.

www.cengage.com/success/Watkins/ELearning3e

☐   I have identified rewards that I can give myself throughout the semester when I am successful.

☐   I have completed the chapter activities.

Additional Resources

🌐 Additional resources on topics covered in this chapter are available at the Premium Website for the *E-Learning Companion*.

Quick Reference Guide

Whether we realize it or not, each of us has a set of learning skills and study habits that we use to succeed in the conventional classroom. To have the same levels of success in online coursework, many of these skills and habits will have to be transformed. For example, you have likely developed throughout your educational experiences a set of skills that you find useful when working on a group project with classmates. Maybe you start off by assigning roles for group members, followed by a discussion of what has to be accomplished and when for everyone to be successful. The same skills can also be applied when the group members are meeting together online; instead of discussing the roles and responsibilities at a small desk, you may be sitting miles apart, at your home computers. Communicating clearly and using the technologies to your benefit will be keys to your success in this new classroom environment.

That being the case, while many of the delivery tools in an online course will be different from those that you experienced in the traditional classroom (for example, verbal discussion being replaced by Internet chat), many of the learning skills and study habits that you have already developed will provide an excellent foundation for your success.

How to Use This Quick Reference Guide

In each section that follows, we provide tips, suggestions, guides, and recommendations for preparing to be successful before, during, and after participation in a variety of online coursework activities. It is impractical (and most likely not that useful) to memorize these tips; rather, keep this book close to your computer so that you can come back to these tips and ideas when you are assigned coursework that requires your participation online. To underscore the tips that you believe will be most useful to you, highlight, underline, and write in the margins.

137

Online Real-Time Chats

Real-time (or synchronous) chats provide you with one of the few online experiences where you can receive immediate replies to your questions or comments, thus allowing for a conversation to develop quickly with your instructor or classmates. For that reason, you will want to take advantage of these unique opportunities.

Before the Chat

☐ *Prepare a List of Questions*
Before the chat begins, identify questions that you would like to ask and receive answers to during the chat. Write the questions in a document that you can cut-and-paste from during the discussion. This will save you the time of typing and editing a question, especially a long question, before sending it. This technique will also help you avoid grammatical and spelling errors.

☐ *Send Additional Questions by Email*
If you have questions for which the timeliness of the response is less important, send them by email or, if you meet on campus, ask them in class.

☐ *Visit the Chat Area the Day Before*
You should check to verify that you have access to the chat area the day before a scheduled chat. If you do not have access, this will give you time to contact technical support. Also, many educational portals will have multiple chat areas, so you want to confirm that you are accessing the correct chat area.

☐ *Create a Good Study Environment*
For example, turn off the television, ask your roommates not to interrupt you, turn off instant messaging programs, and the like. (See Chapter 4.)

☐ *Identify and Organize Any Files*
Files that you may want to reference during the chat should be easily accessible so that you can view them quickly during the discussion.

☐ *Verify Access to Chat Transcripts*
Check with the instructor to find out if you will have access to the transcripts of the chat after it is complete.

☐ *Review Any Rules, Agenda, and/or Etiquette Guide*
Often, instructors will provide guidelines for course chats in the syllabus or in class. These could include rules for indicating when you have a question, etiquette for discussing topics with other students, and so forth. If you are going to lead the chat discussion (such as for a group project conversation), then develop an agenda and a set of rules for the chat. These should be shared with the other chat members prior to the chat session.

STUDENT-TO-STUDENT TIP

Use the chat room for your group projects. It will help you formulate your plans and make your team more cohesive.

During the Chat

☐ *Arrive to the Chat Area at Least 5 Minutes Before*
This will give you time to ensure that your computer and connection are working properly.

☐ *Do Not Greet Everyone*
Most synchronous chat software provides a list of who has entered the chat, so do not greet each new person with a "hello" when they arrive.

☐ *Do Not Respond to Each Comment or Question*
Respond only to those that address you specifically or to which your response will make a valuable contribution to the discussion.

☐ *Keep the Conversation Focused on the Topic*
Post only comments or questions that add value to the discussion.

☐ *Note the Time to Develop Social Relationships*
Online relationships can be developed more effectively in small-group chats, instant messaging, or email, rather than during class time when many students are in the chat area together.

☐ *Address Your Comments or Suggestions*
Identify the individual to whom you would like to respond question when you post to the chat. For example, "Dr. Robinson, in our readings I was somewhat confused by the terms 'cranial' and 'caudal.' Could you explain the difference?" or "Jane, how is your progress coming on the introduction section of our group project?"

☐ *Take Notes*
Especially if you will not have access to the chat transcripts, you should take notes on what is being discussed in the chat, either on paper or in a word processing document.

☐ *Keep Postings Concise*
To the extent possible, keep your questions or comments short and to the point. If your question or comment is likely to take up more lines of text than are visible in the chat interface, then divide the question into two parts.

☐ *Participate*
Improve your comprehension by being an active participant in the discussions. Attempt to find the right balance of joining the conversation without dominating the conversation.

☐ *Cut-and-Paste*
Typically you will want to cut-and-paste links to other websites (that is, URLs) into your postings instead of typing them in; this will reduce the number of inverted letters or missing periods in links.

☐ *Raise Your Hand with a Blank Message*
To gain the attention of the instructor or other host for a chat, simply post a blank message to the chat discussion. This is the equivalent of raising

your hand when your <u>chat</u> <u>software</u> doesn't have other features for gaining the instructor's attention.

☐ *Use Emoticons and Acronyms to Express Your Feelings*
You should use the familiar acronyms/initialisms (Table QR-2) and <u>emoticons</u> (Table QR-3), to add nonverbal communication elements to your <u>emails</u>.

☐ *Do Not Post "I Am Back"*
If you lose connection or leave the discussion during the <u>chat</u>, do not inform everyone when you have returned. If you are absent for a long period of time due to technical problems, write your instructor an <u>email</u> explaining the issues involved. This is one of the times when getting a transcript of the <u>chat</u> session would be useful to determine what information you may have missed.

☐ *Do Not Multitask*
For your college courses, do not attempt to have more than one <u>chat</u> session going on at a time. Your comprehension of the discussion topics will be greatly decreased if your attention is divided among two conversations.

☐ *Keep Private Conversations Private*
If you want to ask a private question or make a comment to an individual student or the instructor, most <u>chat</u> <u>software</u> applications will permit you to "whisper" to other individual members in the <u>chat</u>. You may, however, want to try this function with a "whisper" that is not offensive to anyone in the <u>chat</u> just in case something goes wrong and everyone in the <u>chat</u> ends up viewing your private comments.

☐ *Spelling and Grammar Are Important*
Though people are typically more flexible on spelling and grammar during <u>real-time chats</u>, it is still important to use correct spelling and grammar to the extent possible without slowing the discussion. As a result, you should be careful when typing and may want to use a <u>word processing</u> program to draft your postings before copy-and-pasting them into the <u>chat</u>.

☐ *Leave Misspelled Words*
If you do misspell a word when posting to a <u>chat</u>, do not post another message correcting the misspelling (unless the misspelled word significantly changes the meaning of the message).

☐ *Avoid Sarcasm, Idioms, Slang, and Jargon*
Do not use cultural or regional communication techniques that can easily result in miscommunication.

☐ *Resist Overanalysis*
Try not to read too much into statements made by other students or to take comments too personally. Miscommunications are common in <u>chats</u> because many of the typical nonverbal communication tools (such as eye contact and body gestures) are not available.

☐ *Patience Is a Virtue*
Be patient and ask questions when you are confused or believe that there may be a miscommunication.

Quick Reference Guide

☐ *Cite and Reference*
Provide accurate citation and reference information for any sources of information that you may use in your discussion, including webpage URLs.

☐ *Stay Until the End*
Normally, you will not want to leave the chat until the instructor has posted a message letting everyone know that the course-related chat has ended.

☐ *Do Not Post "Good-Byes"*
It is not necessary for you to announce when you are leaving the chat session. Your classmates and instructor will see your name leave the list of participants when you exit the chat area.

After the Chat

☐ *Review*
Go through the transcripts from the chat (or your notes) to determine if you should follow-up the discussion with email messages to your professor or fellow students.

☐ *Summarize*
Sum up what you learned during the chat and/or what tasks you must complete next. Include this summary in your notes from the chat or along with your copy of the chat transcripts.

☐ *Follow Up*
Immediately after completing the chat, email follow-up questions and comments, as well as your summary of what was discussed. Do this while the conversation is fresh in your mind.

☐ *Improve Your Performance*
Identify strategies that would improve your comprehension and participation the next time you are going to participate in a synchronous discussion. Write these down in a document that can be saved to your course file folder in your computer.

☐ *Keep a Record*
Keep all files related to each chat session in a computer file folder where you can access them when preparing for future assignments, activities, or exams.

> **STUDENT-TO-STUDENT TIP**
>
> Read the discussion questions ahead of time and spend some quality time thinking about the answers to them.

Online Discussion Boards

Asynchronous discussions (normally in online bulletin or discussion boards) offer you the opportunity to carry on a conversation with your fellow students or professor at times convenient to you. Because each participant in the discussion can choose when to reply to the latest addition to the conversation, the flexibility in pace and length of the conversation can vary greatly. You can, however, use this additional time for responding to messages to clarify your comments or questions to ensure that there are not miscommunications.

Before Your Participation in a Discussion Board

☐ *Review Earlier Postings*
Prepare for the discussion by reviewing previous postings to the <u>discussion board</u> related to the conversation topic(s) on which you are going to focus.

☐ *Review Any Rules or Etiquette Guide*
Often, instructors will provide guidelines for participation in <u>discussion board</u> conversations in the syllabus. By following the rules and etiquette guidelines, you can often avoid miscommunications.

☐ *Clarify Expectations*
Determine what the instructor expects of your postings, whether formal or informal, emphasizing quality or quantity, and so forth. Informal postings (like those that you would write to a friend) are common, but most often the clarity and precision of formal communications will be desired for online <u>coursework</u>.

☐ *Examine a Model Posting*
Identify any model postings that an instructor may have provided to illustrate the desired level and types of participation.

☐ *Verify Continuing Access*
Find out from the professor if you will continue to have access to previous discussions throughout the semester (or if older discussions will be removed or no longer be visible to students).

☐ *Create a Schedule*
Schedule times throughout each week of the semester when you will participate in the <u>discussion board</u>s. Include in this plan how much time you will spend responding to postings with your comments or questions. To fully participate in the discussions in most courses, you will want to schedule time at least every other day.

☐ *Create a Good Study Environment*
For example, turn off the television, ask your roommates not to interrupt you, turn off <u>instant messaging</u> programs, and the like. (See Chapter 4.)

During Your Participation in a Discussion Board

☐ *Take Your Time*
Editing and reviewing your additions to the <u>discussion board</u> can help avoid miscommunications. Having time to revise and improve your comments or questions is an advantage of <u>asynchronous</u> discussions that you can benefit from.

☐ *Do Not Respond to Each Comment or Question*
Respond only to those that address you specifically or to which your response will make a valuable contribution to the discussion. Find a balance of quality and quantity with your additions to the discussion.

☐ *Keep the Conversation Focused on the Topic*
Post only comments or questions that add value to the discussion. Often, you will want to <u>cut-and-paste</u> into your message the specific comment or question to which your response is referring.

☐ *Keep to the Topic of the Thread*
Most <u>discussion board</u>s will <u>thread</u> the discussion (that is, illustrate the order of the conversation) so that you can see which postings are replies to which other postings. To the extent possible, try to keep your comments or questions in the correct <u>thread</u>, to provide consistency to the conversation.

☐ *Use the Subject Line*
If your <u>discussion board</u> does not <u>thread</u> the discussion, it is especially important to include in your posting specific information in the subject line regarding the posting to which you are replying. Including a copy of the original posting at the bottom of your posting is often useful in clarifying your response and reducing the chances for miscommunication.

☐ *Write Postings in a Clear and Expressive Manner*
Most often, you will want to write one or two well- structured and thought-out paragraphs in a single posting to an online <u>discussion board</u>. Despite the fact that these paragraphs should have an introduction, supporting facts, and conclusion as in any well-structured writing that you would submit for a grade in a college course, online discussion postings are typically short; most often you will want to limit the paragraphs in your postings to three to five sentences.

☐ *Address Your Comments or Questions*
Identify at the beginning of a posting if you would like a specific individual to respond. For example, "Dr. Robinson, in our readings I was somewhat confused by the terms 'cranial' and 'caudal.' Could you explain the difference?" or "Jane, how is your progress coming on the introduction section of our group project?"

☐ *Provide a Signature*
Although most <u>discussion board</u>s will include your name with the posting, it is always a good idea to include your <u>signature</u> at the end of your messages.

☐ *Participate*
Improve your comprehension by being an active participant in the discussions. Attempt to find the right balance of joining the conversation without dominating the conversation.

☐ *Be Discreet and Polite*
Do not include anything in your <u>discussion board</u> postings that you would not typically write on a postcard; these discussions are rarely private.

☐ *Cut-and-Paste*
Typically you will want to <u>cut-and-paste</u> links to other <u>websites</u> (that is, <u>URLs</u>) into your postings instead of typing them in; this will reduce the number of inverted letters or missing periods in links.

☐ *Spelling and Grammar Are Important*
You should be careful and may want to use a <u>word processing</u> program to draft your postings before copy-and-pasting them into the <u>chat</u>.

☐ *Resist Overanalysis*
Try not to read too much into statements made by other students or to take comments too personally. Miscommunications are common in <u>discussion board</u> conversations because many of the typical nonverbal communication tools (such as eye contact and body gestures) are not available.

☐ *Avoid Sarcasm, Idioms, Slang, and Jargon*
Do not use cultural or regional communication techniques that can easily result in miscommunication.

☐ *Cite and Reference*
Provide accurate citation and reference information for any sources of information that you may use in your discussion, including <u>webpage</u> <u>URLs</u>.

☐ *Post Only Messages That Add to the Discussion*
Avoid short and pointless postings (such as "I agree" or "I really like this") that do not add substantial value to the discussion. Your postings to the <u>discussion board</u> should include examples and descriptive information about your comments or questions. No one wants to take the time to <u>download</u> multiple postings that merely say "Nice work."

After Your Participation in a Discussion Board

☐ *Review*
Go through the many postings included in the discussion to determine if you may have missed any essential comments and/or if any follow-up communications with fellow students or the instructor is necessary.

☐ *Summarize*
Sum up the major topics discussed in the online conversation and what you have learned from the discussion. Write this summary down and keep it for your records.

☐ *Follow Up*
After an online discussion has ended, <u>email</u> follow-up questions and comments as well as your summary of what was discussed.

☐ *Improve Your Performance*
Identify strategies that would improve your comprehension and participation the next time you are going to participate in an <u>asynchronous</u>

discussion. Write these strategies down in a document that can be saved to your course file <u>folder</u> in your computer.

☐ *Keep a Record*
If <u>discussion board</u> postings will not remain available throughout the semester and you would like to keep information contained in one or more the postings, be sure to copy the posting(s) to a <u>word processing</u> document that you can save to your personal computer.

Email

<u>Email</u> is almost certainly the most common online communications tool used in college courses. Despite the fact that you are likely to have a great deal of experience in communicating with friends and family using <u>email</u>, the use of <u>email</u> in completing <u>coursework</u> should not be overlooked in preparing to be successful in college. Avoiding miscommunications and developing positive online relationships through <u>email</u> commonly requires that students pay additional attention before clicking on the Send button.

Before Sending an Email

☐ *Review Any Rules or Etiquette Guide*
Examine any rules or guidelines required by the instructor for <u>emails</u> related to the course (such as subject line requirements, naming attached files, and so on).

☐ *Verify Email Addresses*
Confirm that you have correct <u>email</u> addresses for all those who are to be recipients of the <u>email</u>.

☐ *Identify and Organize any Files*
Files that you may want to reference in an <u>email</u> should be easily accessible so that you can find them. Have access to copies of previous <u>emails</u>, course syllabi, and other files related to the course so that you can quote these resources as necessary in your <u>emails</u>.

☐ *Ask if the Message Is Appropriate*
Before writing an <u>email</u> to an instructor or fellow student, ask yourself if the message is appropriate for the recipient and the context. For example, you would not likely want to <u>email</u> your instructor to tell him or her that you will be missing class because you were out late the night before.

☐ *Relax*
If you are upset or angry, avoid writing any <u>emails</u> to your fellow students or the instructor for several hours.

☐ *Create a Schedule*
Each day you should schedule a time specifically for reading and replying to <u>emails</u>.

During an Email Conversation

☐ *Use the Subject Line*
Include an accurate description of the <u>email</u> contents in the subject line.

☐ *Include the Previous Message in a Reply*
Often, you will want to quote the original message in your reply to avoid possible miscommunications. This can also provide a record of the discussion for your later review. When including an original message in the reply, however, do not alter the original message in any way; typically you will not want to include more than the last message (that is, do not include the previous five messages in your reply).

☐ *Forward Only Course-Relevant Emails*
Avoid forwarding <u>email</u> messages that do not directly relate to the course materials. Forwarding jokes and other miscellaneous <u>email</u>s should be saved for personal <u>email</u>s only.

☐ *Review All Messages Carefully*
Prior to sending <u>email</u> messages, carefully review the message, looking for misspelled words and grammar errors.

☐ *Ask a Friend to Review Important Emails*
For important <u>email</u>s, ask a roommate, fellow student, or friend to review the message. Clear and simple messages communicate most effectively.

☐ *Don't Store All Your Messages in Your Email Inbox*
Your <u>email</u> inbox will quickly become full of old messages and you will have a difficult time accessing important information if you do not develop a <u>folder</u> structure for storing <u>email</u> messages. When a message comes into your inbox, reply to it and save it in an appropriate <u>folder</u> that same day.

☐ *Confirm Software Compatibility for Attachments*
For the recipients to open a file that you have attached, they must have the <u>software</u> application affiliated with the file (for example, the recipient must have Microsoft Word or a compatible application in order to view an <u>attachment</u> with the file extension .doc). You should verify that the recipient has the necessary <u>software</u> before sending a file.

☐ *Describe Attachments*
In your <u>email</u> message, include a description of any attached files (including the name of the file and the <u>software</u> application used to create the file).

☐ *Browse Before You Attach*
Many <u>Web portal</u>s and <u>email</u> <u>software</u> applications require that you first identify the file that you want to include as an <u>attachment</u>; this is often done by clicking on a Browse button and then attaching the file in a second step by clicking on the Attach button.

☐ *Ask Before Sending Big Files*
It is also good etiquette to ask before sending <u>email</u>s with large file <u>attachment</u>s because the receiver may have to request additional <u>server</u> space to make room for the <u>email</u>(s). If you have numerous large <u>attachment</u>s, include those within separate <u>email</u>s.

☐ *Be Cautious When Receiving Attachments*
Files that are attached to <u>email</u>s that you receive can contain files with computer viruses. If you do not know the sender of the <u>email</u> or if you are not expecting an attached file from an instructor or classmate, do not immediately open it. Take the time to <u>email</u> the sender in order to verify that they did intend for you to receive the file and that the file does not contain a computer virus. It is worth the extra time to be cautious because a computer virus can wipe away months of your work in just a few minutes.

☐ *Resist Overanalysis*
Try not to read too much into statements made by other students or to take comments too personally. Miscommunications are common in <u>email</u> because many of the typical nonverbal communication tools (such as eye contact and body gestures) are not available.

☐ *Be Discreet and Polite*
Do not include anything in your <u>email</u>s that you would not typically write on a postcard; these discussions are rarely private.

☐ *Double-Check Recipients*
Always review the To:, Cc:, and Bcc: <u>field</u>s prior to sending any <u>email</u>. Often, in a hurry to complete our work, we will mistakenly add (or omit) an intended recipient to an <u>email</u> message. This can be both embarrassing (such as when an <u>email</u> to another project team member goes to the instructor) and sometimes destructive to the online relationships that you have built.

☐ *Include a Signature*
At the end of every <u>email</u> message, you should include a <u>signature</u> (name and <u>email</u> address).

☐ *Keep the Conversation Focused on the Topic*
Post only comments or questions that add value to the <u>email</u> conversation.

☐ *Avoid Sarcasm, Idioms, Slang, and Jargon*
Do not use cultural or regional communication techniques that can easily result in miscommunication.

☐ *Send Only Emails That Add to the Discussion*
Avoid writing short <u>email</u> messages that do not contain substantial information for the recipient. Rarely will a short <u>email</u> (such as "I agree," "Thank you," or "Me too!") be useful to fellow students or your instructor. Take the time to compose messages with appropriate sentence and paragraph structures.

☐ *Cut-and-Paste*
Typically, you will want to <u>cut-and-paste</u> links to other <u>websites</u> (that is, <u>URLs</u>) into your postings instead of typing them in; this will reduce the number of inverted letters or missing periods in links.

www.cengage.com/success/Watkins/ELearning3e

☐ *Review the History*
When joining in an <u>email</u> conversation that has already been started by others, read the history of original <u>emails</u> that are most often included at the bottom of the <u>email</u> in reverse chronological order. This will provide you with the context of the more recent <u>email</u> messages.

☐ *Remove Email Addresses from Forwarded Messages*
If you are forwarding an <u>email</u> message that contains the names and <u>email</u> addresses of multiple recipients who also received the original <u>email</u>, take a few minutes to remove those before forwarding the message.

☐ *Cite and Reference*
Provide accurate citation and reference information for any sources of information that you may use in your discussion, including <u>webpage</u> <u>URLs</u>.

☐ *Have Multiple Email Accounts*
It is common for instructors to request that you use your college's <u>email</u> system (that is, johndoe@mycollege.edu) because the college is responsible for maintaining access. Use this account for all of your course-related <u>emails</u> and establish an alternate account for personal <u>emails</u>. You can often receive free <u>email</u> accounts for your personal communications (for example, at http://www.hotmail.com, http://www.mail.com, and http://mail.yahoo.com).

☐ *Use Formatting to Emphasize Your Ideas*
Use the bold, underline, and italics features of your <u>email</u> software applications to communicate more effectively.

☐ *Use Emoticons and Acronyms to Express Your Feelings*
You should use the familiar acronyms/initialisms (Table QR-2) and <u>emoticons</u> (Table QR-3), to add nonverbal communication elements to your <u>emails</u>.

☐ *Email Yourself*
Send <u>emails</u> to yourself as reminders of daily tasks to be completed.

☐ *Number Tasks or Lists*
If you include a number of tasks or request for information in a single <u>email</u>, number them or use the bulleted list function of the <u>email</u> application.

☐ *Review One Last Time*
Always review an <u>email</u> message one last time before sending it. Check spelling, grammar, punctuation, and the recipient list, as well as the overall impression of the <u>email</u> message.

After Sending an Email

☐ *Keep a Record*
File copies of all <u>emails</u> related to each college course that you take in <u>folders</u> outside your <u>email</u> inbox. You can delete these at the end of the semester after grades have been received, but until then you may want

to refer to the <u>email</u> messages in preparing for exams or reviewing a conversation for clarity.

☐ *Patience Is a Virtue*
Be patient while waiting for a reply. Instructors and classmates are not necessarily responding to their <u>email</u> messages at the same times you are checking your <u>email</u>.

☐ *Courteous Follow-Up*
If you have not had a response to an <u>email</u> in more than 48 hours, you can write a polite message to the recipient to see if the <u>email</u> was received.

Listserves

College instructors typically use <u>listserves</u> when they want to communicate the same message to all students in a course or when they want to facilitate discussions that can include multiple students. You can use the <u>listserve</u> as an effective tool for communicating with multiple classmates.

Before Participating in a Listserve

☐ *Sign Up for a Class Listserve*
<u>Listserves</u> make it easy to <u>email</u> everyone in your college courses by simply addressing the <u>email</u> to the <u>listserve</u> address. To become a member of most <u>listserves</u>, you will have to subscribe or register, though instructors do sometimes create a <u>listserve</u> for all students in the class so that you do not have to subscribe individually.

☐ *Save Subscription Information*
When you have subscribed (or been registered by your instructor) for a <u>listserve</u>, you should receive an <u>email</u> outlining how to send messages to the <u>listserve</u>, rules, and etiquette guidelines, as well as information for how you can unsubscribe to the <u>listserve</u>. This is useful information that you should save.

☐ *Review Any Rules or Etiquette Guidelines*
Often instructors will provide guidelines for participation in <u>listserve</u> discussions in the syllabus. By following the rules and etiquette guidelines, you can often avoid miscommunications.

☐ *Hang Out Before Participating*
It is usually useful to review several messages posted by group member before sending your own message to the <u>listserve</u>. This will give you the opportunity to identify group norms and informal rules of etiquette.

During Your Participation in a Listserve

☐ *Review the Tips for Sending Emails*
<u>Listserve</u> messages are principally <u>email</u> messages that are sent to a large list of recipients, so the same suggestions and tips for sending <u>email</u>

messages (see the tips earlier in this guide) apply when sending messages to a <u>listserve</u>.

☐ *Check Listserve Replies*
When replying to a message that you received from another member of a <u>listserve</u>, you will want to examine the recipient <u>field</u> to make sure that you are replying to the individual and not to all members of the <u>listserve</u>.

☐ *Don't Use a Listserve for Private Conversation*
If you would like to respond to an individual regarding their posting to a <u>listserve</u>, make sure that you address the reply message to the individual and not the <u>listserve</u>.

☐ *Always Include Your Email Address in the Message*
Often <u>listserves</u> will not indicate your <u>email</u> address in the From: <u>field</u>. For recipients to respond to you individually, always include your <u>email</u> address in the text of the message.

☐ *Send Only Emails That Add to the Discussion*
Avoid sending <u>emails</u> to the <u>listserve</u> that do not add new and valuable information to the discussion.

☐ *Don't Use Vacation Notices*
If you are going to be out of town or away from your <u>email</u> for an extended period of time, do not establish a vacation message (a messaging response automatically sent to everyone who sends you an <u>email</u> letting them know that you are on vacation) without also informing the <u>listserve</u> manager that your subscription should be temporarily suspended.

After Participating in a Listserve

☐ *Save and Review*
Go through the <u>listserve</u> messages to determine if you may have missed any essential comments and/or if any follow-up communications with fellow students or the instructor is necessary.

☐ *Summarize*
Sum up the major topics discussed in the <u>listserve</u> conversation and what you have learned from the discussion. Write this summary down and keep it for your records.

☐ *Improve Your Performance*
Identify strategies that would improve your comprehension and participation the next time you are going to participate in an <u>asynchronous</u> discussion. Write these down in a document that can be saved to your course file <u>folder</u> in your computer.

Online Group Projects

Group projects are commonly used in both high school and college courses, but using online technologies to facilitate the group member roles and responsibilities is likely to be less familiar to most students. With more working adult students, as well as distance-education students, in today's classrooms the traditional strategies for successful group projects are changing, requiring the application of online technologies that provide greater flexibility for individual group members.

Before Your Participation in a Group Project

☐ *Review*
Look at all the information, rules, guidelines, and grading policies regarding the group project prior to beginning any work. These guidelines should also provide information on how groups will be assigned or formed during the course.

☐ *Introduce Yourself*
Take the opportunity to introduce yourself to the other group members. Include in your introduction some information about your schedule for the semester, your goals for the course, and what roles you would like to have in developing a successful team, as well as your contact information.

☐ *Verify Contact Information*
Make sure that you have accurate and up-to-date contact information for all group members. You should keep a *hard* copy of this information in case you have technology problems later in the semester.

☐ *Devise a Communications Strategy*
You will want a plan for the project that includes a schedule of meetings (that is, when and for how long), an explanation of the online communication tool(s) that will be used, and a decision on which group member will lead discussions. For example, a plan may state that your group will use instant messaging for weekly meetings and email for other communications.

☐ *Identify Group Roles*
Prepare a plan for the group project that includes the roles of each member in completing the work (such as leaders, communicators, and task managers), as well as the tasks that must be completed. The importance of group roles in the success of each team member is magnified when a project group moves to an online environment. In many cases, it is best to have one group member who is responsible for communicating with the instructor regarding the group project. This will reduce the number of opportunities for miscommunication.

☐ *Assign Tasks*
Each task should have an individual or team that is ultimately responsible for the successful completion of the task.

☐ *Commit*
All group members should commit to being prepared for each meeting, allotting sufficient time for the group project, communicating with other group members openly, and being consistent in the quality and predictability of their interactions.[1]

www.cengage.com/success/Watkins/ELearning3e

☐ *Select a Software Standard*
To ensure that everyone in the group has access to all important files that will be created throughout the semester, you will want to select a software standard. For instance, even if only one member has an older version of Microsoft Word, then other group members should <u>back save</u> their files to a version that ensures that all group members can access the files.

During Your Participation in a Group Project

☐ *Follow Up on Tasks*
Throughout the group project, all team members must be responsible for successfully completing the required tasks they have been assigned.

☐ *Maintain Your Role*
Throughout the semester, it is essential that all group members continue their functions within the group (such as organizing meetings, taking notes, communicating with the instructor, and keeping copies of all group files).

☐ *Encourage Good Working Relationships*
Do what you can to foster good group dynamics and relationships throughout the project. The importance of group relationships is elevated when group projects are relying on online technologies to facilitate the project.

☐ *Share Calendars Online*
Use shared calendars and <u>groupware</u> (see Chapter 5) to facilitate scheduling meetings, sharing draft documents, and meeting deadlines.

☐ *Patience Is a Virtue, but Keep on Top of Group Members*
Be patient with your classmates, but do not miss agreed-on deadlines.

☐ *Keep a Record*
All files related to the group project (including <u>email</u>s and transcripts of <u>synchronous</u> <u>chats</u>) should be kept in a single location in your computer.

☐ *Back Up Files*
Every week, <u>back up</u> copies of all files related to your group project.

☐ *Review and Edit Each Other's Work*
Review and revise papers, <u>email</u>s, and other communications with group members to ensure clarity and reduce the odds of miscommunications.

☐ *Resist Overanalysis*
Try not to read too much into statements made by others students or to take comments too personally. Miscommunications are common because many of the typical nonverbal communication tools (such as eye contact and body gestures) are not available.

☐ *Cite and Reference*
Provide accurate citation and reference information for any sources of information that you may use in your discussion, including <u>webpage</u> <u>URL</u>s.

Quick Reference Guide

☐ *Follow the Group's Communication Strategy*
Maintain the use of the agreed-on structure for online communications. For example, if the role of one group member is to lead online
<u>synchronous</u> discussions, then do not attempt to take over that
responsibility during a <u>chat</u> session.

☐ *Track Your Progress*
Use technology to share files, provide feedback to group members, track
changes made in a Microsoft Word document, indicate progress being
made on the project, communicate with the instructor, and so forth.

After Your Participation in a Group Project

☐ *Follow Up*
After completing an online group project, send an <u>email</u> to each member of the project group thanking them for the contributions they
made to the project. You do not know when you may be required to
work with these individuals again.

☐ *Keep a Record*
Save copies of all final documents that the group submitted to the professor.

☐ *Improve Your Performance*
Identify strategies that would improve your performance the next time
that you are going to participate in a group project. Write these down in a
document that can be saved to your course file <u>folder</u> in your computer.

Online Exams

Taking an exam is commonly a stressful experience for students, and when
the test is to be completed online, the anxiety can be magnified for students
who are not prepared. In preparing for an online exam, you should prepare
for the actual test items as you would for other similar exams. In addition,
you will want to identify strategies that can effectively reduce any additional
stress of having the test online.

Before an Online Exam

☐ *Review Guidelines*
Prior to completing an online test or exam, review the guidelines for
taking the exam provided by the instructor. Given the limitations
of current technologies, open-book exams that are time limited are
likely to be the most common, though proctored online exams (that is,
in a designated computer lab with a supervising staff member) are
also used at many colleges and universities.

☐ *Verify Format*
Review any information provided by the instructor regarding the format of questions (such as short answer, multiple choice, and essay).

☐ *Take Practice Exams*
Find out from the instructor if there are online practice exams available for you to take prior to the graded exam.

☐ *Confirm That You Have Adequate Software*
Especially if you are going to complete an online exam on a computer other than your personal computer, prior to taking the exam determine if the required software is available on the machine you will be using. Additional software (such as a calculator and <u>word processing</u> applications) may also be useful if permitted by the professor.

☐ *Study*
Prepare for the test questions as you would for a classroom exam.

☐ *Apply Time-Appropriate Constraints*
In preparing for the exam, complete sample test questions within time constraints that match those possibly required for the online exam. For example, if you are going to be required to complete a 30-question exam in 1 hour, then prepare for the exam with no more than 2 minutes to answer each sample question.

☐ *Create a Good Test-Taking Environment*
For example, turn off the television, ask your roommates not to interrupt you, turn off <u>instant messaging</u> programs, and the like. (See Chapter 4.)

☐ *Identify the Ideal Time*
Often, you will be able to complete an online exam at a time that is convenient to you (for example, any time on one of three consecutive days). Identify a time when you will have no interruptions or distractions.

☐ *Prepare Your Resources*
Make sure that you have any permitted resources (such as books, notes, pen, and paper) with you when you complete the exam.

☐ *Relax*
Take a minute to close your eyes and calm down before entering the <u>webpage</u> that contains the exam.

During an Online Exam

☐ *Watch the Time*
If the exam is timed, set a stopwatch or have a clock in view so that you can keep track of how much time you have left to complete the questions. It is often useful to have an alarm or other signal to let you know when there is only 10 minutes left before the exam must be completed.

☐ *Print a Copy*
By printing out the exam, you give yourself several options. You can complete the exam on the paper copy and then transfer the answers over to the online version for submitting to the instructor, or you can keep a copy of each online answer you have selected just in case you lose your connection to the <u>Internet</u> or electrical power.

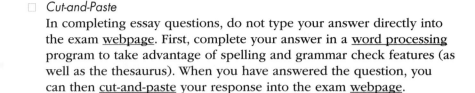

☐ *Cut-and-Paste*
In completing essay questions, do not type your answer directly into the exam <u>webpage</u>. First, complete your answer in a <u>word processing</u> program to take advantage of spelling and grammar check features (as well as the thesaurus). When you have answered the question, you can then <u>cut-and-paste</u> your response into the exam <u>webpage</u>.

☐ *Stay on the Exam Webpage*
Do not attempt to go to another <u>website</u> within the same browser <u>window</u> while you are completing the exam. Avoid clicking on the forward or backward arrows to access information because you will commonly risk losing the answers that you have already entered for the exam. Instead, open a second copy of your <u>Internet</u> browser, when allowed, to search for online information that may be useful in completing the exam (typically done by holding down <u>Ctrl</u> + n at the same time).

☐ *Stay Calm Even if the Technology Doesn't Work*
If a problem does occur with your technology, do not panic. Take careful notes of what has occurred and immediately <u>email</u> your instructor letting him know the specifics of the situation. Be sure to identify any error messages or other information that may have been provided.

☐ *Review the Exam Before Submitting*
Go through the online exam to guarantee that all your intended responses are entered before clicking on the Submit button.

☐ *Submit Only Once*
Typically, you will only want to click on the Submit button once. If an error does occur when submitting the exam, make another attempt and also <u>email</u> your professor about the situation. If possible, include in that <u>email</u> a copy of the answers that you intended to submit from the printed copy of the test you have kept.

After an Online Exam

☐ *Take Notes*
Make note of the questions that you were unsure of for your answer or that you could not answer. Immediately following the exam, review your textbook and notes to determine the correct answer.

☐ *Check Your Grade*
Most online exams will provide you with an immediate score for multiple-choice and short-answer questions. If there was an essay component to the test, you will likely have to wait a few days for those scores to be added to your grade.

☐ *Improve Your Performance*
Identify strategies that would improve your performance the next time that you are required to complete an online exam. Write these down in a document that can be saved to your course file <u>folder</u> in your computer.

www.cengage.com/success/Watkins/ELearning3e

Online Presentations

Of the course activities described in this guideline, online presentations are likely the adaptation most different from the traditional classroom activity. As a result, the use of online presentation is routinely limited and infrequent, often because the instructor is unfamiliar with strategies for making online presentations a successful teaching tool. When required, online presentations are rarely done in a <u>synchronous</u> format unless being done with video or audio conferencing equipment. More commonly, online presentations will require the sharing of Microsoft PowerPoint slide presentations that contain limited amounts of audio information.

Before the Online Presentation

☐ *Review the Guidelines*
Make note of <u>software</u> requirements, submission instructions, and requirements for presentation content.

☐ *Plan Your Success*
Establish a plan for completing the online presentation. Managing your time is essential because the development of a successful online presentation often requires more time and effort than your typical classroom presentation.

☐ *Confirm That You Have Adequate Software*
Verify that you have the appropriate <u>software</u> for completing the presentation.

☐ *Select a Screen Resolution of 800 × 600*
So that most of your fellow students can properly view your presentation, you may want to set your screen resolution to 800 × 600 prior to developing your presentation materials (especially Microsoft PowerPoint files that will be saved in the <u>HTML</u> format). This will be the most compatible screen resolution setting for most presentation <u>software</u> applications and computers.

☐ *Send Files 24 Hours in Advance*
At least 24 hours prior to your presentation, you should provide any materials that you want other students or the professor to review or use during the presentation.

During the Online Presentation

☐ *Confirm That Everyone Has a Copy of Your Presentation*
Especially if you are going to be conducting a video or audio conference to accompany the slide presentation, make sure that everyone can view the slides before starting.

☐ *Use the Technology*
Although presentation slides for the traditional classroom presentation should typically be limited to five words per line and five lines per

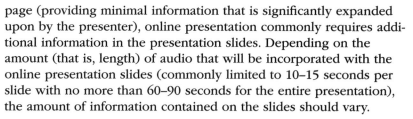

page (providing minimal information that is significantly expanded upon by the presenter), online presentation commonly requires additional information in the presentation slides. Depending on the amount (that is, length) of audio that will be incorporated with the online presentation slides (commonly limited to 10–15 seconds per slide with no more than 60–90 seconds for the entire presentation), the amount of information contained on the slides should vary.

☐ *Avoid Animated Slide Transitions*
Microsoft PowerPoint animations and slide transitions are generally lost when the presentation is saved to an HTML file format (and often when opened on a computer using a previous version of the software). As a result, do not spend a great amount of time working with these features.

☐ *Use Some Personalized Audio*
You can attach audio to accompany your online presentation slides. Audio dialogue to accompany the presentation slides can be inserted into a Microsoft PowerPoint presentation (this function is found in the Insert **pull-down menu** of PowerPoint). Audio files are large, so they should be used sparingly to provide information that requires additional explanation beyond the content of the presentation slides.

☐ *Save as a PowerPoint Show*
You can save Microsoft PowerPoint presentations as a PowerPoint Show (or .pps) file that will automatically start for viewers in the full-screen presentation format.

☐ *Save as a Hypertext Markup Language file*
You can save Microsoft PowerPoint presentations as a PowerPoint HTML (.html or .htm) file that can be used as a website containing the presentation slides.

☐ *Offer Guidelines for Asking Questions*
If you are participating in a live audio or video conference to supplement the presentation slides, then you provide participants with guidelines for asking questions.

After the Online Presentation

☐ *Review*
Consider the feedback provided by the instructor.

☐ *Follow Up*
After completing the online presentation, email follow-up questions and comments to your professor and/or classmates as appropriate.

☐ *Improve Your Performance*
Identify strategies that would improve your performance the next time that you are required to give an online presentation. Write these down in a document that can be saved to your course file folder in your computer.

Online Readings and E-Books

The typical college experience will introduce you to a variety of technologies (for example, <u>synchronous</u> <u>chat</u> and <u>asynchronous</u> <u>discussion boards</u>), but to be successful in most courses, you will still want to be a proficient and effective reader. Increasing your comprehension when reading online materials or e-books is crucial to your success in any online learning experience (also see Chapter 3).

Before You Read

☐ *Review*
Prepare for completing online readings by reviewing the required and recommended reading lists provided by the instructor.

☐ *Determine the Context*
Examine the required list of online readings (as well as other readings) within the context of the semester. This can provide you with a context for how readings relate to previous and future topics to be covered in the course.

☐ *Select a Preferred Monitor Resolution*
Experiment with varying monitor resolution settings (such as, 640 × 480, 800 × 600, or 1024 × 768 pixels) to determine which is best suited for your reading preferences.

☐ *Create a Good Study Environment*
For example, turn off the television, ask your roommates not to interrupt you, turn off <u>instant messaging</u>, and the like. (See Chapter 4.)

☐ *Create a Good Reading Environment*
For example, select a comfortable and supportive chair with appropriate lighting, as well as a computer set at the correct height. (See Chapter 4.)

☐ *Confirm That You Have Adequate Software*
Verify that you have the necessary <u>software</u> for viewing online readings in the multiple formats that may be required (for example, Microsoft Word and Internet Explorer, <u>Adobe Acrobat PDF</u>, and Netscape Navigator).

While You Are Reading

☐ *Define Your Goals*
Based on the context of the reading within the course, you should determine goals for reading the materials, making special note of specific information that you have learned by the time you complete the reading(s).

☐ *Identify the Purpose*
There are typically four potential purposes for reading: (1) understanding and comprehension, (2) evaluating critically, (3) practical application, and/or (4) pleasure.[2]

☐ *Preview*
Examine the entire reading before starting a detailed read.

☐ *Select an Appropriate Pace*
Determine an appropriate pace for your reading. For example, reading detailed technical information to better understand and comprehend the material may take more time than reading similar material for practical application.

☐ *Become an Active Reader*
Ask questions of yourself and take notes as you read through the materials.

☐ *Make a List of Questions*
Identify a list of questions that you should be able to answer when you have completed the reading.

☐ *Look for a Pattern*
When reading materials, it is often useful to look for patterns in the text (such as chronological, place, cause-effect, and comparison-contrast).

☐ *Use the Features of an E-Book Reader*
If you are using an e-book reader (such as an Amazon Kindle, Sony Reader, or other similar device) use the search and note-taking capabilities built into the device to improve your reading comprehension. (See Chapter 3.)

☐ *Take Notes on the Computer or E-Book Reader*
Depending on the permissions authorized by the creator of an <u>Adobe Acrobat PDF</u> document, you may be able to take notes directly on the document. These notes will appear as sticky notes on the document and will not alter the original information. When using Microsoft Word, you can add comments, which will appear to the right or along the bottom of the document (this function is found in the Insert <u>pull-down menu</u> of Word). You can also take notes in a separate <u>word processing</u> file.

HOW TO
10

☐ *Track Changes*
When using Microsoft Word, you can keep track of modifications made to the document by you and other viewers. The insertions or deletions of others will be illustrated in multiple colors, depending on the viewer. This function, called Track Changes, is found in the Tools <u>pull-down menu</u> of Word.

HOW TO
5

☐ *Review Section Titles and Headings*
Using section titles and headings to provide clues about the major concepts or ideas will allow you to focus on the broad content rather than specific words of each sentence.

☐ *Read the Introductions and Summaries*
Use the introductory and concluding paragraphs as guides for your reading.

☐ *Keep a Dictionary Nearby*
Don't let a limited vocabulary reduce your understanding of the materials. You can also keep a <u>word processing</u> program (such as Microsoft Word) running on your computer in order to use its thesaurus (Shift + F7) for

words that may be less familiar, or go to dictionary <u>websites</u> (such as Dictionary.com).

☐ *Use SQ3R*
Use the SQ3R process for increasing reading proficiency: Survey, Question, Read, Recite, Review.[3]

☐ *Take Reading Breaks*
When reading from a computer monitor, take reading breaks at least every 30 minutes to rest your eyes.

After You Read

☐ *Review Your Questions*
Evaluate your notes on the reading to determine if you can answer the questions that you intended to answer by completing the reading.

☐ *Review Your Notes*
Look over your notes for completeness, accuracy, and usefulness before closing the reading materials. Analyze the outline structure underlying your notes in comparison to the reading materials that you have just completed.

☐ *Keep a Record*
When permitted, save copies of online reading, along with your notes, for later review.

☐ *Improve Your Performance*
Identify strategies that would improve your performance the next time that you are required to complete online readings. Write these down in a document that can be saved to your course file <u>folder</u> in your computer.

Online (Electronic) Portfolios

Online (electronic) portfolios are increasingly becoming the means of demonstrating your skills, experiences, and accomplishments in college courses. These collections of assignments and activities, saved in their electronic format either as files on a disk or links on a personal portfolio <u>webpage</u>, provide the professor with multiple measures of what you have learned and what skills you have gained in the course.

Before You Create a Portfolio

☐ *Review the Guidelines*
Instructors will commonly provide you with specific guidelines for online portfolios, including descriptions of each element that must be included as well as grading criteria.

☐ *Examine Sample Portfolios*
Find out if sample portfolios from previous semesters are available to illustrate the instructor's expectations.

☐ *Create a "Look-n-Feel"*
Establish a "look-n-feel" for your portfolio at the beginning of the semester (including color schemes, margins, fonts, and so forth). Use this for all <u>word processing</u> documents, <u>webpage</u>s, and other files that you create for the course.

☐ *Confirm That You Have Access to Adequate Software*
Determine which <u>software</u> applications will be required for creating the elements of the online portfolio (such as Microsoft Word and <u>Adobe Acrobat PDF</u>).

☐ *Identify Any Additional Hardware Requirements*
Determine if additional computer devices will be required for creating the elements of the online portfolio (such as a scanner or digital camera). Often you will be able to check these out from a campus computer lab for use in class projects.

☐ *Confirm Adequate Storage Space on the College's Server*
For an online portfolio, verify that you have adequate space on your college's or university's <u>server</u> for storing the many elements of the portfolio.

☐ *Ask for Help in Creating Webpages*
If you are unsure of your skills for creating the necessary <u>webpage</u>s for an online portfolio, contact your college's or university's technical support services to identify any training that may be available to students.

While You Are Preparing a Portfolio

☐ *Back Up Files*
When creating the elements of your online portfolio, be sure to make backup copies of all files.

☐ *Follow Through with Your "Look-n-Feel"*
Throughout the semester, design all of your assignments and activities to adhere with the "look-n-feel" that you have selected for your portfolio (including color schemes, margins, fonts, and so forth). Though you may not use every assignment or activity for your portfolio, this will save you time.

☐ *Develop a Structure for Linking Webpages*
For an online portfolio, develop an initial <u>webpage</u> that will link the viewer to the various elements of your portfolio. Produce this <u>webpage</u> early in the semester and include the other elements of your online portfolio throughout the semester. Do not leave the creation of the online portfolio until the end of the semester.

☐ *Review Grading Criteria*
Throughout the semester, you will want to make sure that you are on target for success by reviewing the grading criteria because online portfolios often have multiple elements.

After You Have Created a Portfolio

☐ *Keep a Record*
Create a backup copy that includes all elements of your online portfolio.

☐ *Review the Submission Requirements*
Before submitting the online portfolio, examine the submissions requirements to make sure that you are making the project available to the instructor in the file format that she requires.

☐ *Improve Your Performance*
Review the portfolios of other student to identify strategies that would improve your performance the next time that you are required to develop an online portfolio. Write these down in a document that can be saved to your course file folder in your computer.

Turning In Assignments Online

HOW TO
22

HOW TO
29

Using online tools for submitting assignments and activities is quite common at most colleges and universities. Online submissions of coursework typically require that you turn in the necessary file(s) by attaching them to an email message or by uploading them to an educational portal (such as WebCT or BlackBoard). From saving printing costs to flexibility in where you are when you submit the coursework, turning in files online has many advantages for you as a student.

HOW TO
36

Before Turning In Assignments Online

HOW TO
43

☐ *Review the Assignment Requirements*
Especially take note of the required file format, file-naming guidelines, and submission process desired by the professor.

☐ *Don't Submit Anything That Hasn't Been Reviewed*
Ask a friend, roommate, or classmate to review the final draft of any assignment or activity before submitting it to your instructor for grading. This will help you avoid a variety of errors that may cost you points.

While Turning In Assignments Online

☐ *Describe Attachments*
When attaching an assignment or activity to an email, include a description of the assignment or activity being submitted, the name of the file being submitted, and the software application used to create the file (such as Microsoft Word or Adobe Acrobat PDF).

☐ *Submit Only Once*
When uploading an assignment or activity to an Internet portal, click on the Submit button only one time.

☐ *Stay Calm Even if the Technology Doesn't Work*
If a problem does occur with your technology, do not panic. Take careful notes of what has occurred and immediately email your instructor and let him know the specifics of the situation. Be sure to identify any error messages or other information that may have been provided.

☐ *Check Dates on Files*
Double-check that the file(s) you are submitting are the most recent and the ones that you intend to submit.

☐ *Name the File with Useful Information*
Follow any file-naming protocols provided by the instructor. For example, in the file name of each file that you submit for grading, you may be required to include your name, the assignment number, your course section number, and/or the date. (See Chapter 3.)

☐ *Back Save When Necessary*
Often professors will require that you back save your files to a previous version of the application (for example, saving a Word 2007 file as a Word 2003 file instead). If this is required, be sure that you do this before submitting the file for grading.

After Turning In Assignments Online

☐ *Follow Up*
For the first assignment or activity of the semester, you may want to email your instructor and let her know that you have submitted the file (include the time and file name with the email). Once you have successfully submitted a file, this verification is no longer necessary.

☐ *Keep a Record*
Back up all files that you submit for grading.

☐ *Patience Is a Virtue*
If you do not receive immediate feedback regarding the assignment or activity, do not panic. Depending on the size of a class and the length of the assignments, grading can commonly take upwards of a week for many professors.

☐ *Keep Track of Your Grades Throughout the Semester*
Plan two or three times during the semester to review the online grade book for each of your courses. If grades are missing for assignments or activities that you have submitted weeks previously, you should contact your instructor. You do not want to wait until the last week of classes to verify your grades.

Online Whiteboards

Success in most college courses requires that you effectively communicate with your classmates and professor. Often, visual images can be used to avoid miscommunications, convey mathematical formulas, illustrate a relationship, and/or improve comprehension. The online whiteboard is the <u>Internet</u>'s adaptation of the traditional classroom chalkboard.

Before Using an Online Whiteboard

☐ *Determine Your Goals*
Before selecting an online whiteboard as a tool for communicating with your classmates or instructor, determine which messages (or what information) is best expressed through illustrations on the online whiteboard.

☐ *Practice*
Rehearse using the online whiteboard before selecting it as a tool. Using a computer's mouse to draw can be tricky, to say the least.

☐ *Consider a Drawing Tablet*
If you are going to use the online whiteboard extensively in communicating with others, consider purchasing a drawing tablet. Shaped like a pencil and piece of paper, drawing tablets perform the functions of a computer's mouse while providing for accurate and detailed representations.

While Using an Online Whiteboard

☐ *Use to Add to Discussions*
Online whiteboards should be used when you consider it to be the most effective and efficient way to communicate a message. It is often best used as a supplement to other <u>synchronous</u> or <u>asynchronous</u> discussions.

☐ *Make Use of Set Shapes*
The set shapes (for example, circles, stars, and squares) can be useful in drawing many illustrations and easier than drawing those shapes freehand with a mouse or drawing tablet.

☐ *Vary Your Colors*
Use the multiple colors available in most online whiteboards to improve the effectiveness of your communications.

☐ *Add Text*
Commonly, you will want to add text to your online whiteboard illustrations; do this using the computer keyboard rather than drawing letters by freehand.

☐ *Cut-and-Paste*
Most online whiteboards allow you to <u>cut-and-paste</u> (or upload) images (such as pictures, PowerPoint slides, and others) to the whiteboard. You can then add to those images using the whiteboards tools.

☐ *Save Before Starting a New Illustration*
Save all illustrations before beginning subsequent drawings.

After Using an Online Whiteboard

☐ *Keep a Record*
Save copies of the images that you have created in the whiteboard.
Often you will want to <u>email</u> copies of these images as <u>attachment</u>s to
others who participated in the online conversation.

☐ *Improve Your Performance*
Identify strategies that would improve your performance the next
time that you use an online whiteboard. Write these down in
a document that can be saved to your course file <u>folder</u> in your
computer.

E-Research

In the past most college students would spend hours in the library each
week searching for resources for their <u>coursework</u>. For you, however, online technologies can be effectively used to provide flexibility in where you
conduct your research as well as reduce the amount of time necessary for
finding the resources you require.

Before Doing Online Research

☐ *Identify Objectives*
Prior to conducting research online, you should establish a list of
objectives for the research. What information do you want to have
when you have completed your research? What questions do you want
to have answered when you have completed your research?

☐ *Determine What Will Be of Value*
Decide what types of information are going to be of the most value to
you (such as empirical research, eye-witness accounts, statistics, narra-
tives, rationale arguments, and so forth).

☐ *Select Resources of Value*
Establish what types of resources are going to be of the most value to
you based on the information that you want to find (such as academic
research journals, trade publications, books, magazines, statistical
databases, and so forth).

☐ *Contact the Library*
Get in touch with your college or university library to determine
which services and resources they have available online. Typically,
some services and resources will be available online (such as searching databases for journal articles and books), whereas others will only

be offered on-campus (such as access to recent journals or copies of most books).

☐ *Get Training*
Many college and university libraries provide training for students on using the many resources they have available, both online and on-campus. Take advantage of these opportunities early in the semester. Often, online tutorials will also be available to students to supplement training provided by the library.

☐ *Review Guidelines*
Look over the specifications of the assignment or activity related to the research to determine requirements and expectations (for example, are you expected to reference at least five journal articles?).

☐ *Don't Plan to Use Online Resources Exclusively*
Although you will want to use the online resources to supplement and reduce the research that you will still have to do at a library, you should not expect to conduct all of your research online for a course assignment or activity.

While Doing Online Research

☐ *Evaluate All Resources*
Information obtained from online resources, like online databases and webpages, is often reliable but should also be evaluated with the same criteria as for print sources. (See Chapter 3.) 🌐

☐ *Expand Your Search*
Use search tools (such as "and," "or," "not" and so on) to expand your search capabilities. (See Chapter 3.)

☐ *Use General Searches Along with Database Searches*
Search the World Wide Web for articles as well. Often, journal articles that are not available in full text through online databases available through the library can be found online on journal websites as samples or on the author's personal webpage.

☐ *Open Links in New Browser Windows*
Save your starting point when exploring new links in new browser windows (right-click on the link and then select Open in New Window).

☐ *Print Sparingly*
Print only those pages that will be most useful to you. You can select individual pages to print by first previewing them in the print command of your Internet browser.

☐ *Verify That You Have Accurate Reference Information*
Make sure that you have all necessary and correct information for resources that you intend to cite in your coursework (such as the author, publication date, page numbers, accurate title, URL, and date you accessed the Webpage).

☐ *Don't Forget Outside Resources*
Special libraries, government agencies, and advocacy groups make
excellent starting points for topical research.

☐ *Contact the Author if All Else Fails*
If you cannot locate a journal article, then you may want to search for
the author's <u>email</u> address and ask him about receiving a copy of the
article. Often, he will be more than happy to provide you with a copy
of his work in order to assist in your education.

☐ *Don't Be Afraid to Ask for Help*
If you are still having problems finding useful information after significant attempts, contact your college or university library to seek the
assistance of a librarian (or information specialist).

☐ *Take Careful Notes*
Take notes about what you have learned from different online
resources; often, you will want to go back to information that you
reviewed earlier.

After Doing Online Research

☐ *Review the Resources*
Examine the resources that you have obtained to ensure that they provide you with the necessary information for completing the assignment or activity.

☐ *Double-Check Reference Information*
Before leaving a <u>website</u> or library, verify that you have accurate citation information for all resources that you plan to reference in the
assignment or activity.

☐ *Improve Your Performance*
Review your search strategies and identify ways to improve your
online research techniques for the next time that you are required to
conduct research for a course.

Summary

Whether we realize it or not, each of us has a set of learning skills and study
habits that we use to succeed in the conventional classroom. Many of these
skills and habits, however, will have to be transformed for you to have the
same levels of success in an online course. In this case, many of the skills
that you used in preparing for the classroom presentation will continue to
be useful, although you will want to transform those skills for success in the
new delivery system. The study tips offered in this chapter will help you
adjust your learning skills, as well as develop new study habits, for being
successful in online <u>coursework</u>.

Notes

1. Based on Winograd and Moore, 2003.
2. Carter, Bishop, and Kravits, 2002.
3. See Pauk, 2001; Ellis, 2003.

TABLE QR–1   KEYBOARD SHORTCUTS FOR COMPUTERS WITH MICROSOFT WINDOWS*

KEY COMBINATIONS	FUNCTION
Alt + Tab	Switch through the active applications that you are using. For example, allows you to quickly move from one Internet search to another.
Ctrl + n	Open a new document in Microsoft Word or new browser window in Microsoft Internet Explorer or Netscape Navigator.
Ctrl + a	Select all (most Windows applications).
Ctrl + End	Move the cursor to the bottom of the document (most Windows applications).
Ctrl + Esc	Same as clicking on the Start button (most Windows applications).
Ctrl + Home	Move the cursor to the top of the document (most Windows applications).
Ctrl + p	Prints (most Windows applications).
Ctrl + s	Save (most Windows applications).
Ctrl + c	Copy (most Windows applications).
Ctrl + v	Paste (most Windows applications).
Ctrl + x	Cut (most Windows applications).
Ctrl + y	Repeat the last action (most Windows applications).
Ctrl + z	Undo the last action (most Windows applications).

*For parallel functions, use the Apple key instead of Ctrl on Macintosh computers.

TABLE QR-2   USEFUL ACRONYMS/INITIALISMS FOR PERSONAL ONLINE COMMUNICATIONS

ACRONYM/ INITIALISM	MEANING	ACRONYM/ INITIALISM	MEANING
AAMOF	as a matter of fact	IMHO	in my humble opinion
BFN	bye for now	IMO	in my opinion
BTW	by the way	IOW	in other words
BYKT	but you knew that	LOL	lots of luck or laughing out loud
CMIIW	correct me if I'm wrong		
EOL	end of lecture	NRN	no reply necessary
FAQ	frequently asked question(s)	OIC	oh, I see
		OTOH	on the other hand
FWIW	for what it's worth	ROF	rolling on the floor
FYI	for your information	TIA	thanks in advance
HTH	hope this helps	TIC	tongue in cheek
IAC	in any case	TTYL	talk to you later
IAE	in any event	TYVM	thank you very much
IMCO	in my considered opinion	<G>	grinning
		<J>	joking
WYSIWYG	what you see is what you get	<L>	laughing
		<S>	smiling
<Y>	yawning		

Source: Based on http://www.pb.org/emoticon.html.

TABLE QR–3   USEFUL EMOTICONS FOR PERSONAL ONLINE COMMUNICATIONS

EMOTICON	MEANING
:) or :-)	Expresses happiness, sarcasm, or joke
:(or :-(	Expresses unhappiness
:] or :-]	Expresses jovial happiness
:[or :-[	Expresses despondent unhappiness
:D or :-D	Expresses jovial happiness or laughing
:e or :-e	Expresses disappointment
:l or :-l	Expresses indifference
:-/ or :-\	Indicates undecided, confused, or skeptical
:Q or :-Q	Expresses confusion
:S or :-S	Expresses incoherence or loss of words
:@ or :-@	Expresses shock or screaming
:O or :-O	Indicates surprise, yelling, or realization of an error ("uh oh!")

Source: Based on http://www.pb.org/emoticon.html.

How-To Tutorials

List of Tutorials

T1

Overview of Tutorials

The purpose of this portion of this book is to provide you with tutorials for some of the most common tasks used in online learning. It provides guidelines on how to work both with Windows and Macintosh computers, Microsoft Word, Google Docs, Adobe Acrobat, Microsoft Internet Explorer, Netscape, Mozilla Firefox, Blackboard, WebCT, eCollege, and Angel. It also provides a tutorial on how to troubleshoot problems that might occur.

The tutorials do not cover every aspect of each of these areas, but they address the most commonly used functions in online learning. Our hope is that you will use these tutorials as you are working on your computer and have them by your side.

The tutorials have been designed using step-by-step instructions along with pictures similar to what you will see on your computer. The tutorials were also designed using the most common versions of <u>software</u>. However, <u>software</u> versions change frequently. Therefore, your version of the <u>software</u> may be different from the ones pictured in the tutorials. If this is the case, don't fret; in most cases, the tutorials will still provide you with the necessary guidance to help you out.

Check out the Student Premium Website for updated and additional tutorials. The website address is www.cengage.com/success/Watkins/ELearning3e.

Checking Your Computer's Hardware Profile in Microsoft Windows

Before starting a course with online course materials, you should verify the hardware profile for your computer. This is important to know when installing <u>software</u>, troubleshooting technical problems, and verifying that you have the minimum configurations to participate in the online portion of your course. This tutorial is designed for Microsoft Windows XP users but may be applicable to other Microsoft Windows users as well.

1. To begin, in Microsoft Windows XP, click on the Start <u>menu</u> and select Control Panel from the list. A <u>window</u> should pop up that looks similar to the one below:

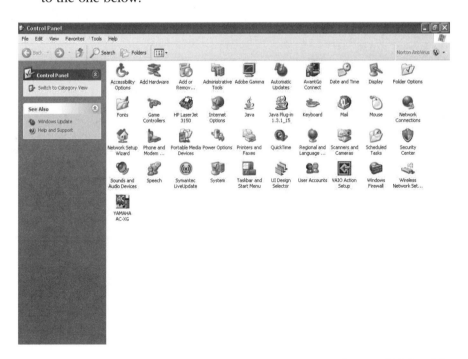

2. Scroll down (if necessary) and double-click on the System <u>icon</u>, and a <u>window</u> should pop up similar to the one below:

3. Note the seven tabs across the top of this new <u>window</u> (System Restore, Automatic Updates, Remote, General, Computer Name, Hardware, and Advanced). Click on the General tab, and you will find information about your <u>operating system</u>, system processor (chip), and RAM.

4. If you click on the Hardware tab and then click on the Device Manager button, you should get a <u>window</u> that looks similar to the one below:

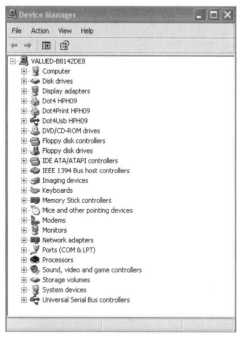

5. In the Device Manager, you can find out a lot about the hardware in your computer. Double-click on any of the items on the list, and you will find out more details about that device. For example, if you want to find out about your monitor, double-click on the word "Monitors" in the list, and you will get more information. You can do this with any of the devices on the list.

Creating Folders and Staying Organized in Microsoft Windows

One of the nicest features of Microsoft Windows is the ability to create <u>folders</u> to organize and save your work. If you do not organize your files in some way, as you add more and more files to your computer, it will be harder and harder to find what you are looking for.

1. To create <u>folders</u> and organize files, begin by clicking on the Start button at the bottom left side of the screen. Then select All Programs from the list, select Accessories, and select Windows Explorer. A <u>window</u> should pop up that looks similar to the one below:

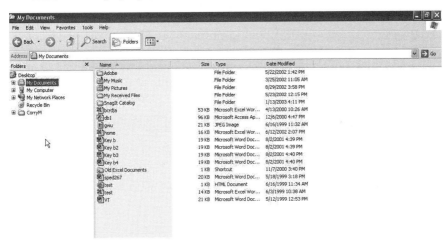

2. The <u>window</u> you are now seeing is divided into two areas. The area on the left lists the drives and <u>folders</u> in your computer. The area on the right will be used to see the details of what is in each of your <u>folders</u>.

3. Because you will most likely have a hard drive in your computer labeled the C: drive, we will use that letter in our examples. If you know that your hard drive is a letter other than C, substitute that letter for the letter C in our examples.

4. In the left-hand side of the screen, try double-clicking on My Computer and then clicking on Local Disk (C:). It should expand and contract the list of current <u>folders</u> on your hard drive.

5. Now let's add a new <u>folder</u> that you will use to save files for a fictional course that you are taking called E-Learning.

6. To create this <u>folder</u>, click on Local Disk (C:) in the left-hand side of the screen. Single-click on the File <u>pull-down menu</u> at the top left-hand side of the screen. Next, single-click on New from the list and then single click on Folder from the list. It should look similar to the screen below:

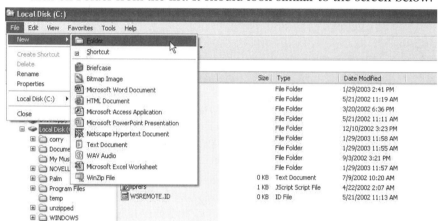

7. Once you do this, on the right-hand side of the screen, a new <u>folder</u> should be created titled New Folder, and the cursor should be positioned on the title. At this point, you can simply type in the name you want for the new folder and press the Enter key. For our example, type E-Learning for the title and then press the Enter key. You should then have a new folder on the right-hand side of the screen titled E-Learning, and your screen should look similar to the one on the following page.

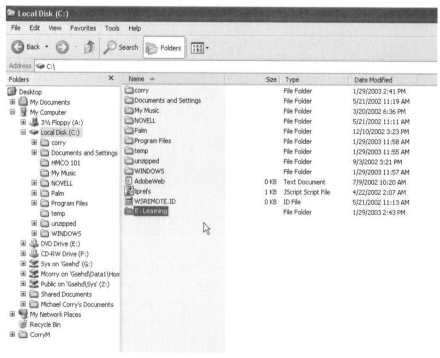

8. Now that you have this new <u>folder</u>, you can save any files that you want into it. You can also move existing files into it by dragging and dropping them into your new <u>folder</u>.

Checking Your Computer's Hardware Profile on a Macintosh Computer

Before starting a course with online course materials, you should verify the hardware profile for your computer. This is important to know when installing software, troubleshooting technical problems, and verifying that you have the minimum configurations to participate in the online portion of your course. This tutorial is designed for Macintosh users.

1. To begin, on your Macintosh computer, click on the Apple <u>icon</u> on the top left-hand corner of the screen. Then click on the Apple System Profiler option.

2. Once you have clicked on the Apple System Profiler option, you should get a new <u>window</u> that has six tabs across the top (System Profile, Devices and Volumes, Control Panels, Extensions, Applications, and System Folders).

3. Click on the System Profile tab, and you will find information about your <u>operating system</u>, RAM and system processor (chip), network configuration (if any), printer (if any), and ROM.

Creating Folders and Staying Organized on a Macintosh Computer

One of the most powerful options in a Macintosh computer is the ability to create <u>folders</u> to organize and save your work. If you do not organize your files in some way, as you add more and more files to your computer, it will be harder and harder to find what you are looking for.

1. To create <u>folders</u> and organize files, begin by double-clicking on the Hard Drive <u>icon</u> on your screen. A new <u>window</u> should open up that lists the various <u>folders</u> on your hard drive.

2. Any <u>folders</u> that already exist on your hard drive are displayed in this <u>window</u>. Now you will be able to create new <u>folders</u> that you will use to save files for different purposes—for example, to organize files for a course that you are taking.

3. To create this <u>folder</u>, click on the File <u>pull-down menu</u> located at the top left-hand side of the screen. Then click on the New Folder option from the list. Once you do this, in the bottom of the <u>window</u> a new <u>folder</u> should be created titled Untitled Folder, and the cursor should be positioned on the title.

4. At this point, simply type in the name that you want for the new <u>folder</u> and press the Enter key. Note that once you type in the new

folder name and press Enter, the <u>folder</u> is then moved into alphabetical order within the list of <u>folders</u>. Now that you have this new <u>folder</u>, you may save any files that you want into it. You may also move existing files into it by dragging and dropping them into your new <u>folder</u>.

Tracking Changes in a Microsoft Word Document

Microsoft Word contains a powerful feature that allows you to track changes made to a document. This feature, like adding notes, is mostly used when more than one person is reading and editing a document. In general, here's how it works. First, one person may write a paper. Then, a second person may review it and make some changes. If the second person uses Track Changes, then all changes that he/she makes to the paper will be marked in such a way that the changes are easy to identify. Then, when the first person gets the paper back, he/she can easily see what changes the second person has made to the paper. The first person then has the opportunity to either accept or reject those changes. As you can imagine, this is very important when doing a group paper.

1. If you want to track the changes you make in a Word document, begin by opening the document. Once you have the document opened, click on the Tools <u>pull-down menu</u> and then select Track Changes. Your selections should look similar to the screen below:

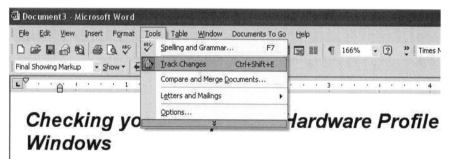

2. Now, try making some edits to your document. You will see two things happening. The first is that all changes are underlined. The second is that a horizontal line appears on the left-hand side of the page where the changes occur. This same thing will occur when someone else makes edits or changes to the document.

3. If you have a document that contains tracked changes, you have the options of accepting or not accepting the changes. To do this, first make sure Track Changes is turned on (as explained above). Then, locate the Review toolbar at the top of your screen. The toolbar should look something like what is below:

4. Using the Review toolbar, you can move from tracked change to tracked change in your document and individually elect to accept or reject each change. You can also accept all the changes or reject all the changes at once. To move forward from tracked change to tracked change, click on the <u>icon</u> with the arrow pointing to the right. If you want to move backward, click on the <u>icon</u> with the arrow pointing to the left. To accept all tracked changes (without reviewing them), click on the <u>icon</u> with the check mark. To reject all tracked changes (without reviewing them), click on the <u>icon</u> with the "x" mark.

5. To turn off Track changes in your document, click on the Tools <u>pull-down menu</u> from the top of the screen. Then click on the Track Changes option, which turns it off.

6. To have Track Changes on for the next person who reads the document, turn it on and then save your document.

Adding Notes or Comments to a Microsoft Word Document

Microsoft Word has a powerful feature that allows you to add notes to the document. This feature, like Track Changes, is mostly used when more than one person is reading and editing a document. This is very useful when doing a group paper.

1. The Adding Notes or Comments feature of Word gives you the ability to add comments to a document without actually changing the text. To do this, start by clicking on the View <u>pull-down menu</u> at the top of the screen. Then click on the Toolbars option and then on the Reviewing option.

Your selections should look similar to the screen below:

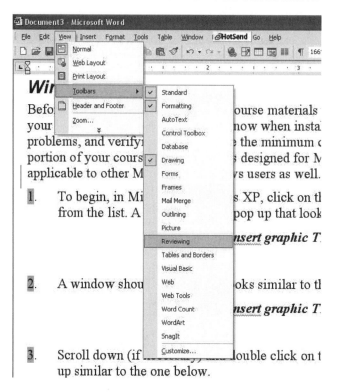

2. Now you should have a new toolbar at the top of your screen. It will look similar to the screen below:

3. To insert a comment, click on the document where you want the comment to appear. Then click on the Insert Comment button on the reviewing toolbar. The Insert Comment button will look similar to the one below:

4. Type in your comment in the area provided. Your comment is now available for others to read.

5. To delete a comment, simply click on the comment and then click on the Delete Comment button on the reviewing toolbar. The Delete Comment button looks similar to the one below:

Working with Documents in Google Docs

Google Docs is designed to allow you to upload existing or create new word processing documents or to upload existing spreadsheets or presentations and then to invite others to join you in editing and publishing those documents, spreadsheets, or presentations. It is a collaboration tool that has many different uses. For our purposes, we will focus on uploading, editing, and sharing a word processing document. The steps for uploading, editing, and sharing a spreadsheet or presentation file are very similar.

1. To upload an existing document into Google Docs, begin by clicking on the Upload button. Your selections should look similar to the screen below:

2. Then click on the Browse button and select the document you would like to edit and share. Once you have selected your document, you need to click on the Upload File button. Your selections should look similar to the screen below:

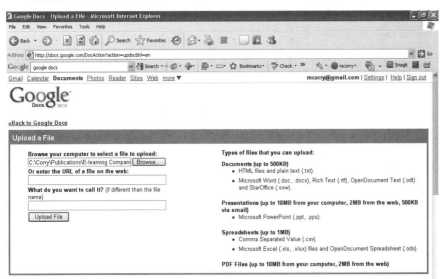

3. The document you selected should now be visible in Google Docs. You should notice that the screen looks like many word processing software screens. Google Docs is set up this way so you can edit, save, and share your documents. It should look similar to the screen below:

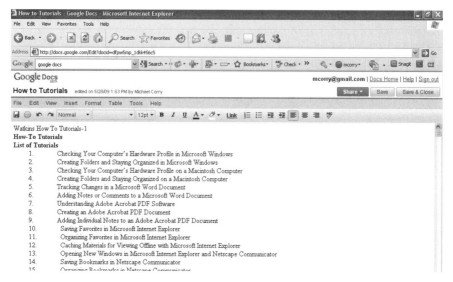

4. Once you have your document in Google Docs you can share it with others. To do this, begin by clicking on the Share button at the top of the screen. Then, select Share With Others. It will take you to a screen similar to the one below:

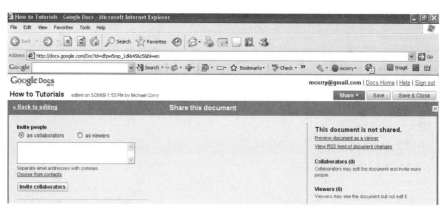

5. You can now invite anyone to view (as a viewer) or edit (as a collaborator) your document. To do this, type in their email addresses into the box provided and then click the Invite Collaborators button. You will be given the opportunity to add a personal note to the email message. Once you click the Send button, the person or people you have invited to view or edit your document will receive an email invitation with instructions on how to access the document you have shared. To

get back to your document, click on the Back to Editing button at the top of the screen. Once you are done editing and saving your document, you can return to the main Google Docs screen by clicking on the Docs Home button at the top of the screen. At the main Google Docs screen you can see all the documents you have uploaded and with whom you have shared them.

Understanding Adobe Acrobat PDF Software

Adobe makes a very useful piece of software called Acrobat that is used in many courses that have online components. The Adobe Acrobat <u>software</u> is used to create PDF files. Therefore, sometimes people call the software Adobe PDF or simply PDF <u>software</u>.

Adobe Acrobat comes in two versions—the full version and the reader-only version. The reader-only version is free and can be downloaded from the Adobe <u>website</u> at

<u>http://www.adobe.com</u>

Many of you may already have downloaded this reader-only version of the software at some point because many documents on the <u>World Wide Web</u> can only be accessed if you have this reader. The reader-only version does exactly what you would think it does: It allows you to read <u>Adobe Acrobat PDF</u> files. But that is all it will allow you to do. It will not allow you to create your own PDF documents or to add personal notes to existing PDF documents.

The full version of the <u>Adobe Acrobat PDF</u> <u>software</u> does allow you to do many more things than just read PDF files. Two of the most important things it allows you to do are to create your own PDF documents and to add personal notes to existing PDF documents. Because the full version contains these important features, your course instructor may require that you have it to participate in the online portions of your course. (*Note:* If you need to purchase the full version of the <u>software</u>, students will often get a significant discount on the retail price of the software. Therefore, consult with your school's bookstore or computer store about getting the discounted price. Also, before you buy the full version of the <u>software</u>, you should consult with your school to find out if they already have it installed on certain computers on campus.)

Creating an Adobe Acrobat PDF Document

Many courses that are completely or partially online will require you to submit documents in <u>Adobe Acrobat PDF</u> format. This format is used because it is a common interface that maintains the settings and formatting of your original document. Creating an <u>Adobe Acrobat PDF</u> document is just like making a photocopy of a piece of paper. The only difference is that with PDF documents you make the copy completely digitally using your computer.

Once you create an <u>Adobe Acrobat PDF</u> copy of your original document, then you can easily attach the <u>Adobe Acrobat PDF</u> file to an <u>email</u> and send it to another student or your instructor(s). You can also put your <u>Adobe Acrobat PDF</u> file into a Digital Drop Box in either Blackboard or WebCT. (*Note:* This tutorial assumes that you have already properly installed the full version of <u>Adobe Acrobat PDF</u> <u>software</u> on your computer. As an alternative, you can upload or create your document in Google Docs (see How-To Tutorial #7) and then Download the document in the PDF format from the File menu.

1. To create an <u>Adobe Acrobat PDF</u> document, start by opening the document that you want to copy or convert into the PDF document. For example, if you have a paper that you wrote using Microsoft Word, you open the file for the paper in Word.

2. Once you have opened your Word file, click on the File <u>pull-down menu</u> at the top left-hand side of the screen. Then click on the word Print in the list. You should get a screen that looks similar to the one below:

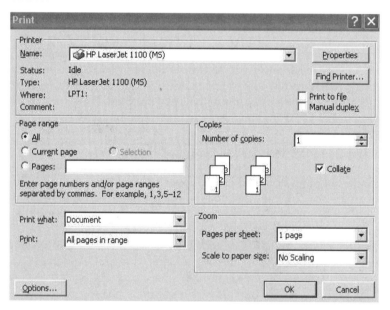

3. In the <u>window</u> that appears, locate the white box to the right of the word Name. The white box should have a down arrow in the right side of the box. Click on the down arrow, and you should get a drop-down list similar to the one below:

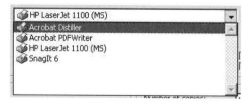

4. Now, single click on the Adobe PDFWriter option on the drop-down list. That option should then appear in the white box. You have now told your computer that you want to print or create an <u>Adobe Acrobat PDF</u> document of your file. To actually create the <u>Adobe Acrobat PDF</u> file, click on the OK button.

5. After you click on the OK button, you should get a screen similar to the one below:

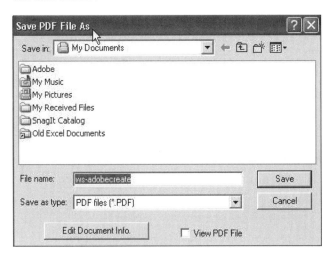

6. Because you are creating a file and not actually printing the document, your computer needs to know what you want to name the <u>Adobe Acrobat PDF</u> file and where to save it. Therefore, on this screen, type in the name for your <u>Adobe Acrobat PDF</u> file and select the folder where you want it saved. Then click on the OK button.

7. After you click the OK button, Adobe Acrobat will automatically open your newly created PDF file so that you can see what it looks like.

Adding Individual Notes to an Adobe Acrobat PDF Document

Adding individual or personal notes to <u>Adobe Acrobat PDF</u> documents can be a great way to share ideas or get feedback or grades on work that you have done. Because of this, it is one of the most common uses of <u>Adobe Acrobat PDF</u> file in online <u>coursework</u>. (*Note:* This tutorial assumes that you have already properly installed the full version of <u>Adobe Acrobat PDF</u> <u>software</u> to your computer.)

1. To add notes to an <u>Adobe Acrobat PDF</u> document, start by clicking on the Start button at the bottom left-hand corner of the screen in Windows. Then click on Programs, click on Adobe Acrobat, and

click on Acrobat Exchange. You should get a screen that looks similar to the one below:

2. Once you have this screen, you need to open the file where you want to add a personal note. You can do this by clicking on the File <u>pull-down menu</u> at the top left-hand corner of the screen. Then select the Open option, select the file you want to open, and click on the Open button. This should open up the PDF document that you wanted. For this example, we have opened up a document that looks similar to the one below:

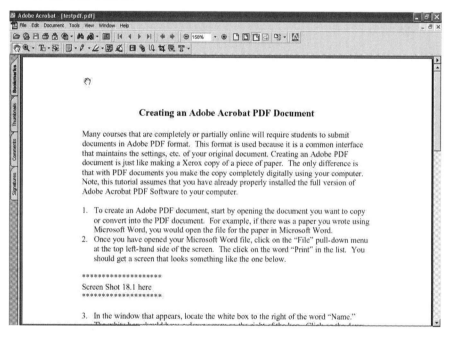

3. Now let's add a personal note to this <u>Adobe Acrobat PDF</u> document by finding the spot on the document where we want the note to appear. The personal note will act just like a Post-it note. You will paste it on the document, but you will not actually change what is in the document. To add a note, start by clicking on the Notes button located on the taskbar near the top of the screen. The Notes button should look similar to the screen below:

4. At this point, your cursor should change shape and look like a cross-hair. Once your cursor looks like a crosshair, position it where you

want the note to appear and click and drag your cursor, making a box about the right size for your note. You should get a <u>window</u> that looks similar to the one below:

5. In this box, type your personal note. Once you are done typing your note, single-click on the top left-hand corner of your note area, and it will close up and look like a Post-it note stuck to the document.

Creating an Adobe Acrobat PDF Document

Many courses that are completely or partially online will require students to submit documents in Adobe PDF format. This format is used because it is a common interface that maintains the settings, etc. of your original document. Creating an Adobe PDF document is just like making a Xerox copy of a piece of paper. The only difference is that with PDF documents you make the copy completely digitally using your computer. Note, this tutorial assumes that you have already properly installed the full version of Adobe Acrobat PDF Software to your computer.

1. To create an Adobe PDF document, start by opening the document you want to copy or convert into the PDF document. For example, if there was a paper you wrote using Microsoft Word, you would open the file for the paper in Microsoft Word.

6. You, or the person reviewing the document, can double-click on the note to open it. You can also add additional comments by double-clicking on it and typing. You can add as many individual notes throughout a document as you like.

7. Once you have added all your notes, make sure that you save the document and notes by clicking on the File <u>pull-down menu</u> and selecting either Save if you want to keep the same name or Save As if you want to change the name of the file.

Saving Favorites in Microsoft Internet Explorer

In Microsoft Internet Explorer, you can make a list of your favorite <u>webpages</u> so that you can easily find them again.

1. Go to the <u>webpage</u> that you would like to add to your Favorites list.

2. Once you have the <u>website</u> on your screen, click on the Favorites <u>pull-down menu</u>. It should look similar to the screen below:

3. Then click on the Add to Favorites option. This will add the <u>website</u> to your list of favorite <u>webpages</u>. To go back and see if it was added, click on the Favorites <u>pull-down menu</u>, and it should appear at the bottom of the list. If at any time in the future you want to visit the <u>website</u>, simply click on the <u>website</u> name in your Favorites <u>pull-down menu</u>, and it will automatically take you there.

Organizing Favorites in Microsoft Internet Explorer

Once you have started to create a list of your favorite <u>webpages</u> in Microsoft Internet Explorer, you can do several things to help you keep the list organized.

1. Click on the Favorites <u>pull-down menu</u>.

2. Then click on the Organize Favorites option. You will get a <u>window</u> that looks similar to this:

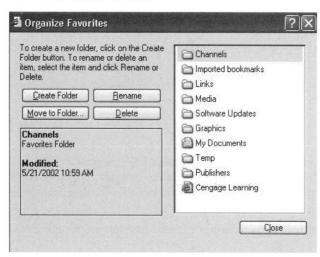

3. All your favorites and any <u>folders</u> containing favorites will be shown on the right-hand side of this <u>window</u>. From this <u>window</u>, you can create a new <u>folder</u> and give it a name. You can then put your links to your favorite <u>webpages</u> into that <u>folder</u>. For example, if you want to create a new <u>folder</u>, begin by clicking on Create Folder; a new <u>folder</u> will appear in the window. Then you give the new <u>folder</u> a name. In this example, we have named this folder Publishers. Now you have a new <u>folder</u> and can add some of your favorites to that <u>folder</u>. It should look similar to the screen below:

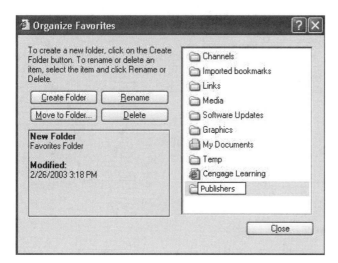

4. To add favorites to a <u>folder</u>, begin by clicking on the favorite and then clicking on Move to Folder. A new <u>window</u> will appear, which will look similar to this:

5. To move the favorite to the new <u>folder</u>, simply click on the name of the folder where you want to keep the favorite and click OK. The favorite will automatically be moved to the new <u>folder</u>. The only thing left is to click on the Close button.

6. In the future, if you want to find your favorite <u>webpage</u>, simply click on the Favorites <u>pull-down menu</u> and then click on either the favorite or the <u>folder</u> where the favorite is saved.

Caching Materials for Viewing Offline with Microsoft Internet Explorer

Microsoft Internet Explorer allows you to cache (or save) Web materials to view at a later time when you are not connected to the <u>Internet</u>. This is important if you want to cache online course materials and then read them at a different time.

1. To cache a <u>website</u> to view offline at a later time, start by going to the <u>website</u> that you want to cache. Then click on the Favorites <u>pull-down menu</u> at the top of the screen and select the Add to Favorites option. You will get a screen that looks similar to the one below:

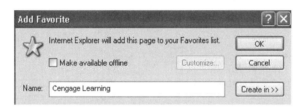

2. Click on the box to the left of the phrase "Make available offline" and then click on the OK button.

3. Before you log off, click on the Tools <u>pull-down menu</u> at the top of the screen and then select the Synchronize option.

You should get a <u>window</u> that looks similar to the one below:

4. Make sure any of the <u>webpages</u> that you want to read offline have a check mark next to them and then click on the Synchronize button. Internet Explorer will then take a couple of minutes to synchronize all the <u>websites</u> that you have selected.

5. Now, go to the File <u>pull-down menu</u> at the top of the screen and select the Work Offline option.

6. You can now log off of the <u>Internet</u>. At a future time, you can simply open Internet Explorer and select the <u>website</u> that you want to view from the Favorites list. Do this by clicking on the Favorites <u>pull-down menu</u> and selecting the <u>website</u> that you want to view. It will open up just as if you were connected to the <u>Internet</u>.

7. One note of caution—the next time you log onto Internet Explorer, make sure that the first thing you do is to go to the File <u>pull-down menu</u> at the top of the screen and select the Work Offline option. This will switch you back to working online. If you don't do this, you will remain in offline mode.

Opening New Windows in Microsoft Internet Explorer and Netscape Communicator

In Microsoft Internet Explorer and Netscape Communicator, many times you will want to have more than one <u>window</u> open at the same time so that you can view more than one <u>website</u> at the same time. This is possible by opening new <u>windows</u>.

1. To open a new <u>window</u> while in Internet Explorer or Netscape, start by clicking on the File <u>pull-down menu</u> at the top of the screen. Then select the New option and then the Window option in Internet Explorer or the Navigator Window option in Netscape. Your selections in Internet Explorer should look similar to the picture below. Your selections in Netscape (not pictured) are very similar.

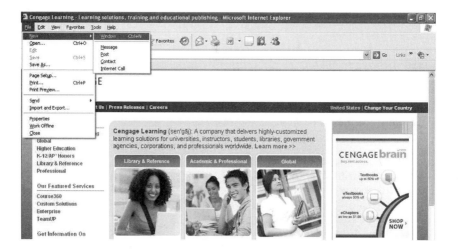

2. Now you should have a new <u>window</u>. The new <u>window</u> will initially look just like the one you left. However, you can type in a different Web address (<u>URL</u>) and go to the new <u>website</u>.

3. You can switch back and forth between <u>websites</u> by clicking on the toolbar <u>icons</u> at the bottom of the page. The toolbar in Internet Explorer should look similar to the picture below. The toolbar in Netscape (not pictured) is very similar. The different <u>websites'</u> <u>icons</u> have the Internet Explorer or Netscape symbol in front of them. (*Note:* You may have many <u>websites</u> open at once.)

Saving Bookmarks in Netscape Communicator

In Netscape Communicator, you can <u>bookmark</u> your favorite <u>webpage</u>s so that you can easily find them again. <u>Bookmark</u>ing is a great tool because it saves you a lot of time by not having to search for <u>websites</u> again and again. It also saves you time because you don't have to type in <u>website</u> addresses. Here's how to <u>bookmark</u> a <u>website</u> in Netscape:

1. Go to the <u>webpage</u> that you would like to add to your Bookmarks list.

2. Once you have the <u>website</u> on your screen, click on the Communicator <u>pull-down menu</u>. Then click on Bookmarks. Your options should look something like the screen below:

3. Then click on the Add Bookmark option. This will <u>bookmark</u> the <u>website</u>. To go back and see if it was <u>bookmark</u>ed correctly, click on the Communicator <u>pull-down menu</u> and then Bookmarks. The name of the <u>website</u> that you <u>bookmark</u>ed should appear at the bottom of the list. If at any time in the future you want to visit the <u>website</u>, simply click on the Communicator <u>pull-down menu</u>, select Bookmarks, and then click on the <u>website</u> that you want to visit, and it will automatically take you there.

Organizing Bookmarks in Netscape Communicator

Once you have started to <u>bookmark</u> your favorite <u>webpage</u>s in Netscape Communicator, you can do several things to help keep the list organized.

1. Click on the Communicator <u>pull-down menu</u> and click on Bookmarks.

2. Then click on the Edit Bookmarks option. You will get a <u>window</u> that looks similar to this:

3. All your <u>bookmark</u>ed <u>websites</u> and any <u>folder</u>s containing <u>bookmarks</u> will be shown in this <u>window</u>. From this <u>window</u>, you can create a new <u>folder</u>, give it a name, and then put your <u>bookmarks</u> into that <u>folder</u>. For example, if you want to create a new folder, begin by clicking on the File <u>pull-down menu</u>. Next, click on the New Folder option, and a new <u>folder</u> appears in the window. Then give the new <u>folder</u> a name. In this example, we have named

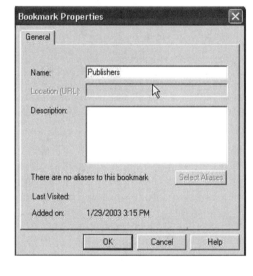

this <u>folder</u> "Publishers." Click OK and you now have a new folder that you may add some <u>bookmarks</u> to. It should look similar to the screen on the right hand side of this paragraph.

4. To add <u>bookmarks</u> to a <u>folder</u>, begin by putting your cursor over the <u>bookmark</u>. Then click and drag the <u>bookmark</u> onto the <u>folder</u> where you want it to be saved. If we were to move a <u>bookmark</u> into the Publishers <u>folder</u>, the end result would look something like the <u>window</u> below. The only thing left is to do is click on the File <u>pull-down menu</u> and then click on the Close option; your

bookmark will be saved in the new <u>folder</u>. It should look similar to the screen below:

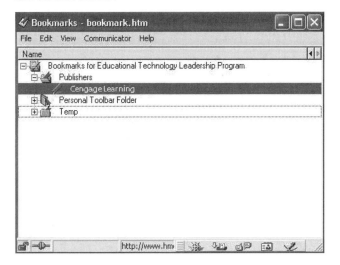

5. In the future, if you want to find your <u>bookmark</u>ed <u>webpage</u>, simply click on the Communicator <u>pull-down menu</u> and then click on Bookmarks. Then click on either the <u>bookmark</u> or the <u>folder</u> where the <u>bookmark</u> is saved.

Opening New Windows and Tabs in Mozilla Firefox

In Mozilla Firefox, many times you will want to have more than one <u>window</u> open at the same time so that you can view more than one <u>website</u> at the same time. This is possible by opening new <u>windows</u> or new tabs.

1. To open a new <u>window</u> while in Firefox, start by clicking on the File <u>pull-down menu</u> at the top of the screen. Then select the New Window option. Your selections in Firefox should look similar to the picture below.

2. Now you should have a new <u>window</u>. The new <u>window</u> will initially look just like your home page. However, you can type in a different Web address (<u>URL</u>) and go to the new <u>website</u>.

3. You can switch back and forth between <u>websites</u> by clicking on the toolbar <u>icon</u>s at the bottom of the page. The toolbar in Firefox should look similar to the picture below. The different <u>websites'</u> <u>icons</u> have the Firefox symbol in front of them. (*Note:* You may have many <u>web-sites</u> open at once.)

You can also open multiple web pages in Firefox by opening new tabs.

1. To open a new <u>tab</u> while in Firefox, start by clicking on the File <u>pull-down menu</u> at the top of the screen. Then select the New Tab option. Your selections in Firefox should look similar to the picture below.

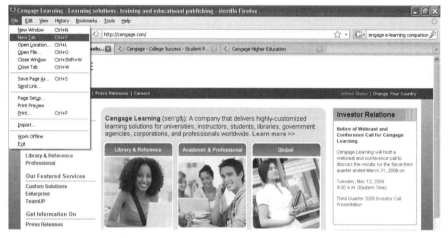

2. Now you should have a new <u>window</u>. The new <u>window</u> will initially be blank. However, you can type in a different Web address (<u>URL</u>) and go to the new <u>website</u>.

3. You can switch back and forth between <u>websites</u> by clicking on the tabs at the top of the page. The tabs in Firefox should look similar to the picture below.

Saving Bookmarks in Mozilla Firefox

In Mozilla Firefox, you can <u>bookmark</u> your favorite <u>webpages</u> so that you can easily find them again. <u>Bookmark</u>ing is a great tool because it saves you a lot of time by not having to search for <u>websites</u> again and again. It also saves you time because you don't have to type in <u>website</u> addresses. Here's how to <u>bookmark</u> a <u>website</u> in Firefox:

1. Go to the <u>webpage</u> that you would like to add to your Bookmarks list.

2. Once you have the <u>website</u> on your screen, click on the Bookmarks <u>pull-down menu</u>. Then click on Bookmark This Page. Your options should look something like the screen below:

3. This will <u>bookmark</u> the <u>website</u>. To go back and see if it was <u>bookmark</u>ed correctly, click on the Bookmarks <u>pull-down menu</u>. The name of the <u>website</u> that you <u>bookmark</u>ed should appear at the bottom of the list. If at any time in the future you want to visit the <u>website</u>, simply click on the Bookmarks <u>pull-down menu</u> and then click on the <u>website</u> that you want to visit, and it will automatically take you there.

Organizing Bookmarks in Mozilla Firefox

Once you have started to <u>bookmark</u> your favorite <u>webpage</u>s in Firefox, you can do several things to help keep the list organized.

1. Click on the Bookmarks <u>pull-down menu</u>.

2. Then click on the Organize Bookmarks option. You will get a <u>window</u> that looks similar to this:

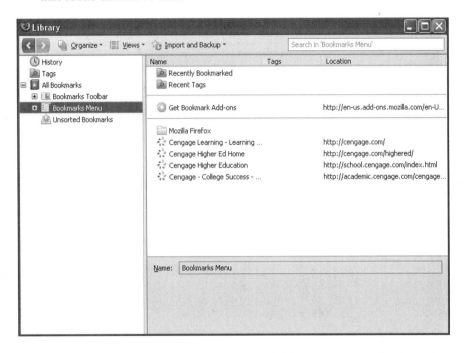

3. All your <u>bookmarked</u> <u>websites</u> and any <u>folders</u> containing <u>bookmarks</u> will be shown in this <u>window</u>. From this <u>window</u>, you can create a new <u>folder</u>, give it a name, and then put your <u>bookmarks</u> into that <u>folder</u>. For example, if you want to create a new folder, begin by clicking on the Organize <u>pull-down menu</u>. Next, click on the New Folder option, and a new <u>folder</u> appears in the window. Then give the new <u>folder</u> a name. In this example, we have named this <u>folder</u> "Cengage." Click OK and you now have a new folder that you may add some <u>bookmarks</u> to. It should look similar to the screen below.

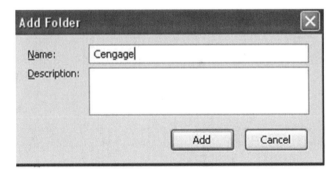

4. To add <u>bookmarks</u> to a <u>folder</u>, begin by selecting Bookmarks Menu. Then click and drag the <u>bookmark</u> onto the <u>folder</u> where you want it to be saved. It should look similar to the screen below:

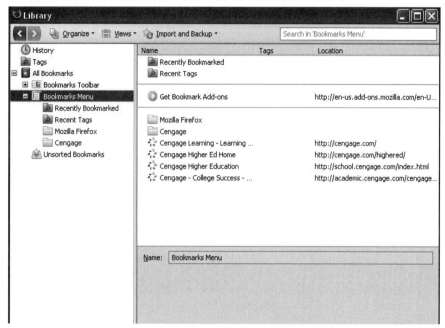

5. In the future, if you want to find your <u>bookmarked</u> <u>webpage</u>, simply click on the Bookmarks <u>pull-down menu</u> and then click on either the <u>bookmark</u> or the <u>folder</u> where the bookmark is saved.

Finding Your Course Materials in Blackboard

Once you have logged in to your course in Blackboard, it is important to understand where you will find your course materials (announcements, calendars, lectures, and so on). The location of these items may vary from course to course, but there are some general guidelines that you can follow.

1. To begin, start by exploring the buttons found on the left-hand side of the screen.

2. Below is a general idea of what you might find when exploring each of these areas.

ANNOUNCEMENTS: This link includes announcements from your course instructor and those people who maintain the Blackboard system for your school. These announcements can be very important, so check them regularly.

COURSE INFORMATION: This link is where you might find general course information such as the name of the course, how many credits it is worth, and when it meets.

STAFF INFORMATION: This link includes information about your course instructor and teaching assistants. Check here for information about office hours.

COURSE DOCUMENTS: This link is where you will find a lot of the materials relating to the course. These items are similar to course lectures, such as papers that you should read and lecture notes from your instructor.

ASSIGNMENTS: This link is where your assignments will be located. Obviously, this is a very important part of the course site.

COMMUNICATION: This link is where you will find things like how to send an <u>email</u> to your classmates or instructor, the virtual <u>discussion board</u>, the virtual classroom or <u>chat</u>, the class roster, and group pages.

DISCUSSION BOARD: This link is a shortcut to the same <u>discussion board</u> that you might find under the Communication button. The Discussion Board is very important because this is where you share thoughts and ideas with everyone in the course by posting messages and replying to others' messages.

GROUPS: If you are assigned to a group, this link is where your group will access important information.

EXTERNAL LINKS: This link is where you will find external links to other <u>websites</u> that are important to your course.

TOOLS: This link allows you to do many things such as putting assignments into the digital drop box, editing your **homepage** and personal information, maintaining your personal and course calendar, checking your grades, and keeping an address book.

RESOURCES: This link is a button that might link you to other general resources that may or may not be specifically course related. For example, some instructors might put recommended readings here.

COURSE MAP: This link provides you with a map of what is in your course. Some people like to use this to navigate quickly through the material that you are expected to cover in the course.

Sending an Email and Adding an Attachment in Blackboard

One of the most important items when working online is the ability to communicate with classmates and your instructor. A great way to do so is by using the <u>email</u> function in Blackboard.

1. To send an <u>email</u> using Blackboard, begin by clicking on the Communication button located on the left-hand side of the screen.

Then, in the middle of the screen, click on the option that says Send E-mail.

2. Once you have selected Send E-mail, in the middle of the screen are several options about who to send your <u>email</u> to. For example, you might have the option of sending it to everyone in the class, or just a certain student or group, or to your course instructor.

3. If you want to send an <u>email</u> to your course instructor(s), begin by clicking on the All Instructors link. You should get a screen that looks like the one below (but with your <u>email</u> address in the From: line and your instructor's name in the To: line).

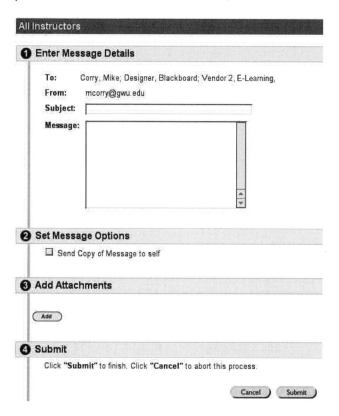

4. At this point, fill in the Subject: line of the <u>email</u> and the Message: area. Now, before you send your <u>email</u>, other options are also available to you, including adding a file <u>attachment</u> to the <u>email</u>. If you wish to add an <u>attachment</u> to your <u>email</u>, click on the Add button under the Add Attachments section. If you do not wish to add an <u>attachment</u> to the <u>email</u>, simply click on the Submit button, and your <u>email</u> will be sent.

5. If you wish to add an <u>attachment</u> to the <u>email</u> message and you have clicked on the Add button under the Add Attachments section, then you should have a screen that looks similar to this:

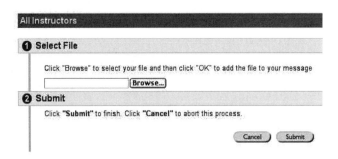

6. Next, click on the Browse button and find the file that you wish to attach. Once you have located and chosen the file to attach, the <u>file name</u> should show up in the box to the left of the Browse button.

7. Then simply click on the Submit button, and your <u>email</u> and <u>attachment</u> will be sent.

Turning In Assignments in Blackboard

As you work your way through college, you will probably be required to turn in assignments online from time to time. Many courses will have you do this using the Digital Drop Box in Blackboard. The Digital Drop Box is like a mailbox slot where you drop off items for your instructor.

1. To submit an assignment using the Digital Drop Box, begin by clicking on the Tools or Course Tools button on the left-hand side of the screen.

2. Then click on the Digital Drop Box option.

3. Once you have selected Digital Drop Box, submit your assignment to your instructor by clicking on the Send File button.

4. At this point, fill in the Title box and the Comments area with information about your assignment. Next, click on the Browse button and find the assignment file that you wish to send to your instructor. Once

you have located and chosen the file to send, the <u>file name</u> should show up in the box to the left of the Browse button.

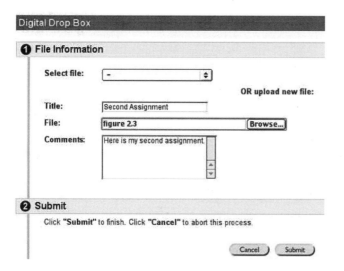

5. Then simply click on the Submit button. Your assignment will be sent to your instructor, and a message will be sent to your <u>email</u> account confirming that your assignment was sent successfully.

Participating in the Virtual Classroom or Chat in Blackboard

One of the most exciting things about Blackboard is the ability to have <u>synchronous</u> conversations with other classmates or your instructor using the Virtual Classroom or Chat function. <u>Synchronous</u> means that the conversations are occurring in real time with all participants in the <u>chat</u> room at the same time.

1. To participate in a <u>chat</u> session, begin by clicking on the Communication button on the left-hand side of the screen.

2. Then click on the Virtual Classroom option.

3. Once you have selected the Virtual Classroom button, click on the Enter Virtual Classroom or Join buttons. You may get a message at this point indicating that it is loading the Chat software. This may take

a couple of minutes. Once the Chat software loads, it should look similar to the following screen:

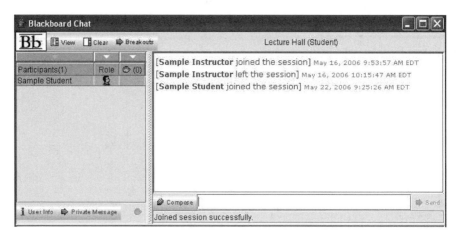

4. To have a <u>synchronous</u> conversation with others who are in the <u>chat</u> room, simply type in your question or comment in the blank box labeled Compose at the bottom of the screen and click on the Send button. Your message will then appear in the box just above where you originally typed it. Everyone in the <u>chat</u> room will then see the message.

5. On the left-hand side of the screen, you will see a list of everyone who is in the <u>chat</u> room. Before you start sending messages, it's a good idea to find out who is there.

6. You can also send a private message directly anyone in the <u>chat</u> room by clicking on the Private Message button. Then type your question in the box that pops open on the screen. Click on the Send button to send the private message.

7. To leave the <u>chat</u> room, click on the "X" at the top right-hand corner of the screen.

Posting to a Discussion Board in Blackboard

One of the most common tools used in online learning is the <u>discussion board</u>. <u>Discussion board</u>s allow students and instructors to carry on conversations over a period of time.

1. To post to the <u>discussion board</u> in Blackboard, begin by clicking on the Communication button on the left-hand side of the screen.

2. Then in the middle of the screen, click on the Discussion Board option.

3. Once you have selected Discussion Board, you will see all the discussion topics or forums that have been created. To post a message to a

particular discussion forum, click on the name of the discussion that you want to post to. This will take you to a screen that will look similar to the one below:

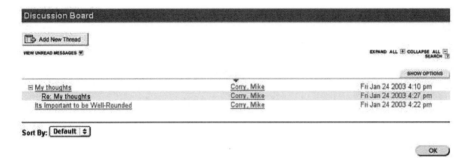

4. In <u>discussion board</u>s, messages are usually organized by <u>threads</u>, a common topic that more than one person wants to comment on. That keeps everyone interested in a certain topic involved by posting messages at the same place to the same <u>thread</u>. If you want to add your own comments or start a <u>thread</u>, click on the Add New Thread button at the top of the screen. You will get a screen that looks similar to the one below:

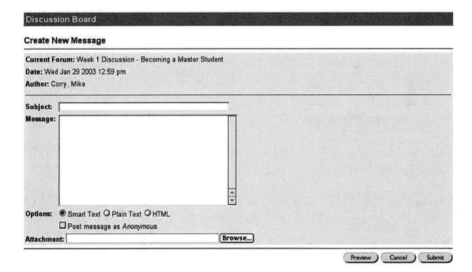

5. In this screen, fill in the Subject: box with the subject of the <u>thread</u> and fill in the Message; box with your first message in the <u>thread</u>. Then click on the Submit button, your <u>thread</u> will be created, and your message added.

6. Now, in the middle of the screen, you can see any <u>thread</u>s and messages that have already been posted to this discussion forum. You may read those messages by simply clicking on the title

of the message. They will look similar to the screen on the following page.

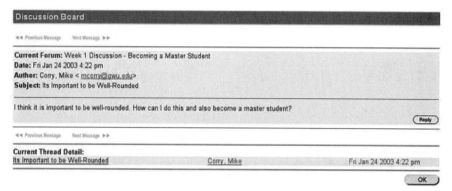

7. You can respond or reply to anyone else's message after reading it by clicking on the Reply button. After you have selected the Reply button, type your message in the message box and click on the Submit button. Your reply to someone else's message will now be posted.

Finding Your Course Documents and Assignments in Blackboard

It is very important for you to be able to find your course materials or documents in any online course.

1. To find your course materials in Blackboard, begin by clicking on the Course Documents or Course Materials button on the left-hand side of the screen.

2. Then in the middle of the screen, you will see the course materials that have been prepared by your instructor:

3. Your course materials may be listed as a series of links to documents. If this is the case, simply click on the title of the document to access it.

4. Another important location in Blackboard that may contain course materials is in the Assignments area. To access the Assignments area, begin by clicking on the Assignments button on the left-hand side of the screen.

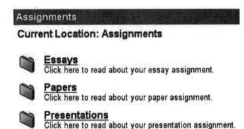

5. Then in the middle of the screen, you will see the assignments that have been prepared by your instructor.

6. Again, your course assignments may be listed as a series of links to documents. If this is the case, simply click on the title of the document to access it.

Finding Your Assignment Grades and Feedback in Blackboard

HOW TO
26

Almost all students want to know about their grades. Blackboard provides a simple way of checking your grades.

1. To find your grades in Blackboard, begin by clicking on the Tools or Course Tools button on the left-hand side of the screen.

2. Then, in the middle of the screen, click on the My Grades option.

📖 View Grades

Item Name	Date	Grade	Points Possible:	Average Score	Weight:
Class Section	7/19/04	–	0	0	0%
P.01.01-Set01	11/18/03	=	16	0	0%
P.01.02-Set01	11/18/03	=	4	0	0%
P.01.03-Set01	11/18/03	=	6	0	0%
P.01.00-Set01	11/18/03	=	26	0	0%
P.02.02-Set01	11/18/03	=	18	0	0%
P.02.02-Set01	11/18/03	=	8	0	0%
P.02.03-Set01	11/18/03	=	16	0	0%

3. Once you have clicked on My Grades, in the middle of the screen, you will see all the information about your grade in the course. This includes both summary information as well as detailed information.

4. Some instructors may also provide feedback on assignments that you submitted using the Digital Drop Box. If this is the case, you can access that feedback by clicking on the Tools or Course Tools button on the left-hand side of the screen.

5. Then in the middle of the screen, click on the Digital Drop Box option. Any feedback sent back to you from your instructor would

be listed in this area. You can access the file by clicking on the name of the file.

 Finding Your Course Materials in WebCT

Once you have logged in to your course in WebCT, it is important to understand where you will find your course materials (announcements, calendars, lectures, and so on). The location of these items may vary from course to course, but there are some general guidelines you can follow.

1. To begin, start by exploring the buttons found on the left-hand side of the screen.

2. Below is a general idea of what you might find when exploring each of these areas:

HOMEPAGE: This link provides a general overview for the course, and the information will vary depending on what your instructor decides to include. Some links that you might find here include those to the start of the course, quizzes, course lectures (content), and external links. (*Note:* Some links on the <u>homepage</u> might be duplicated under other links on the left-hand side of the page—for example, course lectures found in Course Content.)

E-LEARNING HUB: This link is where you might find general information and resources about e-learning. This may include frequently asked questions and answers, articles about e-learning, and how to use WebCT.

CALENDAR: This link will include a calendar that you can use to organize your schedule and the schedule for the course. The calendar might include dates for assignments, readings, and quizzes.

STUDENT HOMEPAGES: This link is where you will find an area where you can create and maintain your own <u>homepage</u>. You can also view the <u>homepages</u> of other students in the class.

DISCUSSIONS: The <u>discussion board</u> is very important because this link is where you can share thoughts and ideas with everyone in the course by posting messages and replying to other's messages.

MAIL: This link is where you can send an <u>email</u> to your classmates or instructor. This is a very important area when communicating in the course.

CHAT: This link is where you can go to participate in a <u>synchronous (real-time) chat</u> with other classmates and your instructor. Again, this can be a very important part of course communication.

COURSE CONTENT: This link is where you will find a large majority of the course materials (lectures, readings, and so on). You will probably spend a lot of time in this part of the course site.

ASSIGNMENTS: This link is where you will find more information about your course assignments. This might include directions, due dates, how to submit an assignment, and others

3. In addition to the links on the left-hand side of the page, many WebCT courses will provide a link at the top of the screen to the Course Map. This will give you an overview of the entire course. You might find the course map useful when trying to navigate through the course.

Sending an Email and Adding an Attachment in WebCT

One of the most important items when working online is the ability to communicate with classmates and your instructor. A great way to do so is by using the email function in WebCT.

1. To send an email using WebCT, begin by clicking on the Mail button located on the left-hand side of the screen.

2. Then in the middle of the screen, click on the Compose Mail Message option. It should look similar to the screen below:

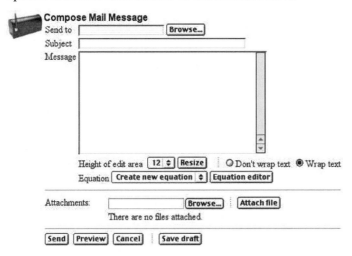

3. Once you have clicked on Compose Mail Message, a new window will open, and you will have several options about who to send your email to. For example, you might have the option of sending it to everyone in the class, to a certain student, to a specific group, or to your course instructor(s).

4. If you want to send an email to your course instructor(s), begin by clicking on the Browse button to the right of the Send to box. You should get a screen that looks something like the one on the right hand side of this page. Click on the name of your instructor and then click on the Done button.

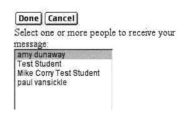

5. At this point, you should fill in the Subject line of the <u>email</u> and the Message area. Now, before you send your <u>email</u>, other options are also available to you, including adding a file <u>attachment</u> to the <u>email</u>. If you do not wish to add an <u>attachment</u> to the <u>email</u>, simply click on the Send button, and your <u>email</u> will be sent. If you wish to add an <u>attachment</u> to your <u>email</u>, click on the Browse button to the right of the Attachments box. If you wish to add an attachment to the <u>email</u> message and you have clicked on the Browse button to the right of the Attachments box, then you should have a screen that looks similar to this:

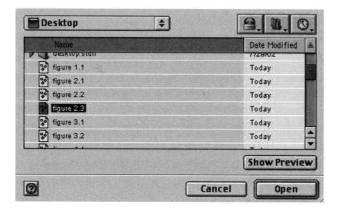

6. At this point, find the file that you wish to attach. Once you have located and chosen the file to attach, click on the Open button and the <u>file name</u> should show up in the box to the left of the Browse button.

7. Now, click on the Attach File button and the name of your attached file should be seen below the Browse button.

8. Then, simply click on the Send button, and your <u>email</u> and <u>attachment</u> will be sent.

Turning In Assignments in WebCT

As you work your way through your course, you will probably need to turn in assignments. Many courses will have you do this using the Upload or Submit features in WebCT.

1. To submit an assignment in WebCT, begin by clicking on the Assignments button on the left-hand side of the screen.

2. Then in the middle of the screen, click on the name of the assignment that you are submitting. You should then see a screen that looks similar to the one below (you may have to scroll down):

Online Becoming a Master Student, 2/e by Gray/Ellis: CORRY01
Home › Assignments › Second Assignment

Assignment: Second Assignment
Return to Assignments

Assignment Information

Maximum grade	100
Due date	March 29, 2003
Instructions	Submit Your Second Assignment Here
Assignment files	None
Submissions	You can only submit your assignment once. No re-submission is permitted.
Notification	The instructor will not be notified via email when you submit this assignment.

Submit Assignment

Status	Not Submitted
Student files	None
	To upload your completed assignment, click **Upload file**.
	[Upload file] [Remove files]
Notification	If you want to be notified when your assignment has been successfully submitted, enter your email address
	[ ]
	After you have uploaded your completed assignment, you must click **Submit assignment**.
	[Submit assignment]

3. At this point, click on the Upload file button. Then click on the Browse button to the right of the Filename box.

4. At this point, you should find the assignment file that you wish to send to your instructor and click on the Open button. Once you have located and chosen the file to send, the file name should show up in the box to the left of the Browse button. Now click on the Upload button. You should get a screen that looks similar to the one below.

Online Becoming a Master Student, 2/e by Gray/Ellis: CORRY01
Home › Assignments › Second Assignment

Assignment: Second Assignment
Return to Assignments

Assignment Information

Maximum grade	100
Due date	March 29, 2003
Instructions	Submit Your Second Assignment Here
Assignment files	None
Submissions	You can only submit your assignment once. No re-submission is permitted.
Notification	The instructor will not be notified via email when you submit this assignment.

Submit Assignment

Status	Not Submitted
Student files	To view a file, click its filename.

Files	Modification Date	Size
☐ figure 2.3	January 29, 2003 1:22pm	42.1 kB

	To upload your completed assignment, click **Upload file**
	[Upload file] [Remove files]
Notification	If you want to be notified when your assignment has been successfully submitted, enter your email address
	[ ]
	After you have uploaded your completed assignment, you must click **Submit assignment**.
	[Submit assignment]

5. Then, simply check the box to the left of your <u>file name</u> and click on the Submit assignment button, and your assignment will be sent to your instructor. If you want an <u>email</u> confirmation, fill in your <u>email</u> address in the appropriate box before submitting the assignment.

Participating in Chat in WebCT

One of the most exciting things about WebCT is the ability to have <u>synchronous</u> conversations with other classmates or your instructor using the Chat function. <u>Synchronous</u> means that the conversations are occurring in real time with all participants in the <u>chat</u> room at the same time.

1. To participate in a <u>chat</u> session, begin by clicking on the Chat button on the left-hand side of the screen.

2. Then in the middle of the screen, you may have several <u>chat</u> rooms available for your use. They should look something like the screen below. Click on one of them. In this example, we are going to click on the Room 1 link.

Room 1

Room 2

Room 3

Room 4

General Chat for Master Student Online 2006-2007

General Chat for All Courses

3. Once you have clicked on Room 1, you will get a new <u>window</u>. It should look similar to the screen below:

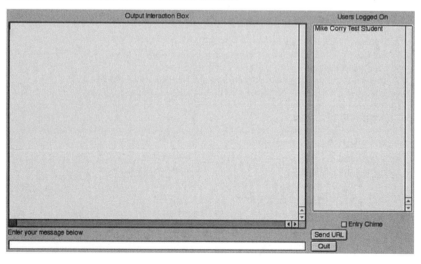

4. The box on the right-hand side of the screen lists the users currently in that <u>chat</u> room.

5. To have a <u>synchronous</u> conversation with others who are in the <u>chat</u> room, simply type in your question or comment in the blank box at the very bottom of the screen and press Enter. The question or comment will then appear above in the Output Interaction Box for everyone in the <u>chat</u> room to see and respond to.

6. At the bottom right-hand side of the screen is the Send URL button. You may go to a <u>website</u> by clicking on that button and then typing in the <u>website</u> address in the blank box that appears. The <u>website</u> will be opened in a new <u>window</u>. Others in the <u>chat</u> room can also view the <u>website</u>, and you can comment on it.

7. To leave the <u>chat</u> room, click on the Quit button at the bottom right-hand corner of the screen.

T30, T31

Posting to a Discussion Board in WebCT

HOW TO
31

One of the most common tools used in online learning is the <u>discussion board</u>. <u>Discussion boards</u> allow students and instructors to carry on conversations over a period of time.

1. To post to the <u>discussion board</u> in WebCT, begin by clicking on the Discussions button on the left-hand side of the screen. You should see a screen similar to the one below:

Online Becoming a Master Student, 2/e by Gray/Ellis: CORRY01
Home ▸ Discussions

Select a topic to see its messages

Compose Discussion Message   Search   Topic Settings

Topic	Unread	Total	Status
All	3	5	
Main	3	5	public, unlocked
Notes	0	0	public, unlocked

2. Then in the middle of the screen, click on All under Topic. Your screen should look similar to the one below:

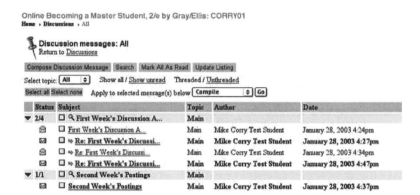

3. You should now see all discussion topics or forums that have been created. If the arrow(s) on the left-hand side is/are not pointing downwards, then click on it, and it will point down. This allows you to see all the postings in the discussion area. To post a message to a particular discussion forum, click on the name of the discussion that you want to post to. This will take you to a screen that will look similar to the one below:

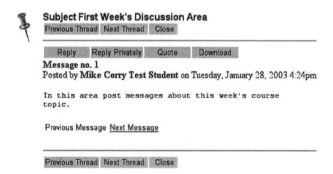

4. Now click on the Reply button and type in your message in the Message box. When you are satisfied with your entry, click the Post button. Your reply to the previous message will be posted, and you will be taken back to the main discussion board screen.

5. In discussion boards, messages are usually organized by threads, a common topic that more than one person wants to comment on. This keeps everyone interested in a certain topic up to date by posting messages at the same place to the same thread. If you want to add your own message or start a new thread, click on the Compose Discussion Message button at the top of the main discussion board screen. You will get a screen that looks similar to the one below:

Compose Discussion Message

Topic   [Main ‡]

Subject [_____]

Message

Height of edit area [12 ‡] [Resize]   ○ Don't wrap text ● Wrap text

Equation [Create new equation ‡] [Equation editor]

Attachments: [_____] [Browse...]   [Attach file]

There are no files attached.

[Post] [Preview] [Cancel]

T31, T32

6. In this screen, fill in the Subject box with the subject of the <u>thread</u> and fill in the Message box with first message in the <u>thread</u>. Then click on the Post button, and your <u>thread</u> will be created and your message added.

7. Now, in the middle of the screen, you can see any <u>thread</u>s and messages that have already been posted to this discussion forum. You can read those messages by simply clicking on the title of the message.

Finding Your Course Content in WebCT

It is very important for you to be able to find your course materials or documents in any online course. In WebCT, course materials or documents can be found fairly easily.

1. To find your course materials in WebCT, begin by clicking on the Course Content button on the left-hand side of the screen.

2. Then in the middle of the screen, you will see the course materials that have been prepared by your instructor.

3. Your course materials may be listed as a series of links to documents. If this is the case, simply click on the title of the document to access it. It should be similar to the screen show below:

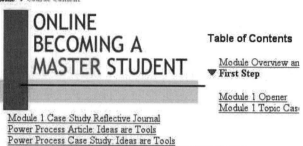

Online Becoming a Master Student, 2/e by Gray/Ellis: CORRY0

Home › Course Content

ONLINE BECOMING A MASTER STUDENT

Table of Contents

Module Overview an
▼ **First Step**

Module 1 Opener
Module 1 Topic Cas

Module 1 Case Study Reflective Journal
Power Process Article: Ideas are Tools
Power Process Case Study: Ideas are Tools
Power Process Case Study: Ideas are Tools Reflective Journal
Module 1 Emotional Intelligence Scenario

▼ **Time**

Module 2 Opener
Module 2 Topic Case Study
Module 2 Case Study Reflective Journal
Power Process Article: Be Here Now
Power Process Case Study: Be Here Now
Power Process Case Study: Be Here Now Reflective Journal
Module 2 Emotional Intelligence Scenario

▼ **Memory**

Module 3 Opener

4. Another important location in WebCT that may contain course materials is in the Assignments area. To access the Assignments area, begin by clicking on the Assignments button on the left-hand side of the screen.

5. Then in the middle of the screen, you will see the assignments that have been prepared by your instructor.

6. Again, your course assignments may be listed as a series of links to documents. If this is the case, simply click on the title of the document to access it.

Finding Your Assignment Grades and Feedback in WebCT

Almost all students want to know about their grades. WebCT provides a simple way of checking your grades.

1. To find your grades in WebCT, begin by clicking on the Assignments button on the left-hand side of the screen.

2. Then in the middle of the screen, you will see all the assignments that you have submitted. If they have been graded, it will say "Graded" under the Status column, and the grade will appear under the Grade column. It should be similar to the screen below:

Online Becoming a Master Student, 2/e by Gray/Ellis: CORRY01

Home ▸ Assignments

Assignments

Current date: January 29, 2003 1:29pm

Title	Availability	Grade	Status
First Assignment	From: Immediately Due: January 28, 2003 5:00pm	98 / 100	Graded
Second Assignment	From: Immediately Due: March 29, 2003 1:00pm	-- / 100	Not Submitted

3. To see more detailed feedback about the assignment, click on the Graded link. There may be instructor comments included in this detailed feedback, or you may want to open the graded file and look for comments there. To open the graded file, click on the <u>file name</u> under the Files column in the Graded Files section of the screen.

Finding Your Course Materials in eCollege

Once you have logged in to your course in eCollege, it is important to know where you will find your course materials (announcements, calendars, lectures, and so on). The location of these items may vary from course to course, but there are some general guidelines you can follow.

1. To begin, start by exploring the buttons found on the left-hand side and at the top of the screen.

2. Below is a general idea of what you might find when exploring buttons found on the left-hand side of the screen:

   ANNOUNCEMENTS: This link will include announcements from your course instructor and those people who maintain the eCollege system for your school. These announcements can be very important, so check them regularly.

   COURSE HOME: This link is where you might find general course information like the course syllabus, calendar, and a glossary of terms related to the course.

   COURSE CONTENT: These links may take on a variety of names, but in general they will be links to course content (for example, Chapter 1).

3. Below is a general idea of what you might find when exploring buttons found on the top of the screen:

   GRADEBOOK: Information in this area might include any grades that you have earned in the course and feedback on assignments from your instructor.

   EMAIL: This is the link to the area of eCollege where you can send <u>email</u>s to your course instructor or other members of the course.

For the most current version of eCollege® products and services, please visit ecollege.com

CHAT: This is where you can communicate in real time with your course instructor or other members of the course.

DOCUMENT SHARING: In this area, students and instructors can upload and <u>download</u> documents for public viewing and to share with each other.

DROP BOX: This area is used for students to submit assignments to their instructors. If the instructor has linked the Drop Box to the Gradebook, your submission will be recorded automatically.

WEBLIOGRAPHY: This area functions like an online bibliography. In many cases, instructors will post links to <u>websites</u> in this area.

Sending an Email and Adding an Attachment in eCollege

One of the most important aspects when working online is the ability to communicate with classmates and your instructor. A great way to do so is by using the <u>email</u> function in eCollege.

1. To send an email using eCollege, begin by clicking on the Email button located on the tool bar at the top of the screen. You will be taken to a screen similar to the one below:

2. The first item on the screen will be a list of Select Recipients from which you will choose either specific individuals, All Class, or groups that your <u>email</u> will go to. (You can create groups, which allow you to send to a large number of people—for instance your class—without having to select each individually.) Chosen recipients will then appear in the Recipients box.

3. At this point, you should fill in the Subject line of the <u>email</u> and the Message area. Before you send your <u>email</u>, other options are also available to you, including adding a file <u>attachment</u> to the <u>email</u>. If you wish to add an <u>attachment</u> to your <u>email</u>, click on the Browse button under the Attachments section. If you do not wish to add an <u>attachment</u> to the <u>email</u>, simply click on the Submit button, and your email will be sent.

4. If you wish to add an <u>attachment</u> to the <u>email</u> message, click on the Browse button next to the Attachments section.

5. Once you have located and chosen the file to attach, the <u>file name</u> should show up in the box to the left of the Open button. Click on the "Open" button to attach the file to your <u>email</u>.

6. Then, simply click on the Send Email button, and your <u>email</u> and <u>attachment</u> will be sent.

Turning In Assignments in eCollege

As you work your way through your course, you will probably need to turn in assignments from time to time. Many courses will have you do this using the Drop Box in eCollege. The Drop Box is like a mailbox slot where you drop off items for your instructor.

1. To submit an assignment using the Drop Box, begin by clicking on the Drop Box button on the top of the screen.

2. In the middle of the screen, you will see that Drop Box will have an Inbox and Outbox listing any items that you may have submitted, along with the time, date, and grade if your instructor has graded it. It should look something like the screen below:

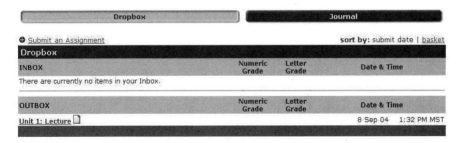

3. Submit assignments to your instructor by first clicking on the Submit an Assignment button. A screen should open that looks like the following:

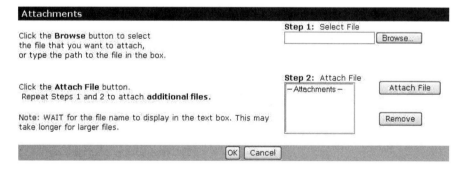

4. Click the Submit to Basket <u>pull-down menu</u> to select the correct assignment. Your instructor should create a basket for each assignment (only those assignments for which your instructor has created a basket can be submitted through the Drop Box). Fill in the Comments area with information about your assignment. To attach your assignment file, begin by clicking on the Add Attachments button. You should get a screen that is similar to the one below:

5. In the Step 1 section, click on the Browse button to select your assignment file. Once the name of your assignment file appears in the box to the left of the Browse button, then click on the Attach File button. Now the name of your assignment file should appear in the box below the Step 2 title. Once you have completed these steps, click on the OK button.

6. Now, simply click on the Submit button, and your assignment and comments (if any) will be sent to your instructor.

Participating in Chat in eCollege

Within your eCollege course, you have the ability to participate in <u>synchro-</u><u>nous</u> conversations with other classmates or your instructor using the Chat function. <u>Synchronous</u> means that the conversations are occurring in real time with all participants in the <u>chat</u> room at the same time.

1. To participate in a <u>chat</u> session, begin by clicking on the Chat button on the top of the screen.

2. In the middle of the screen, the Chat button will be highlighted.

3. Click on the Enter Main button. You will be brought to a screen listing all existing <u>chat</u> rooms. Click on the <u>chat</u> room that you would like to enter. Once you enter into a <u>chat</u> room, it should look something like the screen below:

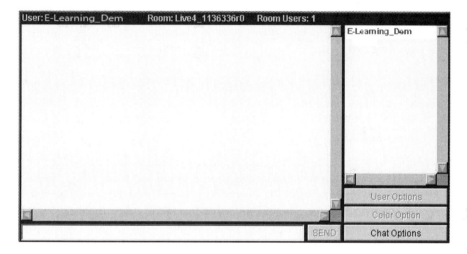

4. The box on the right-hand side of the screen lists the users currently in that <u>chat</u> room. It is always a good idea to know who is in the <u>chat</u> room before you begin your conversations.

5. To have a <u>synchronous</u> conversation with others who are in the <u>chat</u> room, simply type in your question or comment in the blank box to the left of the Send button. Then simply click on the Send button. The question or comment will then appear for everyone in the <u>chat</u> room to see and respond to.

6. You can also send a private message directly to anyone in the <u>chat</u> room by clicking on their name in the list on the right-hand side. A new <u>window</u> will open. Type your private message in the area provided. Then click the Submit button to send the private message.

7. To leave the <u>chat</u> room, click on the Back button at the top left-hand corner of the screen.

Posting to a Discussion Board in eCollege

One of the most common tools used in online learning is the <u>discussion board</u>. <u>Discussion boards</u> in eCollege allow students and instructors to carry on conversations over a period of time in an <u>asynchronous</u> format—that is, the conversation is not occurring in real time. Depending on how your instructor has designed your course, the discussion area could be on the course <u>homepage</u> or within the content/lectures.

1. Once you locate the discussion area, you might see several discussion topics. To begin, click on discussion topic in which you wish to post a message. You should see a screen that looks something like the following:

Discussion

⊕ <u>Respond</u>

▷ <u>Expand All</u> ▷ <u>Show Options</u>	sort by: response | <u>author</u> | <u>date</u> | <u>read</u> | <u>unread</u>	
Responses	**Author**	**Date & Time**
▷ ☑ <u>Discuss how you plan to use yo</u>	Kristina Nelson	2 Aug 05 2:42 PM MST
↳▷ ☑ <u>Kristina wrote, "I think one w</u>	Crystal Neal	5 Aug 05 8:43 AM MST
↳▷ ☑ <u>That sounds like Kristina Nels</u>	Kristina Leonard	9 Aug 05 9:54 AM MST
↳▷ ☑ <u>Hi Everyone,</u>	Jill Legare	12 Aug 05 11:14 AM MST
↳▷ ☑ <u>Jill, I agree...encouraging st</u>	Lisa Siracuse	28 Aug 05 11:27 AM MST
▷ ☑ <u>Concerning Student Retention:</u>	Jeff Borden	2 Aug 05 4:04 PM MST
↳▷ ☑ <u>Hello, Jeff. I liked your dis</u>	Kristina Nelson	3 Aug 05 1:49 PM MST
↳▷ ☑ <u>Hello Jeff and Kristy,</u>	Kristina Leonard	3 Aug 05 4:07 PM MST
↳▷ ☑ <u>No problem, Kristina.</u>	Kristina Nelson	4 Aug 05 1:06 PM MST

2. In <u>discussion boards</u>, messages are usually organized by <u>threads</u>, a common topic that more than one person wants to comment on. That keeps everyone interested in a certain topic connected by posting messages at the same place to the same <u>thread</u>. If you want to add your own comments or start a <u>thread</u>, click on the Respond button at the top of the screen. You will get a screen that looks similar to the one below:

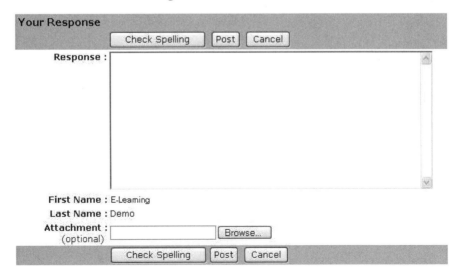

Your Response

Check Spelling · Post · Cancel

Response :

First Name : E-Learning
Last Name : Demo
Attachment : [   ] Browse...
(optional)

Check Spelling · Post · Cancel

3. In this screen, fill in the Response box with the message you wish to post to the discussion <u>thread</u>. Then click on the Post button, and your <u>thread</u> will be created and your message added.

4. Now, in the middle of the screen, you can see any <u>threads</u> and messages that have already been posted to this discussion forum. You can read those messages by simply clicking on the message.

5. You can respond or reply to anyone else's message after reading it by clicking on the Respond button at the end of the message. After you click on the Respond button, type your message in the Response box and click on the Post button. Your reply to someone else's message will now be posted.

T38, T39, T40

Finding Your Course Documents and Assignments in eCollege

HOW TO 39

It is very important for you to be able to find your course materials or documents in any online course. They may consist of lectures, presentations, spreadsheets, and so on.

1. To find your course materials in eCollege, begin by examining the buttons on the left-hand side of the screen on the course <u>homepage</u>. In many courses, the course materials are listed as a series of links to documents.

2. Once you identify the course documents, click on any one that you wish to examine more thoroughly. The course materials that have been prepared by your instructor will be displayed in the middle of the screen.

3. Another important location in eCollege that may contain course materials is in the Assignments area. To access the Assignments area, begin by clicking on the Assignments button on the left-hand side of the screen.

4. Then in the middle of the screen, you will see the assignments that have been prepared by your instructor.

5. Again, your course assignments may be listed as a series of links to documents. If this is the case, simply click on the title of the document to access it.

Finding Your Assignment Grades and Feedback in eCollege

HOW TO 40

Almost all students want to know about their grades. eCollege provides a simple way of checking your grades.

1. To find your grades in eCollege, begin by clicking on the Gradebook button on the top of the screen.

2. Then in the middle of the screen, you will see all the assignments that you have submitted. If they have been graded, the grade will appear under the Assignment column. It should be similar to the screen below:

Gradebook for E-Learning Demo						
	Course Content				**Achieved Points (Average)**	**Points Possible**
	Assessment	Assignment	Assignment	Assignment		
Unit 1	--	*	*	*	*	n/a
Unit 2	50	*	*		50	n/a
Unit 3	--	*	*		*	n/a
Unit 4	--	*	*		*	n/a
Unit 5	--		*	*	*	n/a
Achieved Points	50	0	0	0	50	
Points Possible	n/a	n/a	n/a	n/a	n/a	

* Indicates an ungraded item

3. To see more detailed feedback about the assignment, click on the grade or score in the Gradebook.

Finding Your Course Materials in Angel

Once you have logged in to your course in Angel, it is important to know where you will find your course materials (announcements, calendars, lectures, and so on). The location of these items may vary from course to course, but there are some general guidelines you can follow.

1. To begin, start by exploring the buttons found at the top of the screen.

2. Below is a general idea of what you might find when exploring buttons found on the top of the screen:

COURSE: This tab is where you might find links to general course information like the course syllabus, announcements, calendar, and course activity.

CALENDAR: This tab is where you might find the course calendar. You can view it by day, week, month or year. The calendar may contain links to assignments, tests and other course activities.

LESSONS: This tab may take on a variety of names, but in general it will take you to course content (for example, Chapter 1).

RESOURCES: This tab is a place where you might find links to general course resources like the course syllabus, announcements, calendar, google search, an online dictionary and course activity.

COMMUNICATE: This tab is where you might find links to anything involving communications with the class. This might include email, chat, and links to course announcements and news.

REPORTS: This tab is where you can create a number of different reports. These reports can include grades, class participation, instructor notes, performance objectives, and forum posts.

Sending an Email and Adding an Attachment in Angel

One of the most important aspects when working online is the ability to communicate with classmates and your instructor. A great way to do so is by using the <u>communicate</u> function in Angel.

1. To send an email using Angel, begin by clicking on the Communicate tab located on the tool bar at the top of the screen.

2. Next, click on the link label View Inbox. You will be taken to a screen similar to the one below:

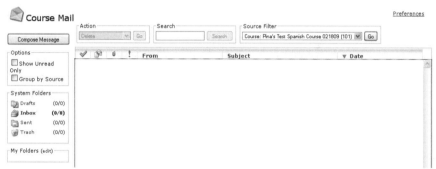

3. Click on the Compose Message link and a new window will open. When you click on the To: button, you will be able to select recipients for your email. You can choose either specific individuals, all members of your class, or groups that your <u>email</u> will go to. Chosen recipients will then appear in the To: box.

4. At this point, you should fill in the Subject line of the <u>email</u> and the Message area. Before you send your <u>email</u>, other options are also available to you, including adding a file <u>attachment</u> to the <u>email</u>. If you wish to add an <u>attachment</u> to your <u>email</u>, click on the Attach Files link in the Attachments section. If you do not wish to add an <u>attachment</u> to the <u>email</u>, simply click on the Submit button, and your email will be sent.

5. If you wish to add an <u>attachment</u> to the <u>email</u> message, click on the Select button next to the Attachments section.

6. Once you have located and chosen the file to attach, the <u>file name</u> should show up in the box to the left of the Select button. Click on the Upload button to attach the file to your <u>email</u>.

7. Then, simply click on the Send Email button, and your <u>email</u> and <u>attachment</u> will be sent.

Turning In Assignments in Angel

As you work your way through your course, you will probably need to turn in assignments from time to time. Many courses will have you do this using the Drop Box in Angel. The Drop Box is like a mailbox slot where you drop off items for your instructor.

1. To submit an assignment using the Drop Box, begin by clicking on the Lessons button on the top of the screen.

2. In the middle of the screen, you will see a link to the Drop Box. Click on that link.

3. A new window will open with your Drop Box. It should look something like the screen below:

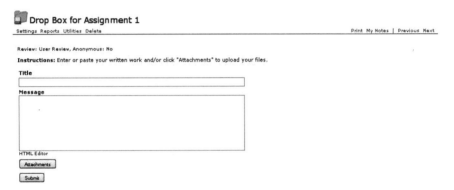

3. Submit assignments to your instructor by first entering the title of your assignment and any message you wish to send to the instructor.

4. Then click on the Attachments button. You should get a screen that is similar to the one below:

5. Click on the Browse button to find your assignment file. Then click on the Open button. Your file name will now appear in the box.

6 The next step is to click on the Upload file button. The assignment file will then be uploaded to the system.

7. Now, simply click on the Finished button, and your assignment and comments (if any) will be sent to your instructor.

Posting to a Discussion Board in Angel

One of the most common tools used in online learning is the <u>discussion board</u>. <u>Discussion board</u>s in Angel allow students and instructors to carry on conversations over a period of time in an <u>asynchronous</u> format—that is, the conversation is not occurring in real time. Depending on how your instructor has designed your course, the discussion area could be on the course <u>homepage</u> or within the content/lectures.

1. Once you locate the discussion area, you might see several discussion topics. To begin, click on discussion topic in which you wish to post a message. You should see a screen that looks something like the following:

2. In <u>discussion board</u>s, messages are usually organized by <u>thread</u>s, a common topic that more than one person wants to comment on. That keeps everyone interested in a certain topic connected by posting messages at the same place to the same <u>thread</u>. If you want to add your own comments or start a <u>thread</u>, click on the Reply button at the bottom of the screen. You will get a screen that looks similar to the one below:

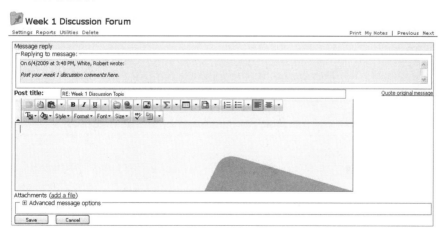

3. In this screen, fill in the box with the message you wish to post to the discussion <u>thread</u>. Then click on the Save button, and your <u>thread</u> will be created and your message added.

4. Now, in the middle of the screen, you can see any <u>thread</u>s and messages that have already been posted to this discussion forum. You can read those messages by simply clicking on the message.

5. You can respond or reply to anyone else's message after reading it by clicking on the Reply button at the end of the message. After you click on the Reply button, type your message in the box and click on the Save button. Your reply to someone else's message will now be posted.

Finding Your Course Documents and Assignments in Angel

It is very important for you to be able to find your course materials or documents in any online course. They may consist of lectures, presentations, spreadsheets, and so on.

1. To find your course materials in Angel, begin by examining the tabs on the top of the screen on the course <u>homepage</u>.

2. Next, click on the Lessons tab to access the course lectures, etc. In many courses, the course materials then are listed as a series of links to documents.

3. Once you identify the course documents, click on any one that you wish to examine more thoroughly. The course materials that have been prepared by your instructor will be displayed.

Finding Your Assignment Grades and Feedback in Angel

Almost all students want to know about their grades. Angel provides a simple way of checking your grades.

1. To find your grades in Angel, begin by clicking on the Report tab on the top of the screen.

2. Then in the middle of the screen, you will see a <u>pull-down menu</u> under the Report column. In the <u>pull-down menu</u> select the Gradebook Grades option. It should be similar to the screen below:

📷 Reports Console

Report Settings	Saved Reports

Choose Report

Category	Report	User(s) Show filter
Learner Profile ▾	Gradebook Grades ▾ 🔲	Busnach, Michael ▾ 🔲

Configure Report   [-] Collapse

Select report view [Chart ▾]   [Run] [Print Preview] [Send Report] [Export] [Save]

3. To see your grades, click on the Run button on the bottom right of the screen. Your gradebook will then be generated.

Troubleshooting Problems

Computers and technology have made it possible for us to do things easier than in the past. For example, we can now pay our bills, send mail to friends, and edit papers much faster and easier than only a few short years ago. However, nothing is perfect and computers are no exception. With that in mind, it is important to understand that at some point you will have problems with your computer hardware or software and you will need to fix those problems or get help to do so. The purpose of this tutorial is to give you some guidance on how to troubleshoot problems that you might face.

1. When it comes to troubleshooting problems, the first place to start is by using the Help function that is available on most <u>software</u>. The Help function usually contains detailed information to help you solve the most common problems associated with the <u>software</u>. It also can provide details about how to do certain tasks within the <u>software</u>. For example, you would use the Help function to figure out how to change the margins in a Microsoft Word document. The Help function is usually found as a <u>pull-down menu</u> on the top of your screen, usually the one farthest to the right. Once you click on it, it will look similar to the following:

2. Once you have clicked on the Help <u>pull-down menu</u>, the best place to start is usually the Contents and Index option. Click on that option. Each <u>software</u>'s Contents and Index area might look a little different, but once you have selected this, then there should be a way to select the Index option. In Microsoft Word, it would look similar to the following:

3. Once you are in the Index area, you can type in a word related to your problem in the blank box at the top. The <u>software</u> will find any related topics and display them in the <u>window</u> in the bottom. Then click on any one of those topics and click on the Display button. The Help topic details will then be displayed. If you don't find the information that you need, simply go to the Index area and type in a different word.

4. If you cannot find the solution to your problem using the <u>software</u>'s Help function, then you should try to get help through your college Help desk. Most schools have their own computer Help desk for students, faculty, and staff. If your problem involves a school computer, <u>software</u>, or <u>Internet</u> access, then you should contact them before contacting the <u>software</u> manufacturer. There is usually no cost to access school Help desks, so you might want to contact them first. In addition, each <u>software</u> manufacturer maintains a Help desk that you can reach either via the telephone or <u>Internet</u>. Accessing the Help desk via the telephone usually involves a charge (except for during the first few weeks you own the <u>software</u>). Access via the <u>Internet</u> is sometimes free, but you may have to wait longer to get your answer. If you choose to use the telephone Help desk option, the phone number will be in your <u>software</u>'s printed documentation. If you can't find that documentation, try locating the number on the manufacturer's <u>website</u>. That is also where you will find access to the <u>Internet</u> Help desk. (*Note:* The Help desk is sometimes called "technical support.")

5. Before you contact any Help desk, you should have certain information available that you will need to provide. Below is a list of the basic information you should have available and how to get it:

VERSION OF THE SOFTWARE: <u>Software</u> comes in many different versions. To find out what version of a <u>software</u> package you own, open the <u>software</u> and click on the "Help" <u>pull-down menu</u> at the top of the screen. It should look similar to the first screen shot on the previous page. Click on the About option and then the name of the <u>software</u>. In the first screen shot above, it says "About Microsoft Word." Once you click on that option, a new <u>window</u> will open and tell you what version of the <u>software</u> you own.

TYPE OF COMPUTER YOU OWN AND THE OPERATING SYSTEM: The type of computer that you own is going to be either a Windows or a Macintosh computer. You can find out how to determine your computer's <u>operating system</u> by referring to "Tutorial 1: Checking Your Computer's Hardware Profile in Microsoft Windows" or "Tutorial 3: Checking Your Computer's Hardware Profile on a Macintosh Computer." An example of an <u>operating system</u> is Windows XP.

WHAT THE PROBLEM IS AND WHEN IT OCCURS: When you contact the Help desk, they are going to ask you to explain what the problem is and when it occurred. It is helpful if you write that information down before you contact the Help desk so that you can communicate it to them clearly.

ERROR MESSAGES: If the reason you are contacting the Help desk is because you are getting an error message, make sure you have written down exactly what the error message says and what you were doing when it appeared.

T47

Glossary[1]

Add-ons See plug-in.

Adobe Acrobat PDF A suite of programs developed by Adobe Systems that allows you to place documents formatted by most word processing (for example, Microsoft Word), presentation (for example, Microsoft PowerPoint), or desktop publishing (for example, PageMaker) programs to be read by users of different platforms (that is, Macintosh or Microsoft Windows) and allows you to view a document exactly as the person wrote it. (Also see How-To Tutorial 8 on page T11.)

apps Short for *applications*, apps commonly refer to software applications that you can download to your smart phone (or iPod) in order to expand the capabilities of your device to include tools ranging from currency converters to maps of the constellations.

antivirus software A utility that checks emails, memory, and disks for computer viruses and removes those that it finds. Because new viruses corrupt, periodically update the antivirus program's virus definitions on your computer, though some programs will now do this automatically over the Internet.

asterisk A character that when used in a search of computer memory (such as a search for a specific file on a CD-ROM) or the World Wide Web acts as a wildcard that can stand for any unspecified file name or search term.

asynchronous Term used to describe communications that do not necessarily take place at the same time, such as email and discussion boards.

attachment A file that is attached to an email or other Internet communication. The contents of an attachment usually do not appear within the body of the email message.

back save To save a file in a format that can be read by previous versions of the software application (for example, to save a document in Microsoft Word 2007 as a file that is compatible with Microsoft Word 2003).

G-1

back up To copy files from one storage area (for example, hard drive, floppy disk, and CD-ROM) to another, to prevent their loss in case of disk failure.

blog Short for "Web log," a <u>website</u> that displays personal journal entries by one or more individuals in chronological (or reverse chronological) order and usually has links to readers' comments on specific postings. <u>Blog</u>s are typically editable <u>webpage</u>s that do not require individuals to know specialized coding (that is, <u>HTML</u>) to post their journal entries.[2]

bookmark A marker used in a program such as a <u>Web browser</u> or a Help utility that allows you to go directly to a specific <u>webpage</u>.

chat To communicate in real-time (that is, <u>synchronous</u>) on a computer network using typed messages. A person chatting with another person or group of people on the network (for example, the <u>World Wide Web</u>) types a message and waits for the other party to type in a response. Also called <u>real-time chat</u> or <u>Internet</u> relay chat (IRC).

Ctrl The control key on PC and compatible keyboards is pressed in combination with another key(s) to produce an alternative function (for example, Ctrl + c will copy highlighted text).

cookie An item (such as a file) that is used to relate one computer transaction with a later one. For example, certain <u>webpages</u> <u>download</u> small cookie files that hold information that can be retrieved by other <u>webpages</u> on the site (such as name, address, recent purchases, and credit card numbers).

coursework The assignments, activities, research, exams, or other tasks that students are required to complete in order to demonstrate their mastery of course topics.

central processing unit (CPU) The part of a computer that interprets and executes instructions.

CPU *See* central processing unit.

cut-and-paste To cut part of a document or a graphic file and then insert and paste it into another place in the document or into another document or file.

desktop In a graphical user interface, an onscreen metaphor for your workspace, just as if you were looking at a real desktop cluttered with <u>folders</u> full of work to do. The desktop consists of <u>icon</u>s that show files, <u>folders</u>, and various documents.

discussion board An electronic communication system that allows users to leave messages, review messages, and upload and <u>download</u> <u>software</u>. Also called a bulletin board system (BBS).

DNS *See* domain name system.

domain name system (DNS) A database system that translates textual network domain names into numeric <u>Internet</u> addresses.

download To transfer a copy of a file from a central source to a peripheral device (such as a CD-ROM or DVD) or a computer. You can download a file from a network file server to another computer on the network (for example, from the <u>World Wide Web</u>) or from a <u>discussion board</u>.

educational portal An educational <u>website</u> considered as an entry point to other <u>websites</u> that commonly include online tools like grade books, <u>real-time chat</u>, <u>discussion board</u>s, online whiteboards, and other course resources.

email A feature that lets a computer user send a message to someone at another computer using the <u>Internet</u>. Email, or electronic mail, can duplicate most of the features of paper mail, such as storing messages in inboxes and outboxes, message forwarding, providing delivery receipts, and sending multiple copies.

emoticons A combination of characters used in <u>email</u> messages, <u>chats</u>, or <u>discussion board</u>s to represent a human emotion or attitude (such as happiness, laughter, and sadness).

field In a database or on a <u>webpage</u>, a space where a single item of information (name, address, telephone numbers, and other information) can be entered into a record.

file directory A way to organize files into a hierarchical structure. The top directory is often called a root directory that is labeled with a letter (such as C: for a computer's hard drive or E: for a computer's CD-ROM drive; though these can be set by the user to be alternative letters). All directories below the root directory are considered subdirectories and represent the file <u>folder</u>s and files contained in the storage device represented by the root directory (for example, C:\ myfiles\ assignment1.doc would represent the file assignment1.doc in the myfiles <u>folder</u> on a computer's hard drive that is labeled with a C: root directory).

file format The format that a program uses to encode data on a disk. Some formats are proprietary, and only the program that has created the file can read a file so encoded. Today, companies often share formats so that users can save files in one program in the format of another company's program (for example, in Microsoft Word you can save the file in the Corel WordPerfect file format).

file name The name given to a file so that it can be distinguished from other files. In most <u>operating systems</u>, you cannot include the following characters in a file name: " " | \ / [ ] , ? * < >

firewall <u>Software</u> (or hardware) designed to prevent unauthorized access to or from a private network or computer.[3]

folder In a graphical user interface, an organizing structure that contains multiple files and is analogous to a directory.

footer In <u>word processing</u>, printed information (especially title, page number, or date) placed in the bottom margin of a page and repeated on every page or every other page of the document. (*Also see* header.)

groupware <u>Software</u> that helps organize the activities of users in a group that uses a network (such as the <u>World Wide Web</u>). Examples of groupware include <u>software</u> that allows users to share calendars, plan meetings, and distribute electronic newsletters.

header In <u>word processing</u>, printed information (especially title, page number, or date) placed in the top margin of a page and repeated on every page or every other page of the document. (*Also see* footer.)

homepage The first screen containing information that you see when you arrive at a <u>website</u>.

host A computer containing data or programs that another computer can access over a network (such as the <u>World Wide Web</u>).

HTML (hypertext markup language) A coding system used on the <u>World Wide Web</u> to format text and set up links between documents.

HTTP (hypertext transfer protocol) A protocol used by the <u>World Wide Web</u> to govern the transfer of data.

icon In a graphical user interface, a picture on the screen that represents a specific file, directory, <u>window</u>, or program.

instant messaging (IM) Creating a private text-based <u>chat</u> room with another individual in order to communicate <u>synchronous</u>ly over the <u>Internet</u>. Most instant messaging <u>software</u> allows you to create a list of friends with whom you frequently communicate and alert you when they are on the <u>Internet</u>.[4]

Internet A matrix of networks that interconnects millions of supercomputers, mainframes, workstations, personal computers, laptops, and handheld devices. The networks that make up the Internet all use a standard set of communications protocols, thus allowing computers with distinctive <u>software</u> and hardware to communicate.

listserve A mailing list manager used for the distribution of <u>email</u> among the list's members.

menu An onscreen list of available options or commands. A bar that you can move from one item to another usually highlights the options.

menu bar A horizontal bar that runs across the top of the screen or the <u>window</u> and holds the names of available <u>menu</u> options.

modem A device that converts data from digital signals to analog signals and vice versa so that computers can communicate over telephone lines, which transmit analog waves.

operating system <u>Software</u> designed to control the hardware of a specific computer system in order to allow users and application programs to employ it easily. The operating system mediates between hardware and <u>software</u> applications.

PDA *See* personal digital assistant.

personal digital assistant (PDA) A lightweight, handheld computer, often featuring <u>software</u> applications that provide calendars, calculators, address books, and other useful resources. New models commonly have an internal <u>modem</u> and cell phone to be used as a link to a larger computer or the <u>World Wide Web</u>.

plug-in <u>Software</u> that you install on your computer in order to expand the features of an application such as a <u>Web browser</u>.

podcast A type of audio file that is shared using the <u>Internet</u> and played using a personal computer, Apple iPod, or other MP3 player. Unlike other <u>download</u>ed or streaming audio files, <u>podcast</u>s enable users to subscribe to a collection of audio files that can be routinely updated and automatically <u>download</u>ed to their computer or audio player.

pop-up menu A <u>menu</u> that appears on the screen in response to a user action (such as a right-click on the mouse) and is separate from the primary application <u>menu</u>s.

pull-down menu A menu that appears directly beneath the item selected on a <u>menu bar</u>.

real-time chat A network of <u>Internet</u> <u>server</u>s through which individual users can hold real-time online conversations. <u>Instant messaging</u> is a type of real-time chat. Also called Internet relay chat (IRC).

search engine A program that allows you to perform searches for data on the <u>World Wide Web</u>.

server In a network, a computer that stores files and provides them to other computers.

shortcut In Microsoft Windows, a file that points to another file (such as a <u>software</u> application, <u>word processing</u> document, or <u>webpage</u>).

signature A short text message that can be automatically included at the end of each <u>email</u> and contains contact information.

smart phone A cell phone that combines the tools of <u>personal digital assistant</u> (PDA) with access to the <u>Internet</u> to provide a flexible and mobile tool for accessing <u>email</u>, <u>surfing</u> <u>websites</u>, and staying organized.

software The programs, programming languages, and data that control the functioning of the hardware and direct its operations.

surfing Browsing through information presented on the <u>Internet</u> by casually following links that you think might lead to something of interest.

synchronous Term used to describe communications that take place at the same time, such as <u>real-time chat</u>s or <u>instant messaging</u>.

thread A series of messages on a certain topic that have been posted on a <u>discussion board</u>, typically using visual indicators to illustrate which messages are replies to which other messages.

Glossary

Glossary

URL (uniform resource locator) The specific name or identifier of a file on the <u>World Wide Web</u>.

vlog Short for "video blog," a specialized type of online journal in which the journal author(s) incorporate video clips (often in addition to text and other content) into their entries.

Web browser A program, such as Microsoft Internet Explorer or Netscape Navigator, that allows you to find and access documents from anywhere on the <u>World Wide Web</u>.

webpage A file on the <u>World Wide Web</u> that is accessible using a <u>Web browser</u>.

Web portal A <u>website</u> considered an entry point to other <u>websites</u>.

Web server A computer on which <u>server</u> <u>software</u> has been installed and that is connected to the <u>Internet</u>, allowing the computer to accept requests for information using the <u>HTTP</u> protocol.

website A set of interconnected <u>webpages</u>, usually including a <u>homepage</u>, generally located on the same <u>server</u>, and prepared and maintained as a collection of information by a person, group, or organization.

wiki A collaborative <u>website</u> whose content can be edited by anyone who has access to it. <u>Wikis</u> are typically editable <u>webpages</u> that do not require the contributors to know specialized coding (that is, <u>HTML</u>) to post their entries or edits.[5]

window A rectangular portion of a display screen set aside for a specific purpose.

wizard An automated instructional guide that is a feature of some Microsoft and other <u>software</u> applications. Wizards can provide application shortcuts for accomplishing specific tasks.

word processing The act or practice of using a computer to create, edit, and print out documents such as letters, papers, and manuscripts.

World Wide Web A collection of <u>Internet</u> servers that support the exchange of files in the <u>HTML</u> format as well as graphics, audio, and video files.

Notes

1. Unless otherwise noted, definitions based on S. Kleinedler, ed., *Dictionary of Computer and Internet Words: An A to Z Guide to Hardware, Software, and Cyberspace* (New York: Houghton Mifflin, 2001).
2. American Heritage® Dictionary of the English Language, 4th edition. © 2006 Houghton Mifflin Company.
3. Definition based on http://www.webopedia.com, accessed March 2003.
4. Ibid.
5. American Heritage® Dictionary of the English Language, 4th edition. © 2006 Houghton Mifflin Company.

References and Recommended Readings

Anderson, T., and H. Kanuka. *E-Research: Methods, Strategies, and Issues.* New York: Allyn and Bacon, 2003.

Blanchard, K. *The One Minute Manager Meets the Monkey.* New York: Quill, 1989.

Carter, C., J. Bishop, and S. Kravits, *Keys to Effective Learning,* 3rd ed. Upper Saddle River, NJ: Pearson Prentice Hall, 2002.

Educational Testing Service, *Succeeding in the 21st Century: What Higher Education Must Do to Address the Gap in Information and Communication Technology Proficiencies.* Princeton, NJ: ETS. Retrieved April 24, 2006, from http://www.ets.org/ictliteracy/succeeding1.html.

Ellis, D. *Becoming a Master Student,* 10th ed. New York: Houghton Mifflin, 2003.

Harnack, A., and E. Kleppinger. *Online: A Reference Guide to Using Internet Sources.* Boston: Bedford St. Martin's, 2001.

International ICT Literacy Panel. *Digital Transformation: A Framework for ICT Literacy.* Princeton, NJ: ETS. Retrieved April 24, 2006, from http://www.ets.org/Media/Tests/Information_and_Communication_Technology_Literacy/ictreport.pdf.

Kleinedler, S., ed. *Dictionary of Computer and Internet Words: An A to Z Guide to Hardware, Software, and Cyberspace.* New York: Houghton Mifflin, 2001.

McVay, M. *How to Be a Successful Distance Learning Student: Learning on the Internet.* Boston: Pearson Custom Publishing, 2000.

Pauk, W. *How to Study in College,* 7th ed. New York: Houghton Mifflin, 2001.

Wahlstrom, C., B. Williams, and P. Shea. *The Successful Distance Learning Student.* Belmont, CA: Wadsworth, 2003.

Watkins, R. "Are You Prepared to be a Successful Online Learner: An E-learner Self-Assessment." In *The 2003 Pfeiffer Annual: Training,* ed. E. Biech. San Francisco: Jossey-Bass/Pfeiffer, 2003.

Watkins, R., D. Leigh, and D. Triner. "Assessing Readiness for E-Learning." *Performance Improvement Quarterly* 17, no. 4 (2004): 66–79.

Winograd, K., and G. Moore. *You Can Learn Online.* Boston: McGraw-Hill, 2003.

Credits

Text Credits

This page constitutes an extension of the copyright page. We have made every effort to trace the ownership of all copyrighted material and to secure permission from copyright holders. In the event of any question arising as to the use of any material, we will be pleased to make the necessary corrections in future printings. Thanks are due to the following authors, publishers, and agents for permission to use the material indicated.

Chapter 6. 6-15, 6-23: Copyright © 2001 by Houghton Mifflin Harcourt Publishing Company. Reproduced by permission from Dictionary of Computer and Internet Words. **6-24, 6-26:** Reproduced with permission from Computer Desktop Encyclopedia (www.computerencyclopedia.com). Copyright © 1981-2003 The Computer Language Co., Inc. **6-6, 6-7, 6-11:** Copyright © 2006 by Houghton Mifflin Harcourt Publishing Company. Reproduced by permission from The American Heritage College Dictionary, Fourth Edition.

How To Tutorials. T11–12: Copyright © Google, Inc. Reproduced by permission. **T14–16:** Adobe product screenshots reprinted with permission from Adobe Systems Incorporated. **T21–22:** Netscape and the Netscape Browser logo are registered trademarks of Netscape Communications Corporation. Used with permission. **T28–33:** Copyright © Blackboard, Inc. All rights reserved. Reprinted by permission of Blackboard, Inc. **T35–41:** Copyright © Blackboard, Inc. All rights reserved. Reprinted by permission of Blackboard, Inc. **T49–55:** Copyright © Blackboard, Inc. All rights reserved. Reprinted by permission of Blackboard, Inc.

Image Credits

Pages T3–T10, Screen shots reprinted by permission from Microsoft® Corporation
Pages T11–T12, ©2009 Google.
Page T14–T17, Reprinted courtesy of Adobe Systems, Inc.
Page T18–T23, Microsoft® Internet Explorer reprinted by permission from Microsoft® Corporation.
Pages T24–T25, © 2008, Netscape Communications.
Pages T26–T29, Portions of this content are © 1998–2009 by individual mozilla.org contributors Content available under a Creative Commons license.
Pages T31–T37, Reprinted by permission of Blackboard, Inc.
Pages T39–T47, Copyright © Blackboard, Inc. All rights reserved. Reprinted with permission.
Pages T48–T54, Copyright © ecollege.com. Reprinted with permission.
Pages T55–T58, Copyright © 2009 ANGEL Learning. All rights reserved.
Pages T59–T60, Screen shots reprinted by permission from Microsoft® Corporation.

C-1

Index

www.cengage.com/success/Watkins/ELearning3e

Important Contact Information

Your College's Technical Support Services (or Help desk)
Website: _____

Email: _____

Phone: _____

Your College's Computer Lab(s)
Location(s): _____

_____

Hours: _____

Phone: _____

Your College's Library
Website: _____

Hours: _____

Phone: _____

Email: _____

Your Internet Service Provider
Website: _____

Email: _____

Phone: _____

Your Computer Manufacturer's Technical Support Services (Help desk)
Website: _____

Email: _____

Phone: _____

Information about Your Computer
Manufacturer: _____

Year purchased: _____

Operating system (including version):

_____

_____

Software programs (including version):

_____

_____

_____

_____

Your College's Academic Advising Offices
Website: _____

Email: _____

Phone: _____

For your lifelong learning solutions, visit **www.cengage.com/custom**

Visit our corporate website at **www.cengage.com**

ISBN-13: 978-1-111-74193-8
ISBN-10: 1-111-74193-X

Custom Edition